THE UNION OF DZOGCHEN AND BODHICHITTA

The Union of Dzogchen and Bodhichitta

by Anyen Rinpoche
Translated by Allison Graboski

Snow Lion Publications
Ithaca, New York • Boulder, Colorado

Snow Lion Publications
P. O. Box 6483
Ithaca, NY 14851 USA
(607) 273-8519
www.snowlionpub.com

Printed in U.S.A. on acid-free recycled paper.

ISBN-10: 1-55939-248-7
ISBN-13: 978-1-55939-248-8

Library of Congress Cataloging-in-Publication Data

Anyen Rinpoche.
   The union of dzogchen and bodhichitta / by Anyen Rinpoche ; translated by Allison Graboski.
      p. cm.
   ISBN-13: 978-1-55939-248-8 (alk. paper)
   ISBN-10: 1-55939-248-7 (alk. paper)
   1. Rdzogs-chen. 2. Bodhicitta (Buddhism) 3. Spiritual life—Buddhism. I. Graboski, Allison, 1974- II. Title.

BQ7662.4.A69 2006
294.3'420423—dc20
                                          2005036836

Designed and typeset by Gopa & Ted2, Inc.

⁘ *Table of Contents*

Tsara Dharmakirti Rinpoche

❖ *Dedication*

For my Root Lama:
You ripened into the great Dharmakaya,
Went to the primordial state where all phenomena are exhausted,
In which all thoughts and duality dissolve like a drawing on water.
I bow at the feet of Tsara Dharmakirti Rinpoche.

Acknowledgments

I WISH TO CONVEY my inexpressible gratitude to my supreme Spiritual Guide, Khenchen Tsara Dharmakirti Rinpoche, along with all the many precious Lamas I have ever had the good fortune to study with, especially Lama Chupur, Dorlo Rinpoche, and Dehor Geshe, whose compassionate guidance, limitless kindness, and sublime wisdom perpetually inspire me.

I also extend my heartfelt thanks to everyone who made the publishing of this text possible; to my exquisite translator, Allison Graboski, without whom this text could not have been written; to my student Lorna Simons, who gave many hours of her time to reading the first several drafts; to Sidney Piburn and Steven Rhodes at Snow Lion Publications, who believed in *The Union* from the beginning, and to Maria Montenegro, a shining star among editors.

⁘ Introduction

THE TIBETAN BUDDHIST perception of time has always been greatly divergent from that of the West. Tibetan Buddhists view time as a cycle called a "kalpa," or "eon," in which the Buddhist Teachings, as well as people's good qualities and their ability to put the Teachings into practice, are impermanent. The modern era is viewed as the end of a cycle of Teachings, or a "degenerate" time as it is translated from Tibetan. Traditionally, this is thought to mean that the purity of the Teachings, as well as people's ability to put them into practice, is at risk of declining. In order to safeguard the purity of the Teachings for as long as possible, many realized yogis and emanations of Buddhas and Bodhisattvas who lived in India and Tibet made prophecies about what this period would be like.

To establish the groundwork for a discussion of the Union of Dzogchen and Bodhichitta, I would first like to discuss three of the prophecies that were made about the modern era. The first prophecy said that during the degenerate age the Teachings of Dzogchen (a method for realizing the nature of mind) would be known to many, while the practice of generating Bodhichitta (the determination to gain ultimate realization for oneself for the sake of benefiting all sentient beings) would be known by only a few. In Tibet, the practices of taking Bodhichitta as the method aspect of the path and Dzogchen as the wisdom aspect of the path have always been practiced as indivisible components of one path. If we examine the history of Vajrayana Buddhism, we will find that this has been consistently the case throughout the ages. Even the great yogis responsible for maintaining the Teachings in India and Tibet, such as Garab Dorje, Shri Simha, and Padmasambhava, meditated on the Outer, Inner, and Secret Teachings in union. It is often said by Tibetans that to practice the Secret Teach-

ings divorced from the Outer and Inner Teachings would be like trying to build a house on a block of ice.

This brings us to the second prophecy. Both Buddha Shakyamuni
and Padmasambhava prophesied that one day the Buddhist Teachings
would pervade the world and that the Teachings would even be practiced in countries that had not traditionally been Buddhist. Personally,
this prophecy has always given me great hope, for it is only through
spiritual awakening that we will find peace not only on a personal level,
but also on a global scale. Indeed, these days there are thousands of
new Buddhist practitioners throughout the world, and a vast redirect-
ing of energy towards spirituality.

Finally, these first two prophecies intersect with yet a third. It was
said that even in this degenerate time many people would be able to
attain realization from the Vajrayana Teachings if they were put into
practice properly. Of course, the word "properly" leaves much room
for interpretation. In a time when Tibetan Buddhism can no longer
rely upon its traditional context to shape the way in which the Teachings are practiced, it may seem unclear exactly how we are supposed to
practice and apply the Teachings in our lives today.

In fact, many of my students have come to me with such concerns
weighing on their minds. They have read about the history of Vajrayana Buddhism and examined the instructions laid out by the foundational texts, but they often tell me that they feel unsure about or even
discouraged by them. They cannot spend their lives in retreat like the
great yogis of the past. And they do not understand how to bring the
nonmaterialistic Teachings of the Dharma into their lives, whose circumstances are necessarily conditioned by the modern culture of mate-
rialism and the established "system." I try to assure students that there
is no need to worry; there are innumerable ways to put the wisdom of
the Buddhist Teachings into practice in their everyday lives. But one
thing is for certain: there is great confusion about how to merge contemporary Western life with the Dharma.

THE UNION OF DZOGCHEN AND BODHICHITTA

The approach I take to Dharma practice is very simple, yet this approach should not be taken to undermine the profundity of the Buddhadharma. This approach is based on the instructions I received from my own root Lama, Khenchen Tsara Dharmakirti Rinpoche, the experiences I have had in my life, and many long years of study and solitary retreat. It is my conclusion that the style of Dharma practice that the great yogis and practitioners of India and Tibet have relied upon up until now has been holistic in nature, and I believe that this approach is still the best one to take today. Logically speaking, the Outer, Inner, and Secret Teachings are fundamentally interconnected and should be adopted and practiced as one path. In fact, they are so fundamentally interconnected that it is actually difficult to give Teachings on one without including the others. This interconnection—along with the "Union" which is the perfect, uncontrived view and the "Union" which is the nature of mind itself—is what I like to call the Union of Dzogchen and Bodhichitta.

Often, when people hear the words "Outer, Inner, and Secret Teachings," they want to associate them with one concept or another, such as the three vehicles of the Hinayana, the Mahayana, and the Vajrayana. When translated from Sanskrit, the words Hinayana, Mahayana, and Vajrayana mean the "lesser, great, and indestructible vehicles," and "vehicle" refers to the method or the path used to cross the ocean of samsara. But associating the Outer, Inner, and Secret Teachings with distinct concepts is not what I have in mind. In fact, associating the Teachings with concepts is precisely what can lead us away from putting them into practice properly. This is because as soon as we begin to talk about the Dharma in terms of duality, it becomes exclusive, such that one necessary component can easily be dismissed, ignored, or subordinated in terms of importance to practice. This suggests that the Dharma is not holistic in nature, but instead that each practitioner may be selective about what they study and practice, thus putting some Teachings into practice while neglecting others, on the basis of assumptions made about the importance of different aspects of the Dharma.

The same thing has happened since the introduction of the Buddhist Teachings into Western pop culture. Many of the more subtle ideas of Buddhist thought, whose understanding requires deep explanations and years of contemplative experience, have been reduced to sound bites and images: simple ideas that are easy to digest and seem easy to realize if we could just remember them. These packaged ideas appear to be spiritual in nature but have lost the essential meaning conveyed by the Teachings *as a whole*. One example of this is the commonly spoken idea that "Everything is One." This idea has its basis in the nature of "suchness," or reality "as it is," which is quite a profound state of realization. However, it has been taken out of context and oversimplified. It is like a beautiful, empty shell that is not capable of pointing us in the right direction or providing us with the means for realization.

In order to truly understand the Union of Dzogchen and Bodhichitta, the Dharma as we have come to know it in the West has to be fundamentally reconsidered. The Union of Dzogchen and Bodhichitta is the path in its totality, a synthesis of the Teachings without losing any of the meaning. Although it is useful in other situations, for this particular discussion, associating the Teachings with dualistic concepts would only distract us from their essential meaning. We must take up the entire path as an interconnected entity of which every single part is given equal importance. This is actually the true meaning of the word "Dzogchen," which can be translated literally as "the great perfection." Some people interpret this to mean that the nature of mind is perfect, or that the realization gained from the Teachings is perfect, and these things may also be true. But actually, Dzogchen is perfect because it is all-inclusive; it is the totality of the path that leads one to realization.

Rather than present the Dharma as a linear path as is often done in many foundational texts, I would instead like to present it here as three facets of an interrelated system whose parts must be practiced simultaneously if they are to lead to the perfect result. These three facets are the Outer, Inner, and Secret Teachings, which are distinguished as separate elements only by the cognitive construct of words, and which completely encompass the wisdom of Tibetan Buddhism. But before I go any further, let me tell you about some of my own experiences with the Union of Dzogchen and Bodhichitta.

From the time I was born, my parents and I lived with a Dzogchen yogi called "Lama Chupur." He was the kind of yogi we call a *drubtob* in Tibetan, or in Sanskrit a *siddha*, or great adept—a yogi who has realized the view of Dzogchen and reached the stage of magical accomplishment. In fact, Lama Chupur's name means "flying over water," and he was given that name after he was seen flying over a wide river near my village. He was the kind of yogi who had spent his whole life wandering around Tibet in search of the Teachings, and he had been the heart student (in other words, had received the entirety of his masters' knowledge and Teachings on realizing the nature of mind) of two of the greatest drubtob masters of his time. So maybe that can give you an idea of what kind of yogi Lama Chupur was.

Lama Chupur came to live in my village after the changes in Tibet. My parents were his students. He recognized me as a *tulku* (reincarnate Lama) from a young age, after which he raised me as both his child and his student. I spent my childhood days in his constant presence, witnessing him and taking instruction from him. I remember that at first glance he did not seem to be meditating on anything special at all. When he gave Teachings, as he often did to the many pilgrims and village people who came to see him, he always gave Teachings on how to generate Bodhichitta and never even mentioned the Secret Teachings. There was a kindness about him that is very difficult to convey with words. He had a marvelously good heart that marked you indelibly whenever you were with him.

Although his words and his ordinary appearance suggested that he was meditating solely on Bodhichitta, sometimes when I looked at him I felt something welling up inside of me. I could tell instinctively by his gaze and the posture he assumed, as well as the clear quality of his mind, that his meditation was much deeper than that. It was not until

I was older and had begun to study with my own root Lama, as well as other Lamas who were staying in retreat in Tibet, that I realized that Lama Chupur had been practicing the Union of Dzogchen and Bodhichitta.

Lama Chupur's story is not unique. My own root Lama, Khenchen Tsara Dharmakirti Rinpoche, was regarded by many Tibetans as the highest authority on the four sects of Tibetan Buddhism. He is the heart student of more than ten renowned Lamas and is the fourth in an unbroken lineage of heart students of Patrul Rinpoche. Yet, many people did not realize the profundity of his meditation because of his humble appearance. Up until the time of his passing, he spent most of his time giving Teachings on Bodhichitta and always presented himself as an ordinary practitioner. But as his heart student who spent more than twenty years under his guidance, I had the chance to experience his transformation. I can say with certainty that I witnessed my own teacher attain the fruit of the Teachings in this very life. When Tsara Dharmakirti Rinpoche passed away at the age of ninety-two, he attained a sign called "Heart, Tongue, and Eyes," which is one of the signs of highest realization that comes as a result of the Dzogchen Teachings. In fact, it is the same sign that came when the omniscient Longchenpa passed away hundreds of years ago. Of course, I did not know the method my teacher used until he gave me the secret oral instructions of our lineage. It was then that I realized that he, too, relied on the Union of Dzogchen and Bodhichitta.

Finally, Tsara Dharmakirti Rinpoche once told me the story of an ordinary old man who lived in Kham, Tibet. He was a poor man with only the clothes on his back who lived in a stone house near a pilgrimage site that many people would circumambulate. Nothing at all about this man seemed special. He was so ordinary, in fact, that until he died, no one even knew his name, much less thought of him as a great Dzogchen yogi. Each day this man would get up, beg for food, and then spend the day saying mantras and holding a Prayer Wheel that he slowly turned in circles. I cannot tell you how shocked his countrymen were when this simple old man attained rainbow body, the sign of one of the highest accomplishments of a Dzogchen practitioner. When my teacher told me this story, I knew once again that the old man's realization had come from practicing the Union of Dzogchen and Bodhichitta.

In my studies, I have read scriptures about yogis who attained the result of the Teachings, but I have also occasionally come across stories of yogis who did not. I always wondered why these yogis did not attain the realization promised by the scriptures even though they spent their whole lives in solitary retreat as they had been instructed. But as I examined further, I realized that they had neglected to practice the Union of Dzogchen and Bodhichitta and had fallen into the wrong view. Thus, it was not their heroic effort that had failed them, but rather the view and style of practice they had undertaken from the outset.

Especially in this day and age, there are many kinds of meditation we can choose to practice. But meditation does not have some inherent quality that promises to rid us of self-attachment, which is the only way we can achieve liberation. Rather, whether or not we achieve liberation depends solely on the type of meditation we choose to practice and the diligence with which we proceed. Thus, the yogis who did not attain liberation practiced a style of meditation that did not rid them of self-attachment, but rather led them to develop negative habitual tendencies and eventually take a lower rebirth. Working with the mind is an extremely delicate art; we must be very careful not to make a mistake about what and how we practice.

This text presents my own holistic view of the Teachings, the Union of Dzogchen and Bodhichitta, as passed on to me by my Lamas, as well as developed through my own contemplative practice and study of the Buddhist canon. In this unprecedented time where so many are able to benefit from practicing the Buddhist Teachings, I urge you to practice the Union of Dzogchen and Bodhichitta and attain the results promised by the Teachings. May this text bring benefit to beings everywhere.

—Anyen Rinpoche

CHAPTER 1
Religion and the Modern World

T HESE DAYS, the word "religion" connotes many things in the West. For some, it suggests a tradition that is outdated or patriarchal, for others it signifies political or social oppression, and for still others it is associated with the cause of war. Religion divides some people from their families or condemns their lifestyle. No wonder many people want nothing to do with religion. But actually, in the traditional Buddhist view, worldliness and religion are said to be like fire and water. The reason that we view worldliness and religion this way is simple. Buddhist meditation is the method for becoming a decent, sane, and eventually, enlightened being. Pursuing worldly life is the method for obtaining a comfortable existence, accruing wealth, success, and looking good in the eyes of others. The great sage and translator Vairochana said,

Worldly life is the great prison of samsara.

This idea of separating worldliness and religion can be found in other spiritual traditions as well. For example, it is said in the Christian tradition that one cannot be devoted to both God and wealth. This idea probably rings true to almost anyone who has had any kind of religious upbringing. However, the Teachings of all religions are subject to misinterpretation, and religion can be exploited just like everything else.

We can see this same tendency to exploit or distort ideas and systems in how legal systems function within societies. Laws were first conceived as a means of conducing to a harmonious society. People wanted to make rules that would maintain a sense of order, and in the case of most Western governments, social equality. But often businesses, individuals, or even lawyers exploit laws to gain a personal advantage. This may make us angry or cause us to feel that the laws have been corrupted. However, we cannot say it is the laws alone that are at fault.

When combined with worldly life, religion can become a means to gain power and control over others or, as in the current climate, destabilize the global political situation. There have been many examples of "nonreligious" activity in the modern era, all in the name of religion. Some people want their group to dominate a government or a certain geographical area, while causing other groups of people to perish. All that can really be said about this kind of behavior is that it shows that the practitioners of the religion have been corrupted by self-attachment, and the fault of pride. However, when we feel discouraged by this contradictory display of so-called spirituality, it is actually we who are at fault. We have taken religion and worldliness to be one and the same enterprise, and begun to fall into the same old cynicism that pervades much of the modern era. It is to our advantage to recontextualize the world "religion" and place it in the sphere of authentic spirituality.

Even in Buddhist practice, there are many ways in which the Dharma can be used in contradiction to its primary purpose. For example, if people who had little experience in the practice of meditation told many people that they were accomplished practitioners who had experienced all sorts of magical phenomena, they would be using the Dharma to make themselves appear special, thereby also accelerating the degeneration of the Dharma and harming the longevity of the Teachings. Although in traditional Tibet there was no mixing of the worldly and the spiritual realms, the West has an established and wonderful tradition of religious service. Engaged Buddhist practice, or actively using our practice to benefit those around us, is one of the best ways we can carry out our vow of Bodhichitta and put the Teachings of the Six Paramitas into practice. It is like a shade of gray between the two extremes of religion and worldliness, but even this type of practice depends upon our strong determination not to let ourselves get sidetracked by mental afflictions like pride, greed, or desire. Most of us live within society instead of removed from it, so we must maintain the distinction between spirituality and worldliness in our own minds in order to keep our motivation pure.

THE BUDDHIST TEACHINGS

The Buddhist Teachings themselves were, from the beginning, not a political or doctrinal endeavor, but a spiritual one. This can easily be seen by examining the lives of Buddha Shakyamuni and Padmasambhava; both were the sons of kings, yet gave up their worldly lives and status to pursue a life of contemplation that was focused on the development and expression of enlightened wisdom. The primary aim of the Buddhist Teachings is to liberate the mind, which allows an individual to express limitless altruism, and to benefit beings who remain suffering. Though vast in scope, the Teachings can be summarized in this short verse spoken by Buddha Shakyamuni:

> Do not commit negative actions.
> Perform abundant acts of virtue.
> Completely tame the mind.
> These are the Buddhist Teachings.

The first two lines should always be understood to have a very black and white relationship. They mean that not only should we avoid harmful actions and do helpful ones, but that by eradicating the root of all negative actions, the entire sphere of our activity naturally becomes virtuous. Consequently, if we do anything that harms another, we have stepped out of the sphere of virtue. Of course in Buddhism, we always measure the positivity or negativity of any action by the motivation or intention with which it is carried out. It is said,

> The virtuous or nonvirtuous aspiration is more important
> Than the appearance of virtue or nonvirtue, no matter
>   how great or small.

Thus, the karma accumulated by any action we perform, whether it is virtuous or nonvirtuous, depends upon our motivation. That is why even a small act done with an excellent motivation can be more beneficial than a great deed done with a mediocre or weak motivation. I once heard a story about the powerful motivation of one monk who lived in my homeland years ago. At the time the story took place, Tibet had gone through great change. Some of the new leaders of our village had gathered about thirty monks together and had begun to give them orders. They told the group of monks that they must slaughter several hundred yak and sheep in a pasture outside the village. Of course, it is against a monk's vows to kill, so this was a horrendous order. One particular monk in the group thought long and hard about what to do. He knew that all of the monks would be punished if they did not do as they were told. But if they killed the animals, each and every one of them would break their monastic vows and their Tantric vows or Samaya. So the monk decided to kill all of the animals himself. That way, he would be the only one to break his vows, and the rest of the monks would be spared from collecting such heavy negative karma. It was this monk's deep feeling of compassion and cultivation of Bodhichitta that led him to kill the animals, although it might have appeared to be quite the contrary. There are many such examples of pure motivation in the history of Tibetan Buddhism, which serve to remind us that appearances can deceive.

ESSENTIAL SPIRITUALITY

The first two lines of Buddha Shakyamuni's words are one way of expressing the essential meaning of the Buddhist Teachings in a universal, that is to say, nonsectarian, way. Yet another way is by using the idea of the Union of Dzogchen and Bodhichitta. Any religion or spiritual path that encompasses the good qualities of the Union of Dzogchen and Bodhichitta could be said to capture the essential meaning of the Buddhist Teachings. These good qualities can be concisely summarized as delivering the "two benefits for self and others." In other words, they give us the method for developing universal love and compassion, which then inspires within us the determination to gain the fully realized state so that we can be of ultimate benefit to others, that is, so we can help others to be free from samara's endless sufferings and problems. Finally, the Teachings then lay out the complete method for attaining the enlightened state by realizing the perfectly uncontrived view, and the nature of ultimate reality.

If we are currently interested in several different spiritual paths but do not know whether or which one to choose, these two ways of summarizing the essential meaning of the Buddhist Teachings are a powerful tool for examination. We can use them as a measure of the transformative or transcendental power of a certain type of practice, to help us decide whether or not it is suitable for us, given the goal we have in mind. No matter what practice we plan to engage in, having a period of examination is extremely important.

The renowned Dzogchen yogi Longchenpa once described the attitude a spiritual practitioner should take in life. He said that a spiritual practitioner should never engage in nonreligious activities, and this included the attitudes they took towards other religions and spiritual paths. No matter what religion they practiced, they should examine it first to understand its strengths and weaknesses. After examining the religion, they should not be angry if they found something that they did not like or did not wish to practice. Instead, they should put that religion or specific practice aside, cultivate a feeling of equanimity towards all religions, and avoid feelings of judgment and resentment.

In Tibet, children are taught from the time they are very young to examine not only the quality of a Lama who comes to teach, but also the Teachings they give. So this type of examination is very natural to Tibetans. However, it is a skill new Buddhists must acquire along the way if their practice is to be successful. In Tibet we say that our spiritual practice should not be like a hound chasing hungrily after a deer. In other words, we should definitely first examine carefully what it is we are going to practice before we actually engage in it.

Many students who come to see me want to begin a practice before they have a clear understanding of what meditation and the Buddhist path actually entail. As far as spirituality goes, this can lead to instability in both the short and long run. If they go after the practice of meditation like the hunting dog pursuing a deer, they may stick with it for a while. But one day, as a result of not having established within their minds the proper foundation, they will find that they lack the faith, diligence, and endurance required to continue practicing. Although they never intended to, they will throw away their meditation, and what's more, tell everyone they know what is wrong with the Teachings they have been given. Of course, since we know that countless beings have attained liberation by practicing these very Teachings, it would be impossible that there is actually something wrong with them. Instead, this is what I would call the fault of the person claiming to practice the religion.

ABANDONING NEGATIVITY AND ACCUMULATING VIRTUE

Karma is accumulated through body, speech, and mind. As for positive and negative actions, they must be discussed in relation to these three levels. First, there are the ten nonvirtuous actions. There are three negative actions of body:

+ killing
+ stealing
+ sexual misconduct, which includes adultery

There are four negative actions of speech:

+ lying
+ slander
+ harsh speech
+ meaningless talk, which includes gossip

There are three negative actions of mind:

+ covetousness
+ ill will or malice
+ holding mistaken views

But more important than the definitions of these categories is the simple idea that our intentions or motivation in relation to others should always remain positive and altruistic. Through the practice of meditation, we learn to become mindful of our intent at every moment, and thus avoid negative conduct. But even this mindfulness is not the same as true realization. Transcending the root of all negative action is only accomplished by cutting through the ignorance that leads to self-attachment. This can be done through practicing the Union of Dzogchen and Bodhichitta.

In order to accumulate virtue, we practice the Six Paramitas. "Paramita" (from Sanskrit, literally "beyond what is measured") implies "gone to the other shore" when translated from Tibetan. "The shore" refers to the far shore, or the shore that is beyond the ocean of suffering that is samsara.. In English paramita is often rendered as "perfection." The Six Paramitas are briefly explained in this short quote from the great Middle Way scholar Nagarjuna's *Jewel Garland* (*Ratnavali, Rin po che'i phreng ba*):

> Generosity is completely giving your wealth to others,
> Ethical discipline is benefiting others,
> Patience is abandoning anger,
> Heroic effort is continually accumulating virtue,
> Meditative concentration is one-pointed meditation free of
>   mental afflictions,
> Wisdom is the method for realizing ultimate reality.

But before we even take our first step on the path, it is important to think about what we are aiming to accomplish with our practice. Actually, this is important not only for our Dharma practice, but in any endeavor we undertake in our lives. Coming from a land as rural and undeveloped as Tibet, I have personally been quite surprised at the diligence with which people in the West work to acquire material wealth. This is because I come from a culture where we are taught that inner development is more important than material wealth. Tibet is a land with a long history of yogis and Dakinis who set aside all worldly comfort to focus on liberation for themselves and others. Westerners are often quite shocked when they first learn about the hardship yogis are willing to undertake to achieve realization. Though the traditions of excellence and the goals we set for our lives may differ, the determination of the human mind and its power to accomplish marvelous things are prominent in both cultures. The material success of the West shows the strength of the human mind, and this same strength can be applied to the practice of Dharma.

Over the past several years I have had the chance to speak with many students who are just entering the path. They are worried about their lives, their jobs, and their families as related to their spiritual practice. They wonder what will happen to them if they become "Buddhists." I have been asked about certain situations a number of times, most commonly if a prospective student will have to give up their material wealth, or become a monk or a nun after entering the Buddhist path. Of course it is not up to me to answer these questions. Each individual must decide for themselves how they will practice, and how much time and energy they will devote to spiritual practice. There are all kinds of people in the world, and each one of them is living in unique circumstances with unique abilities and talents. Some people, like many of the Lamas I studied with in Tibet, have vowed to stay in retreat their whole lives and devote themselves solely to realizing the nature of reality. I, myself, take the Bodhisattva vow quite seriously. I do not care how many times I will have to take rebirth in samsara; but I am determined that every single being will one day attain liberation from suffering.

It is quite possible to practice the Dharma even if we do not feel able to make this kind of commitment. The important thing is to look ourselves squarely in the eye and be honest about what kind of practice we can commit to in our lives. If we are dishonest in the beginning, we will not be able to sustain our spiritual practice over a long period of time. By starting out gradually, we will probably find that our capacity and willingness to incorporate the Dharma into our lives increases. Buddha Shakyamuni would not have given eighty-four thousand different kinds of Teachings if all human beings were the same in their level of under-standing and aspiration, and if the same type of Teachings appealed to everyone.

No matter what role we decide Buddhism will play in our lives, we must rely on the root teaching of Bodhichitta, or the mind of enlight-enment, when we enter the Buddhist path. It is said in the Teachings that even one with the wisdom of Mañjushri cannot attain enlighten-ment without generating Bodhichitta. The Teachings of Bodhichitta, as well as the Six Paramitas, are what are called the "method" or "skill-ful means" aspect of the path. As far as Vajrayana Buddhism as a whole is concerned, without the method for realization provided by the Teachings of Bodhichitta, it would be impossible to attain realization from the Dzogchen Teachings. In other words, the path of Vajrayana Buddhism is one path that joins method and wisdom indivisibly.

THE FOUR SEALS

As stated in the scriptures, a Buddhist is not defined by his or her outer appearance, or the family, or of birth, but rather by acceptance of what are called "the Four Seals":

1. **All products are impermanent.** ("Product" refers to any kind of compounded phenomenon or thing that arises in dependence on causes and conditions.)

No matter how hard we think about the world around us, there is not one thing that is born, produced, or created that will not abide for some time and then die, disintegrate, or otherwise come to an end. We could try long and hard to find a single person who did not one day have to die. From the moment of our conception, we have been mov-ing day by day towards our death, and all human beings share the uncertainty as to when the moment of death will come.

The same is true for the society, country, and even period in which we live. Although many of us may live in rich and powerful countries that seem like they will stand the test of time, modern day archeology has revealed to us what before we only suspected. Beneath the layers of earth that have built up over time lie the ruins of other civilizations, led by powerful kings and warriors who also seemed invincible. We can see their remains in museums, old paintings, archeological sites, and even on television. It is sometimes eerie to read epics and poems from the past, many of which speak of gaining immortality and enduring throughout the ages. But actually, the only difference between the dreams we have at night and our worldly, human lives is how long they last.

Finally, we can find myriad examples of impermanence in the physical world around us. It does not matter if we analyze a cycle like a period of one year, where one season surely follows another, or a shorter period of time such as a day, where afternoon always follows morning. As far as our world is concerned, the only constancy we can find is its impermanence. Contemplating impermanence is of great importance for developing an understanding and foundation for the Outer, Inner, and Secret Teachings, for it is the intellectual basis for the realization of emptiness.

2. **All afflicted phenomena cause suffering**. ("Afflicted phenomena" refers to the individual's sense faculties, consciousnesses, and a perceived object that come together and result in the generation of a mental affliction.)

Just as the nature of fire is heat, so the nature of mental afflictions is suffering. According to the Buddhist Teachings, there are said to be eighty-four thousand different mental afflictions, classified from gross to extremely subtle. Among the grossest of all eighty-four thousand kinds of mental afflictions are the five worst ones of attachment, anger, jealousy, pride, and ignorance. If those five had to be reduced to the three worst ones, attachment, anger, and ignorance would remain. Finally, if those were reduced to the singlemost crucial affliction to overcome, that would be ignorance, which is responsible for giving rise to all the others. Therefore, it is ignorance that is the root of all suffering. It is this ignorance that yields the perception of self and other, and in fact, the perception of all kinds of duality.

Although it is possible to explore the nature of each of these mental afflictions individually, for the purposes of this text I will examine only one. I think that perhaps the most vivid example of this idea in the modern world is what is popularly referred to as true love, which is celebrated in Western culture as the pinnacle of all emotions. Love is traditionally described in songs and poetry as the meaning of life, the happy ending to be found in a world full of disappointment. The great poet William Shakespeare spoke of the ideal of love in his famous "Sonnet 116," in which he says that "love is not love" if it cannot endure hardship, and that love endures not for just "brief hours and weeks, but bears it out even to the edges of doom." It is such a beautiful idea; no wonder we still continue to read and celebrate this poem today.

But despite this idea of love as something that is everlasting and permanent, we know from experience that this is not the case. Ordinary beings cannot separate love from attachment, for this is what characterizes humanness. Love, not as the ideal, but as the expression of attachment, always holds the promise of suffering within it. For example, some loves go unrequited and cause the lovers a lifetime of sorrow. Lovers become filled with jealousy and rage through betrayal and misunderstanding. Some lovers disagree with their families about their choice of partners and eventually become estranged from their lover or their kin. Often when relationships end, people harbor bitter resentments that last a lifetime. Finally, although most people believe that their marriage or relationship will last forever, even the most devoted partners have no choice but to separate at the time of death.

An alternative reading of "Sonnet 116" is that authentic love is the kind of loving-kindness we say a Bodhisattva generates towards all sentient beings. Despite having to face pain, suffering, and hardship, a Bodhisattva does not change their wish to benefit others. And even if they must go to the "edges of doom," they are willing to endure it so long as they can continue to benefit beings.

3. **All phenomena are empty and selfless**.

Because we have already accepted that all produced or composite things are impermanent, we can take this logic one step further and say that all phenomena are empty of existing in and of themselves without depending for their existence upon causes and conditions. This is what we mean when we say things are "selfless." There are two kinds of selflessness: the selflessness of the individual and the selflessness of phenomena. This could also be phrased as the lack of inherent existence of the person and the lack of inherent existence of all things. In Buddhism, for example, the individual is understood to be made up of five "aggregates," of which one is physical and four are related to mind: 1) form, that is, the body, 2) sensation, 3) perception, 4) conditioning factors, and 5) consciousness. First, to understand the selflessness of the individual, we should make an examination of ourselves. As we investigate the body and mind, we should try to find an abiding self. For example, we might first assume that the self abides in the body. Upon examining the body, we find that it is made up of innumerable smaller parts like flesh, blood, bones, skin, ligaments, and tendons. We would not say that any one of them was the self. On the other hand, if one of them were the self, it would logically be possible for an individual to have thousands of selves. And, if the body or any part of the body actually was the self, the consciousness would die along with the body. All of these results pose problems for the existence of an actual, abiding self.

Through this investigation, it is easy to see that the body is not in fact the self. Rather, we apprehend a self based on the collection of parts that form the body. The root of this apprehension is ignorance, and the result is the suffering of self-attachment experienced by sentient beings in their everyday lives.

In the same way we examined the nature of the body, we can examine the nature of phenomena. We have already established that all composite things are impermanent, but like our apprehension of the self, what makes those things appear to be fixed or unchanging is our ignorance of their true nature. By thoroughly contemplating impermanence through careful observation, we can logically realize that all phenomena are empty and impermanent. However, it is only through the practice of meditation, especially on the Secret Teachings, that this understanding becomes a reality.

4. **Nirvana is peace.**

Nirvana is the state free from suffering, which is what Buddhism defines as peace. It is not outer or worldly peace, but peace within the mind. Indeed, one with true peace of mind is able to work with any situation, which is why the Buddhas are extremely resourceful at alleviating the suffering of ordinary beings. However, I do sometimes meet students who want to practice Buddhist meditation but do not actually believe that the state of nirvana exists. It is possible to begin the practice of Buddhism with such doubts. But it is crucial for one who practices Buddhism to contemplate this idea extensively and come to understand that a state free from suffering can actually be attained, or they will find that they are unable to sustain their practice in the long run.

THE HISTORY OF THE BUDDHIST TEACHINGS

The activity of the Buddhas is said to be inconceivable. That is why when we examine a Buddha or a great master of meditation, it is difficult to comprehend exactly why they have chosen to give certain Teachings or manifest a certain appearance at a given time. Another way of saying this is that the enlightened ones respond to the confusion of the beings they meet, and express the wisdom of the Teachings in innumerable ways. Moreover, it is normal for different people to glean different meanings or have different understandings of the world around them, based on their own aptitude and personality. This accounts for the fact that there are many different types of Buddhism, and most sects do not even agree exactly on what Teachings Buddha Shakyamuni gave. This is true even in terms of how Buddhists interpret the life of Buddha Shakyamuni, which is described differently by each Buddhist tradition.

However, there are twelve events that occurred in the life of Shakya-muni that all sects of Buddhism do agree upon. The history that follows is this universally accepted version of the life of Buddha Shakyamuni.

In one of Buddha Shakyamuni's past lives, he was a student of Kashyapa Buddha, the third Buddha of this kalpa. During that lifetime, he took full monastic vows and received from his teacher instructions on the methods for attaining liberation. The realization that resulted from his practice caused him to take birth in Tushita heaven as a Bodhisattva named Dampa Dokkarpo. In that lifetime, Dampa Dokkarpo reached the state where he would only have to take birth in samsara one more time before he reached enlightenment. He chose the circumstances of his next life carefully, deciding to take birth as Shakyamuni, the son of a king, who lived in a central land and had an unusual aptitude for meditation (1). When Mayadevi, the woman who would be Shakyamuni's mother, was practicing meditation on an auspicious day, he entered her body through an opening beneath her right arm (2). He took birth from the same opening without causing her even the slightest pain or discomfort (3). As a young boy, Shakyamuni mastered his studies easily, as well as the worldly arts and sports. He was said to be uncommonly skilled at both, and was second to none during the course of his worldly life (4). After finishing his studies, Shakyamuni married a woman named Yasodhara and was crowned the king of the land. From that day until he was twenty-nine years old, he lived a life of luxury and ruled as the king (5).

One day Shakyamuni went out beyond the palace grounds and saw one example of suffering at each gate as he rode around the four sides of his estate. Riding past the first gate, he saw a child being born, and thus realized the suffering of birth. Riding past the second gate, he saw a gathering of elderly people, and thus realized the suffering of old age. Riding past the third gate, he saw sick people lying in the street, and thus realized the suffering of sickness. Riding past the fourth gate, he saw someone dying and realized the suffering of death.

Based on his realization of these four kinds of suffering, Shakya-

muni knew with certainty that he would never be free from the suffering of samsara despite his wealth and high status. So he decided to
renounce his worldly life and become a monk (6).

Shakyamuni sought out instructions from the Brahmanical teachers of his day, traveling to different places, and taking up intensive
meditation and practicing austerities for six years. He became dirty and
disheveled, and after a while he was as thin as an ordinary beggar (7).
One day, a woman offered him milk taken from a thousand cows and
mixed with honey. After he drank it, he became strong again and his
skin was said to gleam like gold (8). After Shakyamuni regained his
health, he traveled to Bodhgaya in central India. On the way, he
stopped and begged a merchant for a grass mat, which the merchant
gave to him. Shakyamuni took the mat with him and when he reached
Bodhgaya, he set it at the base of a Bodhi tree. Then, he vowed not to
arise from his meditation until he reached enlightenment, even if he
died in the process.

But before Shakyamuni reached enlightenment, he was tested by the
four maras, or temptations, who tried to seduce him into generating
attachment for his worldly life and to cause him to take rebirth again
in samsara. But Shakyamuni's resolve was unaffected by the myriad
appearances they created before him. As a sign of his developing wisdom, a coiled hair had grown on his forehead between his eyes. Light
emanated from this coiled hair and he defeated the maras (9). Following this, Shakyamuni completed the purification of his cognitive obscurations and attained perfect enlightenment (10). At first, he thought
that no one would want to follow the path he had discovered, since it
was difficult to understand and to practice. He went alone into the
forest, where he meditated until Brahma and a retinue of gods
approached him and begged him to teach the Dharma. Heeding their
request, Buddha Shakyamuni began to teach the Dharma (11). Finally,
Buddha Shakyamuni passed away at the age of eighty-one and entered
parinirvana (12).

The history of the Buddhist Teachings can also be told from the
Outer, Inner, and Secret perspectives. However, it does not matter

from what perspective they are examined; all three exist in union and are separate only in their explanation.

From the Outer perspective, Buddha Shakyamuni was born as an ordinary individual who underwent the hardships and sufferings of human life to lead others to liberation. Through his extraordinary aptitude for meditation and his strong determination, he attained enlightenment and began to teach others to practice the Dharma. From the Inner perspective, Shakyamuni was a Bodhisattva who was not compelled to take birth in the desire realm, but did so because of his deep wish to relieve the suffering of sentient beings. From this perspective, he had the appearance of an ordinary being although his mind was one with the Bodhisattvas. From the Secret perspective, Shakyamuni was an expression of the primordial wisdom of Samantabhadra, who emanated as a human to benefit ordinary beings by giving the three kinds of Teachings to beings according to their faith and capacity for practice.

✦ CHAPTER 2
✦
✦ *Relying upon a Spiritual Friend*

MANY WESTERN BUDDHISTS have the perception that relying on a qualified Lama, that is, a Spiritual Friend, puts them in a situation of having to relinquish their free will and all control over their lives and having to do what someone tells them merely for the sake of doing it. I think this may be because there is no traditional kind of relationship in Western culture that is similar to the kind of relationship shared between a Lama and student of, in particular, Vajrayana Buddhism. Needless to say, this tends to breed grave misunderstandings. First of all, I think it is important to understand the feeling that most students of Buddhism traditionally have towards their Teachers. Rather than feelings of blind and unquestioning faith, or nagging suspicion about their Teacher's motives, the feeling of the true student toward the true Lama is a feeling of deep love and respect, and a trust that goes beyond that of normal familial or friendly relationships. For lack of a better way to explain what I mean, I will use my relationship with my own Lama as an example.

I remember the first time I ever heard anyone speak about my root or main Lama. It happened when I was just five years old. At that time in Tibet, we did not speak freely about religion, and did not even utter aloud the religious title "Rinpoche." So the day when I first heard my parents and Lama Chupur, the Dzogchen Lama who had raised me since birth, talking about my Teacher, I was not yet aware that he was even a Lama at all. They spoke about him simply as "Menpa Chudrak." Chudrak is my teacher's name when spoken in Tibetan. "Menpa" means doctor, for my Lama is a renowned healer, having healed himself from cancer in his younger years as well as having been healed twice by dreams and visions when he was deathly ill on other occasions. But even more amazing than that is the fact that my Lama never studied medicine at all. His ability as a healer arose directly from his practice of the Medicine Buddha, and the clear wisdom of his mind.

To be honest, at that early age I did not even know the meaning of the word "menpa" and I had never heard of a Lama named Chudrak. But just the same, when I heard his name uttered, I fell speechless and was filled with a feeling so deep I cannot even begin to put it into words. My body began to shiver, and tears made their way down my cheeks. I knew that I had to meet this man, whoever he was. Lama Chupur immediately noticed my unusual reaction, and made sure that I would meet Tsara Dharmakirti Rinpoche as soon as possible.

After I turned seven, my parents took me to meet my "Menpa Chudrak" for the first time. From the first moment I saw him, there was nothing anyone could do to convince me that he was an ordinary human being; everything about him was special and extraordinary. Because of the situation in Tibet at that time, my teacher was living in a one-room wooden shack and tending sheep in a meadow just like an average Tibetan, but I knew different. I was able to stay with him for one month before I was forced to return to my village with my parents. I had only known my Lama for a few weeks, but I can honestly say that it was harder for me to part from him than it would have been to leave my own parents.

For several years while I attended school, I was not able to see my Lama again. But he was with me in my mind's eye no matter where I went. If I tripped and fell down or even got a tiny splinter, his name would come to my lips as I prayed for him to watch over me. Then one day, after the situation in Tibet had become more relaxed, my Lama came to give Teachings at the monastery in my village. I wept as soon as I heard his voice, and when he had finished giving Teachings, he asked that I be sent back with him. So it was then that I finally went to live with my Lama.

Once I got to my Lama's homeland, he had the difficult job of teaching me the proper conduct of a young Lama and scholar. Because he considered me one of his very few close students, he was extremely hard on me. I could actually say that he was harder on me than he was on most of his other students. Because of his kind heart and deep wish for my spiritual progress, he wanted me to be perfect. Keep in mind that the appearances and manner of giving instructions by Tantric Lamas can be very different from those of an ordinary person. They will go to any length to show us how to abandon our mental afflictions and dualistic perceptions. Although the motivation behind this is extremely compassionate, kind, and unselfish, it can be extremely difficult to bear; at times it is painful, and at others quite embarrassing.

I could have come to the conclusion that my Lama was acting in a way that came from his own ego rather than being for my benefit. But because of the relationship I had with him, it was easy for me to see that he was always acting on my behalf. He used each and every situation, each and every moment, to push me towards realization. Thus, I can honestly say that there was not a single moment when my teacher was acting out of a desire to control or otherwise manipulate me. He was teaching me to subdue myself, and this is the essential lesson for any yogi. Without the training and the deep faith that I developed in him, I would never have been able to receive the secret oral instructions of our lineage, and learn the method for realizing the nature of mind. When I reflect on my life, it is so easy to see now that everything I have become I owe to him.

The kind of faith and devotion I feel for my Teacher may seem unusual to people in the West, who have never experienced this kind of relationship. But it is not at all unusual in my homeland, where the Teachings and the blessings of the lineage have been passed on for more than a thousand years. In fact, this kind of relationship is extremely important throughout the entire path, especially when we begin the practices of Tantra. I could go so far as to say that without this type of relationship with a qualified Lama, realization of the Dzogchen Teachings would be impossible.

In thinking about reliance on teachers, we can realize that it is not only in our spiritual lives that we need to rely upon teachers. In our everyday lives there are many things we have to do in order to survive, and all of these skills are taught to us. The traditional arts like woodworking, ceramics, and calligraphy are also learned from teachers. And how many people would understand the intricacies of science or technology without a teacher of some kind?

Of course, there are all kinds of teachers. Some teachers are extremely skilled in what they teach, and others are not. Some really know how to reach their students, and others do not. Many students listen to their teachers carefully and study according to what their teachers tell them. But it is the rare student who rejects all of their teacher's experience and advice and still manages to master a difficult course of study.

Coming from traditional Tibet, you can imagine my surprise when I began to meet and talk with Western students who believed it was possible to master the art of meditation and realize the nature of mind simply by reading books. I do not mean to say that study and examination are not helpful and important, but spiritual practice that is based solely on this cannot lead to perfect realization. I sometimes tell these students that I am so sure this is not possible that I would cut off my own head if someone were able to do it. This may sound like an extreme assertion, but I assure you I would not make it if I was not absolutely sure it was true. If it were possible to master even worldly knowledge from books, then why would the tradition of education and schooling have been invented at all?

Another surprising attitude I have encountered in the West is that of people who began to study Buddhism with a Teacher, and then somehow felt that they had graduated from the program and no longer needed one. This is naturally the case in certain contexts in the West, where students complete a program of study, are given a Bachelor's or a Ph.D., and then go on to guide themselves through a career. But in some ways, the need for a Teacher as one progresses along the Buddhist path is even greater toward the end than in the beginning. And with all the possibilities for making a wrong turn, especially when attempting to practice Dzogchen—in which we must master the view of Trekchod and the practice of Todgyal, proceeding without a Teacher is not something I consider to be a possibility at all.

SCRIPTURE, LOGIC, AND EXAMPLE

Traditionally, Buddhists establish the need to study and practice under the guidance of a qualified Lama from the point of view of scripture, logic, and example. First, from the point of view of scripture, the Dzogchen master Jigme Lingpa said,

> In order to attain all of the perfect qualities,
> You should rely upon the ones of the highest birth.
> Just like a sandalwood tree in the forest
> With its dampness, branches, and leaves
> Imbues ordinary trees with the scent of sandalwood,
> You will become like whatever you rely upon.

We do not even have to think in terms of a Spiritual Teacher to see the truth of this verse. We respond to the conditions of the world around us, and become like our surroundings. In the spirit of this idea, it is said in the *Collections of Sutra (mDo btus)*,

> An excellent student who possesses devotion
> Should always rely upon a skilled Spiritual Teacher
> Because the Teacher's good qualities will arise in him.

And, with his uncommonly skillful use of contemporary language, Chögyam Trungpa Rinpoche once expressed this same idea when he said that the wisdom of Vajrayana Buddhism was "contagious." That is, we have to catch it from someone who has it.

Second, the logic behind following a qualified Lama is expressed by this traditional argument:

> Regarding an individual who wishes to attain enlightenment,
> Because he does not know how to gather
> The accumulations and purify the obscurations,
> Such a one should rely upon a Spiritual Friend;
> Take the Buddhas of the past as an example.

The meaning of this passage is, of course, that there has never been a Buddha who attained enlightenment without relying upon a qualified Lama or Spiritual Friend.

Third, the necessity to practice under the guidance of a qualified Lama can be explained metaphorically. The Spiritual Friend can be likened to a guide who leads us to the far shore of the ocean of samsara. If we were going on safari in the jungle, we would never attempt it on our own. The jungle is full of wild animals and all manner of unknown situations. Not only would it be dangerous, but we might also never arrive at our destination. We would want to take a guide with us, someone who spoke the language, knew the terrain, and would be able to warn us of and help us cope with the dangers. The same can be said for the jungle of the samsaric mind, and the Spiritual Friend, who has the experience from their own practice and realization, as well as having been guided along the path themselves. If we want to know the shortest or easiest way to go, it is better to ask the advice of one who has gone before us.

Traditionally, the Spiritual Friend is also likened to the captain of a ship, who makes sure the boat arrives at its proper destination. Taking this metaphor a little further, I would say that this is true when working with the Outer and Inner Teachings, where the boat is moving slowly and steadily towards its destination with no real threat to its safety. Even if the wind picks up or there is a storm, it is still going to get there eventually.

But when we begin to practice the Vajrayana, or Tantric, Teachings, and especially Dzogchen, instead of going by boat it's like taking a jet, or perhaps a better image is the space shuttle, which will get us there fast for sure. But if we do not take up a holistic view of the path, and fail to entrust ourselves to the careful guidance of a qualified Spiritual Friend, we will very likely crash. There have been many such stories told in my country. Such a crash would not be the gentle bump of a leisurely boat, but would be a devastating crash that demolished everything.

THE GOOD QUALITIES OF A SPIRITUAL FRIEND

Of course, choosing a Spiritual Friend can be quite an ordeal if we are not sure how to go about it. But let me give anyone who is currently searching for a Teacher just one warning. As easy as it is to follow a good Teacher and gain his or her good qualities, it is just as easy to follow a teacher without the proper training or qualifications and acquire negativity. In other words, we had better know well whom it is we are following. The qualities necessary in a qualifed Lama are summarized in this verse from the great master Shantideva's text *Embarking on Bodhisattva Activities (Bodhisattvacharyavatara, Byang chub sems dpa'i spyod pa la 'jug pa)*, available in various English translations such as that entitled *Guide to the Bodhisattva's Way of Life*:

> The Spiritual Friend is always
> Skilled at the meaning of Sutra and Tantra
> And has the supreme conduct of a Bodhisattva.
> [His or her instructions] are more important than life itself.

Concerning a Spiritual Friend who does not have these qualities, the master Jigme Lingpa said,

> In particular, following one without the excellent qualities,
> Whose mind is devoid of Bodhichitta, and who aspires to
>   worldly fame
> Is a grave mistake, like following a blind leader.

I have noticed a tendency in the West to skip over this very important part of the path, perhaps because many of the Western Buddhists

I meet are puzzled by the idea of how to examine a teacher to determine whether they are qualified to lead us on the path. I think this may relate to something I noticed when I first came to the West from Tibet. In general, the people I have met in the West tend to trust easily, and form relationships much more quickly than is done in Tibet. Actually, it is the Tibetan way to carefully examine first, and only then to give another, and in this case a Teacher, one's trust. As much as is possible, I would encourage students who want to take up the path, and especially those with their eye on learning the practices of Tantra, to learn the ways of examining a Spiritual Friend.

Although the scriptures go into great detail on the subject of what to look for in a Spiritual Friend, I will try to simplify them as much as possible so they are easy to understand and can be put into practice immediately. Speaking strictly from the perspective of defining a Spiritual Friend, traditionally we say that a qualified Lama is one who has had vast experience and training in the three areas of 1) listening, 2) contemplating, 3) and meditating. As for "listening," he or she has received and studied many Teachings and has gained wisdom and intelligence from extensive reflection upon Teachings heard and read in scripture or related texts. Thus, the qualified Lama has gained the additional quality of being able to answer questions about the way to practice the Dharma so that if a student has questions or doubts, the Teacher knows exactly how to answer or put those doubts to rest. Through meditation, the Spiritual Friend has exerted great effort to eliminate mental afflictions and self-attachment, while at the same time cultivating universal love and compassion. Finally, such an individual has become established and skillful in the meditation on the perfect, uncontrived view and is progressing on the path towards enlightenment.

From the perspective of the Vajrayana Teachings, a Spiritual Friend belongs to an unbroken lineage of empowerments, transmissions, and oral instructions that originated with Buddha Vajradhara and continues to the present day. Furthermore, a qualified Teacher has kept pure his or her Tantric Samaya, or spiritual commitment. He or she has received empowerments, transmissions, and oral instructions within a

lineage in which no break or interruption has occurred from generation to generation. Such a Teacher is skilled in the meaning of Sutra,
and especially in the profound Teachings of Tantra, and takes a holistic view of the path. Like the great Lamas I described in the opening
section, a qualified Teacher vividly embodies, by presence and example, the Union of Dzogchen and Bodhichitta.

After receiving such an explanation, simplified though it may be,
students still sometimes ask me how it is possible to know for sure if
a Lama has these qualities or not. The answer to this question is actually quite simple. In general, we say there are two signs that show the
presence of these qualities. A subdued mind shows that the mental
afflictions and self-attachment have been diminished or eradicated.
Deep humility and pure perception are signs that the Spiritual Friend's
meditation is established and profound.

If a Lama does not have these qualities, we should simply not cultivate a Lama-disciple relationship with them and carry on respectfully.
The master Sakya Pandita said,

> One who is a Lama,
> But does not practice according to the Dharma,
> Should be viewed with equanimity.

We should not scorn, disrespect, bad-mouth, or otherwise generate
any negativity towards such a teacher, since doing any of these will
only harm us in the end. Instead, we should continue in our search to
find a Spiritual Friend who suits us, and work on developing faith and
pure perception.

The Outer, Inner, and Secret Spiritual Friend

In the scriptures there are said to be six kinds of Spiritual Friends, but
these six can be condensed into just three: the outer, inner, and secret
Spiritual Friend. An outer Spiritual Friend is a teacher who is well-
known throughout the world, who has given Buddhist Teachings

widely and instructions on how to take up the path. The easiest example of this type of Spiritual Friend would be Buddha Shakyamuni, who gave extensive Teachings on the path after he reached enlightenment. The inner Spiritual Friend is any teacher who has created good conditions for our practice. Such a teacher might have given us an empowerment, taught us the meaning of a scripture, taught us to read and write, or given us a teaching about how to put the path into practice.

Based on the causes and conditions created by the outer and inner Spiritual Friends, it becomes possible to rely upon a secret Spiritual Friend. The secret Spiritual Friend is the one we sometimes call the "root" Lama or "uncommon" Spiritual Friend. This type of Spiritual Friend is said to be endowed with the three kindnesses because he gives us 1) the empowerments, 2) Teachings on Sutra and Tantra, and 3) the secret oral instructions.

If we spend a long period relying upon one Spiritual Friend with whom we have a very deep relationship, it is also possible that this one teacher becomes the outer, inner, and secret Spiritual Friend all at once. This is based on their granting of the Outer and Inner Teachings to us, their instructions and efforts to help us perfect our conduct, their tireless attention to our studies, and finally, once we have built the proper foundation, the granting of the three kindnesses.

Not only is it important for a student to examine the Spiritual Friend before taking up the practices along the path, it is also equally important for the Spiritual Friend to examine the student in order to assess their habits and potential as a practitioner. Tantric Lamas are extremely attuned to the minds of students and, some even say, are able to see through them, so to speak, with only one look. As it is said in the *Sutra of the Ten Dharmas (Dashadharmakasutra, Chos bcu pa)*:

> Whether or not one is endowed with the
> Virtue, wisdom, and tendencies of a Bodhisattva
> Can be seen by examining the signs,
> Just as smoke signifies fire
> And a water bird points to a lake.

The "virtue, wisdom, and tendencies of a Bodhisattva" include qualities like compassion, faith, diligence, logic, and intelligence. Based on
the student's behavior and the appearance of these qualities, it is easy
for a Lama to decide how to work with a particular student and to what
extent they will allow the relationship to develop.

However, if we wish to meditate on the Secret Teachings, there are
several additional qualities a Spiritual Friend will look for. From *Vajrasattva's Phantasmagorical Net Tantra (rDo rje sems dpa'i sgyu 'phrul dra ba)*:

> [One who makes] offerings to the Teacher,
> [Who is possessed of] diligence and clear discriminating
>   intelligence,
> [Who] keeps the Tantric Samayas,
> [Who] understands the practices of mantra and mudra,
> And [who] possesses all the articles necessary [for Tantric
>   practice].

"Offerings to the Teacher" can be described in terms of the outer,
inner, and secret types of offerings, although I should probably add
that the very best offering consists of all three. Outer offerings are
those of service and material wealth, so that the Spiritual Friend can do
the work that he or she is trained to do which is beneficial to the local
and global community, as well as maintain a lifestyle that is focused
completely on the Dharma. Inner offerings are those of faith, devotion, and diligence in practicing the Teachings that have been given.
Finally, the secret offering is to abide in the perfect, uncontrived view
in accordance with the oral instructions.

Next, we need "diligence and clear discriminating intelligence" in
order to understand the Spiritual Friend's instructions properly and
then put them into practice. Third, we need to have the correct understanding of the Tantric Samayas, or commitments, and how we are to
keep them. It is said in the scriptures that an individual who keeps pure
Samaya does not need to worry about their ability to realize the Teachings; the power of their Samaya will act to spark their realization.

Finally, we need to receive and properly understand the oral instructions, and then to obtain the ritual articles required to put them into practice.

It is said in the Tantric Teachings that it is rare to meet a student such as the one described in this passage above. However, I believe that by the powerful nature of dependent arising, anyone who has true faith and a genuine wish to put the Teachings into practice will always find the proper Spiritual Friend who will help them out of extraordinary compassion. Once we have established a relationship with our Spiritual Friend, it is up to us how hard we work to realize the Teachings we are given. If we really want to gain realization from the Teachings, we have to make sure that we are not just a facsimile of a Dharma practitioner. The Dharma is not about making ourselves look like we are something we are not. Rather, the Teachings, our meditation, and the Spiritual Friend must be able to reach us and fundamentally cause us to change our minds for the better.

DEVELOPING FAITH

The refuge vow is often said to be like the gate to attaining the wisdom of the Buddhist Teachings. But true refuge can only be taken through the development of faith. It is said in the Sutras,

> A person without faith
> Cannot attain a virtuous result,
> Just as a seed that has been scorched
> Cannot yield a green sprout.

And the master Jigme Lingpa said that "faith is the root of all Dharma."

I am sure that at least a few people are thinking to themselves that they do not like the idea of faith, or do not know exactly what faith is. Like Tibet, the West has its own long religious history, and thus the words "religion" and "faith" also have all kinds of connotations. For example, I once spoke to a woman who said to me that faith was something belonging to those who do not have the ability to think logically or critically about themselves or the world around them. Another man referred to faith as a "crutch." In addition, the scientific worldview, which has until recent advances in quantum physics tended to minimize the exploration and role of mind, has also added some complications to the matter, since many people these days seem to believe that science and faith are at irreconcilable odds. So I would like to recontextualize the word "faith" so we can develop it and apply it in our practice.

First of all, when talking about faith, we should distinguish between two main types. The first is a natural kind of faith, which arises as a result of the culture we are born into. For example, Tibetans, who are raised with faith in the Buddhist Teachings, do not have to make any particular effort to accept these Teachings as being the path towards enlightenment. However, if we are not born into the culture of the religion we wish to practice, we must gradually cultivate a type of faith that is closer to the meaning of the words "trust," "belief," or "conviction," which develops through a thorough personal examination of the Teachings. We should accept a teaching when it seems real and true to us, having stood the test of our scrutiny, and not before. On the other hand, once we have examined a teaching and found it to be satisfactory, we should try to incorporate the teaching into our everyday lives rather than just set it back on the shelf as something we accept but do not or cannot apply. The coldness of cynicism can be a terrible obstacle to the cultivation of faith.

Actually, examination is a theme that comes up over and over again in Buddhism. Rather than the idea found in many religions of separating faith from intellect, in Buddhism it is essential to combine these and allow each to act as a good condition to further develop the other. So, within the context of Buddhist practice, we should always understand the word "faith" to require the application of logic, intellectual inquiry, and reason. In fact, without the use of the intellect, it would be quite impossible to comprehend how to correctly put the path into practice at all.

The prominence of science and scientific advancement in the modern day has been equally divisive, causing many people to feel they must choose between a scientific worldview and a religious or spiritual one. I sometimes ask people what differences they perceive between science and religion. Some people answer that science is logical, impartial, objective or factual, and based on what can be observed. However, Buddhism also has these same qualities. As far as the Middle Way, or Madhyamaka, view is concerned, it is established by perfect logic and acts as the foundation for the uncontrived view. Furthermore, meditation itself is the very art of impartiality, which observes only what is there, using it to further the realization of the nature of mind.

But some still might not be satisfied with this answer. To them I pose only one question. All of the hypotheses formed as part of the scientific method that await proof or disproof—do they not require an initial assumption, and in a sense a sort of faith, before they can be further investigated? The very premise that something might be proved to be true following examination, analysis, and experience is exactly the same paradigm we are using when we begin to practice meditation. Just as scientific data are collected, in meditation we gain experience and confidence through careful observation of the mind, and thus begin to develop actual faith in the process we have engaged in. Because science as we currently know it can only study those things that can be observed with the five senses and not the mind itself, no scientific discovery will be able to match what yogis realize through the art of meditation. No scientific discovery can lead us to liberation from samsara, or free us from its recycled problems and suffering. This realization can only occur in the realm of mind. So although science and Buddhism can be seen as parallel fields in many ways, science is actually limited, while spiritual realization is limitless, since it addresses mind and not just matter.

Sadly, faith seems to be something that is lost on people who do not feel it. Someone who has never experienced faith, either naturally or through examination, might feel that faith does not exist, or is just a figment of the imagination whose purpose is to give reassurance or consolation. Many people believe that spiritual or religious faith is exclusively blind faith, but according to the Teachings, an individual lacking the type of faith that works in conjunction with reasoning is the one considered to be blind.

Faith is defined in many ways in the Teachings, but it can generally be described as a continuum along which one gains more and more certainty. The first stage in the development of faith is called "pure faith." This is a kind of faith that is hard to put into words, that is more visceral than anything else. It occurs, for example, when we visit a sacred place, see a holy person or such a person's photograph, hear a Teaching that uniquely touches our heart, or meet our Spiritual Friend for the first time. We have a feeling inside of us that something has touched us deeply—that we are somehow moved, though we may not be not sure what has come over us. Some people like to refer to this type of faith as a "spiritual awakening."

Next, based on the experience of pure faith, we begin to examine the meaning of the Buddhist Teachings and the nature of the world within and around us. Slowly, we begin to recognize the Truth of Suffering and the Truth of the Cause of Suffering and develop a "longing faith" in which we want very much to be liberated from this difficult life of suffering in samsara. As the word "longing" suggests, this type of faith grows stronger and stronger over time. Third, based on our wish to be free of the suffering of samsara, we begin to feel "convinced faith"—a deep certainty about the Truth of the Cessation of Suffering and the Truth of the Path to Cessation. In other words, we begin to trust that there is a method for being liberated from samsara, and also a state that is free from suffering. Finally, based on the development of convinced faith, we come to have "irreversible faith," the kind of faith that we would stake our life upon. No matter what situation we are facing, we would rather die than renounce the Dharma, for we know it is the only way we can find true peace.

There is a famous story told about irreversible faith. The story goes that a yogi was told by invaders to his village that he must give up his faith in the Dharma or die. The man thought for a moment, and then calmly replied that his faith had arisen as a result of his examination and practice. Therefore, while it would be possible for him to renounce his faith in words, he could not do so within his mind. What a wonderful example he gave us to aspire to!

In order to develop irreversible faith, it is said that four conditions are necessary. First, we need to rely upon a Spiritual Friend. Second, we need people who are also working towards the goal of liberation who can be our companions on the path. Third, we need a proper understanding of the good qualities of the Three Jewels. Fourth, we need a clear understanding that suffering or perpetual dissatisfaction is samsara's nature, and a clear wish to be freed from that condition. Furthermore, for those of us who wish to practice the Dzogchen Teachings, faith is especially important. Faith is the basis for pure perception, which is one of the main roots of realization.

OUTER, INNER, AND SECRET REFUGE

When we take the refuge vow, we are allying ourselves with the Three Jewels, and adding the quality of confidence to our faith. But in order to make this vow deeply and from the heart, we must understand what it is that we are taking refuge in. In other words, what are the good qualities we are allying ourselves with when we take the refuge vow? In Tibetan, the objects of refuge are said to be the "rare and supreme"— Buddha, Dharma, and Sangha.

First, let's move to a concise explanation of the good qualities of the Buddha. The sage Jigme Lingpa said that the good qualities of the Buddha were "beyond description." However, they can generally be classified as of two types: the quality of abandonment of afflictions and the quality of realization of all positive dharmas. When Buddha Shakyamuni took up the path, he generated Bodhichitta and then gathered the two accumulations of merit and wisdom. As a result, he was able to perfectly abandon the two categories of obscurations and to realize the nature of reality. The first of the two categories is the mental affliction obscurations. By abandoning the totality of the mental afflictions, Buddha Shakyamuni was able to eradicate the cause for taking rebirth in samsara. However, it is not possible to reach full enlightenment through abandoning the mental afflictions alone. It is also necessary to abandon the cognitive obscurations, the second category. A simple way to understand the cognitive obscurations is that they are what cause us to have the perception of the three spheres (agent or doer, object, and recipient of the action), in other words, a dualistic view of subject and object.

Next, the quality of the Buddhas' realization can be seen from two different points of view. First, it can be seen from the point of view of "ultimate wisdom," or having realized the nature of mind and remaining in the uncontrived natural state, which is free from all impurities. Second, it can be seen from the point of view of "conventional wisdom," or having a penetrating and complete understanding of the nature of all phenomena.

There are also said to be eight good qualities of the Dharma, but these eight can be summarized as the two truths: the Truth of the Path and the Truth of Cessation. The Truth of the Path is the method by which the Buddhas are able to abandon the two types of obscurations and gain realization. It includes the practices of generating Bodhichitta, gathering the two accumulations, and taking up the Six Paramitas. The resulting state of perfect liberation is what is referred to by the Truth of Cessation.

Finally, there are eight good qualities of the Sangha, which can be summarized as the two qualities of awareness and liberation. Generally, we say that Sangha members create good conditions for us to gain realization on the path. The quality of awareness refers to their awareness of the nature of mind. More specifically, it is their recognition of the nature of mind as ultimate Bodhichitta. Next, based on their recognition of the nature of mind, they are able to completely self-liberate mental afflictions and the cognitive obscurations.

According to the Teachings, it is actually the Sangha of the Arya Bodhisattvas that fully embodies these good qualities. The Arya Bodhisattvas have attained a stage of realization called the "first Bhumi," or "level," which is the first of ten stages of progressive realization on the

Mahayana path. An Arya in the Mahayana context is an individual who, having generated Mahayana Bodhichitta, has a direct realization of emptiness and therefore has achieved the Path of Seeing. This level is also marked by the abandonment of all but the most subtle mental afflictions. Ordinary beings cannot be said to fully embody these qualities since they are limited by mental afflictions and have not yet realized emptiness directly. However, because ordinary beings cannot see Bodhisattvas on the first Bhumi, we also recognize the followers of Buddha Shakyamuni's Teachings as the Sangha, no matter what stage of realization they have reached. More specifically, we recognize practitioners of the Mahayana, who begin with the aspiration of Bodhichitta and take up the path of the Six Paramitas with the goal of liberation for all beings, as the Sangha.

This has just been a very brief introduction to the good qualities of the Three Jewels, so that we can begin to form a general idea of what is meant by the objects of refuge, and see why they are worthy of our trust. Though this may seem elementary, having a proper understanding of the Three Jewels is of great importance both for practitioners who are just taking up the path and for those who are experienced and established in their practice. This is because taking refuge in the Three Jewels is like the switch that controls the flow of energy into our spiritual practice.

The Teachings say that there are three kinds of motivation we could have when taking the refuge vow, according to our capacity. First is the lowest or most ordinary kind of aspiration, which is that of taking refuge out of a wish to attain happiness in this life. Taking refuge is in this case seen as a way to avoid the sufferings of human life, and to avoid taking birth in the lower realms. Second is the aspiration developed by beings that have realized the sufferings of samsara and wish to attain liberation for themselves from cyclic existence. They take refuge to deliver themselves from the ocean of suffering, without any motivation to liberate others who remain in samsara. Finally, the aspiration developed by beings of the highest capacity is the wish to attain complete Buddhahood, not just freedom from samsara, in order to be able to free all beings suffering in samsara.

Once we have cultivated the motivation that is suitable to our own personality and goals for practice, we should take the vows of outer, inner, and secret refuge. However, we should note that each of these styles of refuge has their own view of the objects of refuge, and also their own way to practice it. It sometimes surprises students when I tell them that by relying solely on the practices of outer, inner, and secret refuge, it is possible to attain liberation.

Outer refuge is the style we are probably all familiar with. We view the Buddhas as the ones who showed us the path to liberation, the Dharma as the path towards liberation, and the Sangha as our companions on the path. The complete instructions on how to meditate on outer refuge can be found in Patrul Rinpoche's foundational text *The Words of My Perfect Teacher*. Generally speaking, we cultivate strong feelings of faith and devotion, visualize the field of refuge in the sky above us, and recite this prayer, which I will further explain below:

> In the Buddhas of the Three Roots, the true Three Jewels,
> In Bodhichitta, nature of the channels, energies, and
>   essences,
> And in the mandala of the essential nature, natural expres-
>   sion, and compassion
> I take refuge until I reach the heart of enlightenment.

However, we should not confuse doing the practice of refuge with receiving the refuge vow, which we receive from our Spiritual Friend. If we are serious about our commitment to the Dharma and about having a lasting relationship with a Spiritual Friend, it is said in the Teachings that receiving the refuge vow creates a link between student and Teacher, both in this and in future lifetimes.

From the point of view of inner refuge, or the common aspect of the Secret Teachings of Mahayoga, we recognize the one who has the qualities of the Buddha, the Dharma, and the Sangha as our own secret Spiritual Friend. This is because our Spiritual Friend has attained the perfect oral instructions and their result, given us the precious Teachings, and also pushed us towards realization. Not only that, but we have had the good fortune to meet our Spiritual Friend in the flesh, which makes him or her more precious and beneficial for us than any other Buddhas or Bodhisattvas we might pray to or read about. So, we take refuge in the Spiritual Friend as the embodiment of the Three Jewels, offering our body, speech, and mind. According to inner refuge, we take up the path by relying upon the Tantric deity. Finally, we rely upon the Dakini as the friend, or the one who creates good conditions for realizing the path. A moving account of Yeshe Tsogyal's own recognition of her master, Padmasambhava, as the essence of all the Buddhas will be given in Chapter 9.

From the point of view of the uncommon secret refuge in the Indestructible Vehicle of the Secret Mantrayana, we aim to gain mastery over the channels, energies, and essences, which is done by practicing what is called *tsa lung* in Tibetan. The Teachings of tsa lung are part of the secret Teachings, and rely upon two paths called *taplam* and *drolam*. When taking up these two paths, we visualize the channels as the Nirmanakaya, train in the energies as the Sambhogakaya, and purify the essences as the Dharmakaya. A further explanation of taplam and drolam will be given in Chapter 9.

CONDITION AND RESULT REFUGE

In addition to the presentation of inner, outer, and secret refuge, refuge can also be classified as condition refuge and result refuge. Condition refuge depends on our faith in the Buddhist tradition. We think of the good qualities of the Buddhas and Bodhisattvas and the effort they made over many eons to attain realization. We focus on our wish to become like them, and use this aspiration as the basis for refuge. We continually try to deepen our faith in the Buddhas and Bodhisattvas, and thus our faith in the Three Jewels becomes a good condition for our continued practice.

To practice result refuge, we take refuge from the perspective of the result to be achieved, recognizing the three kayas in conjunction with the three qualities of the nature of our own mind. We recognize the mind's empty nature as the Dharmakaya, the mind's clear expression as the Sambhogakaya, and the mind's all-pervading capacity as the Nirmanakaya. After we recognize the nature of mind as the three kayas, we take up the uncontrived view, which is the Union of Dzogchen and Bodhichitta, in order to attain realization. An in-depth discussion of the view as the Union of Dzogchen and Bodhichitta will follow in Part II of this volume. Of course, if we wish to practice result refuge, as well as inner or secret refuge, it is imperative that we receive both the vow and the proper oral instructions from the qualified Spiritual Friend.

◆ CHAPTER 3
◆
◆ *Taking up the Path*
◆

No one has ever attained the final result
Without relying upon the holistic path.

THESE WORDS, spoken by Terton Karmalangwa, remind us
that the path we must practice is the Union of Dzogchen
and Bodhichitta. However, even as I write this, I realize that the level
of discipline needed to practice the path can be deceiving. Many people hear the word "Dzogchen" and immediately think of words that
are now strongly associated with it, such as "uncontrived" and "effortless," and think this means there is nothing to contemplate, study, or
practice. The instructions that say there is nothing to take up or abandon easily can be, and sadly often are, taken out of context and made
to sound as if we do not have to practice any path at all, or do anything
that requires effort, for that matter. In fact, it sounds so easy that many
people do not realize the importance of taking Bodhichitta as the
method, nor do they realize that their practice is missing a most essential element if they fail to do so.

There are numerous paths detailed in the Buddhist canon, and it
would take years and even lifetimes to study each and every one of
them. The reason there are so many paths is because different methods appeal to different people, who are influenced by their own habitual ways of thinking and the goals they wish to achieve through
practice. However, no matter what path we study, we will find one thing
to be true in every case. The purpose of giving Teachings on the path
is to provide us with the means for attaining the skills and experience
we need to reach liberation. So, if we wish to practice the Union of
Dzogchen and Bodhichitta, we must first understand exactly what the
"path" is when put into this context.

THE WORLDLY AND TRANSCENDENTAL PATHS

In the most general way of speaking, the path is divided into the worldly path and the transcendental path. The worldly path is so named because it does not give us the means to transcend samsara. As I said earlier, it is actually possible to practice meditation without practicing in a way that can cut through the root of self-attachment. In this case, the Teachings of the worldly path rely upon a type of shamatha, or meditative concentration, which enables its practitioners to abandon only the coarsest of mental afflictions. And even this abandonment is only temporary. Eventually, such practitioners' concentration will break or be interrupted, and they will be unable to continue abiding in shamatha. They will generate attachment for samsara, and be forced to take rebirth yet again. We can also think of the worldly path as that practiced by a person who only wishes to attain happiness for this life-time and avoid taking rebirth in the lower realms.

For most of us, it is because we experience suffering and wish to transcend it that we are motivated to take up a spiritual practice. After all, if we were perfectly happy with all the cards life dealt us, it would never occur to us to change. So, if we are weary of the perpetual trials of life in samsara, then it follows that we must search for the cause of our suffering and the method to transcend it. It is said in Maitreya-natha's *Sublime Continuum* (*Uttaratantra, rGyud bla ma*),

> Just as a patient needs to know how to eliminate the cause
>   of their illness
> And must rely upon a doctor in order to get well,
> [So also one must know] what path will eliminate the cause
>   of suffering
> And lead to the attainment of happiness,
> [As well as] what to abandon, what to realize, and what to
>   rely upon.

The Buddhist Teachings often compare the experience of samsaric suffering to an illness that each and every sentient being is forced to live with. When thought of in this way, we see that samsara's suffering is no ordinary illness, but more like a chronic disease, causing constant and relentless problems and more grief than even the most terrible diseases we can think of, since we have no hope of curing a chronic condition by taking ordinary medicine. Ordinary medicines or worldly solutions might suppress the symptoms of our many different problems, but they can never bring lasting relief. The only thing that can cure this chronic disease of samsara's suffering is a practice that cuts through the root of ignorance; and this is the Union of Dzogchen and Bodhichitta.

There are three realms of samsara: the desire realm, the form realm, and the formless realm. Within each of these realms there are several classes of beings. For example, the desire realm consists of six classes of beings, of which certain types of gods, human beings, and animals are three of those classes. It is said that beings that live within the desire, form, and formless realms of samsara constantly experience some form of suffering, depending upon their karma. For example, human beings experience three types of suffering. One is the suffering of suffering, which is just what it sounds like: a many-layered kind of suffering. It is like the straw that breaks the camel's back: we just have one experience of suffering on top of another with no end in sight. For example, we may have a terrible illness like cancer, but even the severe pain of that illness cannot stop some other problem from happening, like getting pneumonia on top of that. We are forced to live with the feeling that the weight of our suffering is too great to bear, and that we do not know how we will go on.

Second, we experience the suffering of change. For example, because we humans have both body and mind, we experience suffering in both. The pain we feel in one seems to move or change into the other. For example, if we break our leg, we will experience not only some physical pain, but also the mental distress or unhappiness of not liking to feel helpless, or being unable to go to work or move around. Another way the scriptures present the suffering of change is by saying that because our mental afflictions are impermanent, feelings of pleasure and pain ebb and flow like the tide, and we have no chance to secure lasting happiness; in one moment we might be happy, but when the situation changes from pleasure or comfort to pain or discomfort, we become unhappy.

Finally the third kind of suffering, called "pervasive suffering," is experienced at every moment (but rarely perceived) by all samsaric beings. That is, not only is it experienced by desire realm beings but it is also experienced by form and formless realm beings, since pervasive suffering is the root of the other two. Beings born in the form and formless realm got there through attaining a high level of stability in their practice of meditative concentration by relying upon Teachings of the worldly path. Unlike sentient beings born in the desire realm, they do not experience the coarse sufferings of the body and mind. Despite this, they still experience many subtle types of suffering and when their meditative concentration is disrupted, they are forced to take rebirth. Pervasive suffering is the suffering of our very condition, which is inescapable. For example, our bodies have the nature of suffering. Notice that we never get younger or healthier, but instead we grow older and weaker and no one and nothing, including the most sophisticated scientific advances, can stop this from eventually happening.

By contemplating the three types of suffering, we can easily see that suffering is something that must be experienced by each and every being within samsara. This is the first of the Buddha's Four Noble Truths, which is the Truth of Suffering. When we examine the cause of our suffering, we realize that it is created by our mental afflictions, the root of which is ignorance. This is the Second Noble Truth, or the Truth of the Origin of Suffering. On further contemplation, we realize that if we were able to cut through the root of this ignorance, we would be completely free from suffering. This is the Third Noble Truth, or the Truth of Cessation. However, if we want to attain cessation and abandon the origin of suffering, we must rely upon the path. Thus, the Fourth Noble Truth is the Truth of the Path, in reliance upon which that cessation of the condition of suffering in samsara can be attained.

The paths that enable us to transcend samsara and thus attain liberation from suffering are called "the Transcendental Paths." They include the two Hinayana paths of the Hearers and Solitary Realizers, as well as a variety of paths that are included within the Teachings of the Mahayana. The practitioners of all three vehicles accept what are called "the five Paths": the Path of Accumulation, the Path of Preparation, the Path of Seeing, the Path of Meditation, and the Path of No More Learning. Although the five paths have the same names and sequence in all vehicles, they are understood differently according to the varying capacities of the followers of those vehicles. Usually, the Teachings of the five Paths are given in conjunction with the Teachings of the Bodhisattva Bhumis. As I said earlier, which level, or Bhumi, a Bodhisattva has attained correlates with their level of realization.

Within the Hinayana presentation, there are only eight Bhumis, while in the Mahayana there are ten. According to the Buddhist Teachings of India and Tibet, the five Paths were presented in a wide variety of ways by different lineages of Teachings. However, all of these can be condensed into the presentation of the five Paths given as the common method, or the Outer Teachings, and the uncommon method, which contains the Inner and Secret Teachings.

Understanding the five Paths takes a great amount of listening, contemplation, and meditation. In fact, the five Paths have been the subject of many philosophical treatises throughout the centuries. That is to say, it would be impossible in this text to explain in detail all of the practices to be undertaken in relation to the five Paths. So, my goal here is to provide only a brief introduction to the common and uncommon methods for taking up the five Paths. Based on this introduction, I think it will become even more apparent why the practice of Dharma requires enduring faith, study, and diligence.

After reading the introduction provided in this text, some students might wish to study the five Paths more deeply. From the point of view of the Outer Teachings, an extensive explanation of the five Paths is conveyed by the root text and autocommentary of the great Chandrakirti's *Entering the Middle Way* (*Madhyamakavatara, dBu ma la 'jug pa*). In addition, from the point of view of the Inner and Secret Teachings, the five Paths are conveyed through the Teachings of many other masters, including the great Longchen Rabjam and also in the master Jigme Lingpa's *Treasury of Precious Qualities* (*Yon ten rin po che'i mdzod*), and in the *Secret Essence Tantra* (*Guhyagarbha Tantra, gSang ba'i snying po rgyud*).

The explanation of the uncommon methods must be passed directly from a Spiritual Friend to the student. So, I would advise any students wishing to take up these paths to seek out and rely upon a qualified Spiritual Friend in order to understand exactly how to put them into practice.

THE FIVE PATHS (COMMON METHOD)

From the perspective of the Outer Teachings, the five Paths are the journey we undergo when we take up the practices called "the Thirty-seven Branches to Enlightenment" as the method to realization. On the first four of the five paths we gain the skills and good qualities of the Thirty-seven Branches, and on the fifth and final path we attain the result.

The first of the five paths, the Path of Accumulation, can be described as the time from which we first generate aspiration Bodhichitta until we first experience the warmth of the second path, the Path of Preparation. "Accumulation" refers to the ocean of merit that must be accumulated during this stage. It is said in the Teachings that the virtue we accumulate is like heat, which slowly begins to melt away the ice of our mental afflictions. However, in this first of the five Paths we only have enough merit to begin to melt away the coarse afflictions that lie on the surface, so our purification does not go very deep.

By listening to, contemplating, and meditating on the nature of selflessness, we realize the impermanence of all phenomena. Using this realization as a basis, we meditate on the first twelve Branches of Enlightenment: the Four Close Contemplations, the Four Things to Be Abandoned, and the Four Limbs of Miracles. As a result, we attain the level of clairvoyances and meditative concentration that are characteristic of this stage of realization, as well as purifying our coarse mental afflictions.

The Warmth experienced as we complete the Path of Accumulation and enter the Path of Preparation is a sign, or the first seed, of the wisdom that will dawn during the third path, called "the Path of Seeing." The Path of Preparation is marked by four stages, called "Warmth, Peak, Patience, and Supreme Dharma." During these four stages we move from an awareness of the empty nature of outer phenomena (Warmth) to the realization that not only are all outer phenomena empty projections of the mind, but that the mind itself is empty (Supreme Dharma). Supreme Dharma occurs at the instant just before we attain the Path of Seeing. During the four stages of the Path of Preparation we meditate on the next ten Branches of Enlightenment. In the first two stages of the Path of Preparation we meditate on the five Powers, and during the last two, the five Forces. This leads us to attain the levels of wisdom and meditative concentration characteristic of the Path of Preparation.

The Path of Seeing is the stage in which we clearly and directly realize the emptiness of self-existence, and attain the first stages of conventional and ultimate wisdom. We also attain liberation from samsara. The name "Seeing" refers to the fact that we can finally see what we could not see before. In terms of the Bodhisattva Bhumis, the attainment of the first Bhumi corresponds with our entering the Path of Seeing, and we pass through the remaining nine grounds as we progress towards enlightenment.

On the Path of Seeing we practice the next seven Branches of Enlightenment, called "the Seven Limbs of Enlightenment." As a result, we abandon the "fetters" (the name of the mental afflictions to be abandoned at this stage) and also the coarsest of the cognitive obscurations. In terms of our earlier metaphor, on the Path of Seeing our virtue is really starting to heat up! It should be noted that there are many different views on the exact methods that are used to abandon the fetters, as well as much debate about which fetters can actually be abandoned on the Path of Seeing. However, as a result of our progress on this path, we attain the wisdom and what are called "the twelve sets of a hundred good qualities" that are characteristic of this path, as well as taking our first step on the ground of nirvana.

Although we definitely enter the Path of Meditation as we progress along the Path of Seeing, it is difficult to locate a clear-cut border between these two paths. This is because on the Path of Meditation we are simply continuing to practice the view of suchness that we realized on the Path of Seeing. However, we are able to increase our good qualities and realization once we reach this stage. On the Path of Meditation we take up the final eight Branches of Enlightenment. These are the practices of the Eight Noble Paths, which result in the abandonment of all but traces of the mental afflictions as well as the majority of the cognitive obscurations. The Path of Meditation is characterized as the path in which we attain all of the uncontaminated good qualities. For example, before we reach the Path of Seeing, due to not yet having had a direct realization of emptiness, our virtues are said to be "contaminated." On the Path of Meditation we attain a type of meditative concentration that is said to be indestructible, or diamond hard, and which serves as the antidote to the subtlest remaining traces of the two types of obscurations. We gain perfect realization of both conventional and ultimate wisdom. This perfect realization is what we call "gone beyond abandonment and realization," or the Path of No More Learning.

FIVE PATHS (UNCOMMON METHOD)

The uncommon methods to take up the five Paths, which include the Inner and Secret Teachings, were taught by the master Longchenpa by combining the methods given in the Sutra and Tantra systems, and using the four chakras as a basis. The result of gaining mastery over the uncommon methods is the attainment of the Four Types of Vidyadharas, or "awareness holders." These four will be explained in more detail in Chapter 9.

First, we take up the practice of tsa lung at the chakra of emanation, which is located at the navel. Mastering tsa lung at this level is equivalent to completing the Path of Accumulation. Upon attaining mastery of tsa lung at the emanation chakra, we will attain all of the signs of accomplishment of the first path and gain the results of clairvoyances, meditative concentration, and the ability to perform miracles that are characteristic of this stage.

Next, we practice tsa lung at the level of the chakra of phenomena, which is located at the heart center. Gaining stability in tsa lung at this level is equivalent to completing the four stages of the Path of Preparation. First, we meditate on the five Strengths in order to attain the first two types of wisdom to be gained at this level. When we reach the stage of Warmth, we attain the "Wisdom of Appearances," after which our doubts and conceptual thoughts cease. At the stage of Peak we attain "Blazing Wisdom," which causes our roots of virtue to become stable and continuous. After we have attained the first two types of wisdom, we realize that all phenomena are like appearances in a dream. Next, we meditate on the five Forces, which leads us to realize the next two types of wisdom. At the stage of Patience we realize "Attainment Wisdom," which cuts our karmic link to the lower realms. Finally, at the instant of Supreme Dharma we realize "Close Wisdom," which is so named because of how close we are to realizing emptiness directly and entering the Path of Seeing. Based on Close Wisdom, the totality of our root of virtue is dedicated only towards full enlightenment. Upon gaining stability in the practice of tsa lung at this level, we further develop our skills in the clairvoyances, the ability to perform miracles, and meditative concentration.

Third, we take up the practice of tsa lung at the level of the chakra of enjoyment, located at the throat. Upon gaining stability in tsa lung at this level, we attain the first Bhumi and enter the Path of Seeing. The wisdom we attain on this path is different from the previous two. We could consider the wisdoms attained on the Path of Accumulation and the Path of Preparation as merely metaphorical, because we have not yet realized suchness or the emptiness of inherent existence directly. But on the Path of Seeing we directly realize the nature of

suchness and gain the twelve sets of a hundred good qualities characteristic of this path. Also, we are able to visit a pure land where we
receive Teachings from the Sambhogakaya Buddhas of the five Buddha families. Finally, we gain the result of the Completely Ripened
Vidyadhara and the Immortal Life Vidyadhara.

Last, we take up the practice of tsa lung at the level of the chakra of
great bliss, which is located at the crown of the head. Upon gaining
mastery in tsa lung at this level, we attain the nine levels of the Path of
Meditation and the remainder of the nine Bhumis, one with each level.
By doing so, we attain the result of the Mahamudra Vidyadhara. After
we complete the nine levels of this path, we are said to have "gone
beyond" the first four paths, having "dried up" the energy of our mental afflictions so that all that remains is wisdom energy. At the completion of the Path of Meditation we enter the Path of No More
Learning and attain enlightenment. We also gain the result of the Spontaneously Arisen Vidyadhara.

The Inner Teachings also give a second explanation of the ten Bhumis from the point of view of the three channels. In general, it is said
that the left, right, and central channels combined have a total of
twenty-one "knots" that cause us to be bound in samsara. As is said in
the Tantras,

> [We are] bound by the knots in the central, right, and left
>   channels
> To the confused appearances of samsara.
> Freeing them is the wisdom of nirvana.

By taking up the practice of tsa lung, we begin to undo the knots in
the channels two at a time. When the first two knots are untied at the
navel, we attain the first Bhumi. We work up the channels in sequence
towards the crown of the head, attaining one more Bhumi for every
pair of knots that are untied. When we untie the final knot at the crown
of the head, we attain enlightenment, becoming one with the Dharmakaya Samantabhadra.

Samantabhadra

After reading the explanation of the common and uncommon methods, I realize that it may appear that the common method contains what we all understand to be the method aspect of the path, or the engaged practice of Bodhichitta. However, it is important to develop our understanding of method past the surface level. Our practice of the Inner and Secret Teachings should not be divorced from the practices and conduct presented in the Outer Teachings. Rather, the Inner and Secret Teachings were given with the knowledge that they must be put into practice in conjunction with the Outer Teachings.

Because of the practice we develop by training in the Outer Teachings, we gain experience and habits that, based on our diligence, become so second nature we could call them "effortless." In fact, we could even recognize this habituation to a particular technique of meditation as what is meant by "effortless" in the context of the Dzogchen Teachings. So if we are putting the Outer Teachings into practice properly, we should already have a great deal of insight about the method aspects of the Inner and Secret Teachings.

In general, there are two ways we can think of the common and uncommon Teachings. As the words suggest, "uncommon" contains "common." If we took away the common and tried to understand only the uncommon, we would find our understanding was incomplete and full of holes—and the energy that we put forth to realize the nature of mind would leak out of these holes if we were not careful. But we could also say that we must make our practice of the "common" uncommon upon embarking on the practices of the Inner and Secret Teachings.

PART II ✦
✦
The Inner Teachings: A Holistic Reading ✦

◆ CHAPTER 4
◆
◆ *Bodhichitta: The Root of All Practice*

L ONG AGO there lived a poor beggar woman named Gamo, whose greatest wish was to make an offering to Buddha Shakyamuni. However, she had nothing to offer, and she did not even have enough money to buy the butter she would need to make a single lamp. Rather than feeling frustrated and angry with her misfortune, Gamo realized that the poverty she found herself in was a result of bad karma she had accumulated in the past, and this only increased her longing to create better conditions for herself in the future. Thus, Gamo began to feel certain that no matter what hardship she must undergo, the most important thing she could do would be to gather the two accumulations.

One morning, Gamo rose early and went out into the marketplace to beg so that she would be able to make an offering to the Buddha. She spent the entire day begging, but she did not even have the merit to receive much of a reward for her effort. That night at sunset her bowl held only a few coins. She emptied the coins into her hand and walked to the far side of the market where a merchant lady was selling butter.

When she showed the merchant the few coins, the merchant said, "You will not be able to buy much butter with that," and proceeded to measure out only a tiny amount of butter for Gamo. It was not even enough butter to make one lamp. Gamo's eyes filled with tears as she gazed at the butter sadly.

"What's wrong?," the merchant asked. Gamo explained to the merchant that she had spent the whole day begging, yet she still could not afford to buy the butter she needed to make an offering. When Gamo had finished her tale, the merchant took pity on her and added a bit more butter to the amount she had already sold her. "It is not much," the merchant said, "but I think this should be enough butter to make one lamp."

Gamo's heart soared. She took the butter to a temple near where Buddha Shakyamuni was living and carefully prepared her offering. Then, as she lit the lamp, she began to pray deeply from her heart, "Any other beings who are living in poverty such as I am, may this simple offering be enough to gather the accumulations so that all of them may be freed from the suffering of samsara. By this merit may the wisdom of my mind burn like the flame of this lamp, so that I may liberate beings from suffering until samsara is completely empty." After Gamo prayed, she left the temple and went to sleep.

The next morning, Maudgalyayana, one of Buddha Shakyamuni's closest students, went into the temple to clean up the offerings made the night before. All of the lamps had burned out except for one, which was still burning brightly. In fact, the butter in that particular lamp did not seem to have been consumed at all. It was still as full as it had been when it was first offered. Maudgalyayana thought to himself, "There is no need for a lamp to burn during the day." He tried to blow out the lamp, but found that he could not. He tried several times to put out the lamp without success, but as he did so Buddha Shakyamuni sensed what was happening and went to the temple immediately.

When the Buddha arrived in the temple, he told Maudgalyayana, "No matter how hard you try, you will not be able to put out the flame of that lamp. Even if you dumped a bucket of water on top of it, the flame would keep on burning. Such is the nature of an offering made with the aspiration of Bodhichitta." It was said that in a future rebirth Gamo attained enlightenment as the Buddha named "The Light of the Lamp" and liberated countless beings from suffering.

As shown by Gamo's great accumulation of merit in this story, it is imperative that no matter what practice or path we wish to take up, we nourish it with the root of Bodhichitta. The master Jigme Lingpa said,

Planting in an excellent field
Yields an abundant harvest of virtue,
Just as the wishing tree of Bodhichitta
Yields fruit again and again until the attainment of the
    peaceful state.

ASPIRATION AND ACTION BODHICHITTA

Bodhichitta is the one practice we cannot do without. Even if we have been given the precious oral instructions on realizing the nature of mind, they will not be the sufficient cause for realization if we have not learned to generate Bodhichitta. The great Dzogchen yogi Patrul Rinpoche said,

> If we have only one thing, the precious Bodhichitta is enough.
> If we have nothing else, we must have the method of the
>   precious Bodhichitta.

We should learn to develop Bodhichitta in a twofold way: through our aspirations and through our actions. Aspiration Bodhichitta is our initial wish that all sentient beings be liberated from the vast ocean of samsara's suffering. Action Bodhichitta requires that we first generate aspiration Bodhichitta, and practice the Six Paramitas as the method to establish the two benefits of 1) attaining Buddhahood oneself to 2) be of ultimate benefit to others. The way to practice aspiration and action Bodhichitta was taught by the omniscient Patrul Rinpoche, who said,

> The instructions for aspiration [Bodhichitta] are to practice
>   the Four Immeasurables;
> The instructions for action [Bodhichitta] are to practice the
>   Paramitas.

THE FOUR IMMEASURABLES

The Teachings say that taking up the practices of the Four Immeasurables is essential for the attainment of liberation. Although these four practices seem quite ordinary, they are actually the means for attaining the extraordinary result if we rely on the Union of Dzogchen and Bodhichitta. Practicing the Four Immeasurables is the cause for attaining the extraordinary result of the four kayas, sometimes referred to the four "bodies" or aspects of the Buddha: the Dharmakaya, Sambhogakaya, Nirmanakaya, and Svabhavakaya. Specifically, meditating on immeasurable compassion is a cause for the attainment of the Dharmakaya, or the Body Which Is the Nature of Truth. Meditating on immeasurable love is a cause for the attainment of the Sambhogakaya, or the Body of Perfect Enjoyment. Meditating on immeasurable joy is a cause for the attainment of the Nirmanakaya, or the Body of Emanation. And finally, meditating on immeasurable equanimity is a cause for the attainment of the Svabhavakaya, or the Essence Body of a Buddha.

Besides planting the seed for attaining the four kayas, the practice of the Four Immeasurables also gives us a noticeable benefit in this life, by enabling us to effectively cut through many of our mental afflictions, and thus to tame our mind. In fact, the amount of negativity our minds tend to produce decreases in direct proportion to how much we practice. As our negativity decreases, our minds begin to gain stability. This stability acts as a good condition for any other type of meditation or contemplation we wish to practice thereafter.

Immeasurable Equanimity

When we take up the Four Immeasurables, we should begin with the practice of immeasurable equanimity. First, we should contemplate the strong emotional attachment we feel to our parents, children, spouse, family, and friends. Then, we should think of the strong hatred and anger we feel towards our enemies or people we don't like. Our resentment and aversion towards those we dislike is often so strong that we feel disappointed if anything good happens to them.

After we have realized that we, too, have this tendency of favoring our loved ones and resenting those we dislike, we should also realize that attachment and aversion cause us to accumulate negative karma.

Next, we should add the element of impermanence to our contemplation. For example, if we could be absolutely certain that the people we love today would always be our loved ones and the people we call our enemies now would always be our enemies, it might not seem such a terrible thing to accumulate negative karma based on our relationships with them. But accumulating karma based on the feelings we have towards our enemies and friends becomes completely illogical when we realize that they are impermanent, just like everything else.

Look at the current news about our own society to find countless examples of this kind of impermanence. For example, we often see cases where one day someone's enemy becomes the next day's friend or today's lover becomes tomorrow's most bitter enemy. The news reports stories about parents who have killed their children, and children who have killed their parents; husbands who have killed their wives, and wives who have killed their husbands. In some countries, the divorce rate is as high as fifty percent, and many children and parents turn against each other when families divide.

If we examine global politics, we find this same trend. Two countries may have sworn to be enemies to the bitter end, but based on economic factors they may end up working together to create a better relationship. They might even form a strong alliance, defying past expectations and beliefs. Alliances are built and fall apart. The political face of the world changes. Our own outlook, friends, families, and even the nature of our resentments change. Once we have realized how uncertain the relations between enemies and friends are, we should abandon this way of thinking and meditate on all beings as being equal in their wish to be happy and free of suffering.

Immeasurable Love

To meditate on immeasurable love, we should first examine the longings of our own heart. If we do, we will find that our greatest wish is to have a life full of lasting happiness that is free of suffering. Based on our own feelings, it is not difficult to then understand that all sentient beings have this same wish to be happy and free of suffering. So, in this type of meditation we turn the focus towards all sentient beings, with whom we share the same hopes and dreams, and cultivate feelings of love towards them. As the supreme Shantideva said, it is we who demolish our chances for happiness through our habitual feelings of selfishness:

> Although we wish for happiness, by our ignorance
> We destroy our happiness as though it were our enemy.

Immeasurable Compassion

To meditate on immeasurable compassion, we should begin by thinking of a being who is enduring a suffering so severe that it is difficult for us to sit still while imagining it, for example, someone who is drowning or has caught on fire. Once we have cultivated a strong wish for them to be free of this suffering, we should work to expand this wish from that one being to all sentient beings, who are forced to bear the excruciating suffering of samsara endlessly. Once we have cultivated a feeling of compassion so deep that we are moved to tears, we should rest in the uncontrived, natural state.

Immeasurable Joy

To meditate on immeasurable joy, we should focus on a being who is experiencing deep joy and happiness. We should truly rejoice in their happiness, and then work to expand our feeling of rejoicing until we are rejoicing in the happiness of all beings within samsara. We should wish them two kinds of joy: joy in their worldly life, and also lasting joy, which is the attainment of liberation from suffering.

Through our practice of the Four Immeasurables we are directly training in the Union of Dzogchen and Bodhichitta. We start with a focused style of meditation, working with the appearance, or method, aspect of the path. Then, from our focused meditation, we move into an unfocused style of meditation, thus working with the emptiness, or wisdom, aspect of the path. However, although it seems that we are first relying upon the appearance of equanimity, love, compassion, or joy and then moving into the emptiness aspect, this is not actually a linear process. Actually, the proper way to meditate would be as the word "union" suggests: we simply leave the contrived object of our focused meditation in its own place, while abiding in the uncontrived view.

By relying upon the motivations of equanimity, love, compassion, and joy we use in contemplating the Four Immeasurables, we can also practice Tonglen, which translates from Tibetan as "sending and receiving." When we practice Tonglen, we are sending our roots of virtue and joy to others and taking, or receiving, their suffering. The basic idea is that we want to give away whatever good we have to others, and take their sufferings upon ourselves. As beginning practitioners, we do this to reverse the habitual tendency we have of always making ourselves the most important—which actually causes us to focus so much upon ourselves that we implode into terrible unhappiness

When we practice Tonglen, we are cultivating the heroic attitude of a Bodhisattva, whose capacity to benefit beings is completely limitless. By engaging in this type of mind training, along with practicing meditation upon the emptiness of self-existence, we are not only entering, but are walking the Bodhisattva path. Because of this, Tonglen is said to be an essential practice for a practitioner of Vajrayana Buddhism.

We practice Tonglen by adopting three main attitudes: first, contemplating the self and others as equal; next, exchanging the self and others; and finally, of giving more importance to others than to self. However, while the practice itself is quite straightforward, I have observed that some students experience confusion when they first receive Teachings on how to put Tonglen into practice. For example, some have asked me whether they can be harmed by taking on the suffering of others. This doubt is caused by two main misapprehensions about the practice of Tonglen. The first is that the suffering we receive when we practice Tonglen is tangible and real, and could thus do us actual harm. To understand why this is a misapprehension, we should come back to the Union of Dzogchen and Bodhichitta. While suffering appears, its nature is completely empty. How could something that is completely empty cause us any harm at all? In general, it is good to combine the practice of Tonglen with meditation on emptiness and impermanence so that we can train ourselves in this view of appearance and emptiness as indivisible. In particular, this technique is important if we begin to feel a glimpse of fear as a result of our practice. If we are truly giving ourselves to the practice, we may indeed feel some resistance to the idea of taking another's suffering upon ourselves, to say nothing of taking on the suffering of all sentient beings. It is good to keep in mind that this is simply our self-attachment at work, and to reflect on emptiness until the feeling passes, and return to our practice when our motivation is pure.

The second misapprehension is the reason we are training in Tonglen. At first, it appears that we are training in Tonglen for the benefit of others, because through this practice we cultivate a wish to take on their suffering. This is true to a certain extent. However, until we reach the first Bodhisattva Bhumi and have a direct realization of emptiness, we are unable to take on the suffering of others directly. It is only at that stage that the practice of Tonglen would enable us to benefit others directly. However, in the early stages we are not able to directly take on the suffering of others.

So, if we cannot directly take on others' suffering, we may wonder why it is important to practice Tonglen at all. The answer is that it is actually we who benefit the most from our practice in the beginning stages. Suffering is caused by ignorance, by which we generate self-attachment and the fixation on the three spheres. Tonglen is a skillful method by which we are able to cut through this self-attachment. For those students who wish to read about the practice of Tonglen in more detail, there are many excellent guides about the practice in English, especially the Teachings given by Chögyam Trungpa Rinpoche and his student Pema Chödrön, along with those by Sermey Khensur Lobsang Tharchin.

ENGAGING IN THE PATH

Regarding the way to engage in the path, the omniscient Longchenpa said,

> If [one wants to practice] the superior Vajrayana on a great
>   wave of virtue,
> Begin by generating Bodhichitta, and then meditate on the
>   view.
> Afterwards, completely dedicate the merit.
> These three are essential for walking the path to liberation.

We call these three stages outlined by the great Longchenpa the "three excellences." By basing our meditation upon these three excellences, we are ensuring that all of the right elements have been included in our practice. So, if we follow Longchenpa's simple instructions, we do not have to worry about whether or not we are practicing in the proper way. That is to say, relying upon the three excellences guarantees that we have taken up the Union of Dzogchen and Bodhichitta. As we read the following Teachings on the Six Paramitas, we should notice the way they utilize the three essential elements of aspiration Bodhichitta, the perfect, uncontrived view, and the dedication of merit.

THE SIX PARAMITAS

Taking up the Six Paramitas is the way to practice action Bodhichitta. Although each of the Paramitas—giving, ethical discipline, patience, heroic effort, meditative concentration, and wisdom—could be practiced without the motivation of aspiration Bodhichitta, it is our aspiration to dedicate our actions to the enlightenment of others that makes them transcendental. On the path, we must gather the two accumulations of merit and wisdom in order to gain the result of enlightenment. The accumulation of merit is the method aspect of the path, and is accomplished by first generating aspiration Bodhichitta, and then practicing the first five Paramitas: giving, ethical discipline, patience, heroic effort, and meditative concentration. The accumulation of wisdom is accomplished by generating aspiration Bodhichitta and practicing the Paramita of Wisdom. "Wisdom" is another way of saying the uncontrived view, or the primordially pure natural state that is the realization of the Dzogchen Teachings. Thus, gathering the two accumulations in conjunction with the three excellences is the perfect means for practicing the indivisible path, which is the Union of Dzogchen and Bodhichitta.

The Paramita of Giving

When we practice the Paramita of Giving, we need both the proper aspiration and the proper conduct to ensure that we are engaging in the Paramita correctly. First, we generate aspiration Bodhichitta, thinking to ourselves, "I offer this act for the benefit of all beings suffering in samsara." There are several ways to classify the practice of giving. One classification is the three of giving, giving completely, and giving ultimately. Here, "giving" means offering our material wealth to others, even if we only offer them a single penny or a cup of tea. "Giving completely" means that we give others all the material wealth we possess, right down to the food on our plates or the clothes on our backs if necessary. "Giving ultimately" is the most difficult kind of practice. It means that we offer our own flesh and blood to others, and are willing to die for their sake. This type of giving requires a very advanced level of realization and should not be engaged in by beginners.

For most students who are just starting out on the path it is difficult to practice more than the generosity of giving, since our self-attachment is so pronounced. However, no matter how much or little we find that we are able to give, we should always pray that one day we will be able to offer our material wealth, roots of virtue, and even our own lives for the sake of others. Generating this kind of aspiration enables us to reduce our own self-attachment, and also our feelings of pride and dissatisfaction.

Some students may wonder why, when there are Six Paramitas, giving was presented first. Buddha Shakyamuni taught that although there are all kinds of suffering, many of these, such as poverty and disease, can be alleviated by the practice of giving. The great sage Chandrakirti said,

> The cause for easing suffering
> Arises from the practice of generosity.

Whether or not our giving practice becomes a transcendental Paramita depends on the method we use when we practice. If we practice giving without relying upon the three excellences, we have offered something—but it is not a transcendental offering. To practice transcendental giving, Chandrakirti said we must be free of the perception of the three spheres:

> [If we realize that] the actor, object given, and receiver
>   are empty,
> Our giving becomes a transcendental Paramita.
> If we attach to these three as being real,
> It becomes a worldly Paramita.

So, after generating aspiration Bodhichitta and giving whatever we are able, we should rest in the uncontrived view that is beyond the three spheres. This is the proper way to combine the wisdom and method aspects of the Union of Dzogchen and Bodhichitta. Finally, we should dedicate the root of virtue for the attainment of enlightenment of all sentient beings. This dedication of merit is from the *Prayer of Arya Maitreya* (*'Phags pa byams pa smon lam*):

> Since things do not exist as entities,
> May my wealth appear spontaneously.
> Since all things totally disintegrate,
> May I perfect the Paramita of Giving.

The result of practicing the Paramita of Giving is the attainment of wealth in this and future lives.

The Paramita of Ethical Discipline

To practice the Paramita of Ethical Discipline, we must abandon our faults and engage in virtuous conduct. We begin the practice of discipline by generating aspiration Bodhichitta, and then work to purify our outer and inner conduct. A Bodhisattva who is a monk or a nun should use their monastic vows as a guide when practicing this Paramita. But Bodhisattvas who have not taken monastic vows should develop their discipline by properly studying and observing their Bodhisattva vows, as well as through familiarizing themselves with the Teachings of aspiration and action Bodhichitta through practicing the Four Immeasurables and the Six Paramitas.

If we truly wish to practice the Union of Dzogchen and Bodhichitta, it is possible to do so at every moment of the day, no matter what we are doing. To do this, we not only need to receive Teachings on the methods for practice, but we also need to develop mindfulness, devotion, and pure perception. By using the following summary of instructions given by the great Longchenpa, it is possible for us to engage in the Union of Dzogchen and Bodhichitta while developing the Paramita of Ethical Discipline. After reading Longchenpa's instructions, what it means to develop pure perception should seem a little clearer. In other words, we are using ordinary, impure appearances to train in the fact that they are of the nature of primordial purity. Longchenpa summarizes:

> When entering though a doorway, practice Bodhichitta by
> wishing that all sentient beings attain enlightenment.
> At night before going to sleep, wish that all sentient beings
> attain Buddhahood.
> When dreaming, wish that all sentient beings realize the
> nature of reality to be like a dream.
> When seated, wish that all sentient beings attain the inde-
> structible seat of Buddhahood.

When lighting a fire, wish that this fire might burn through the mental afflictions of all sentient beings.

When the fire is burning, wish that the wisdom of all sentient beings might burn like the roaring flames.

When eating, wish that your food might become the "food" of meditative concentration that can be eaten by all sentient beings.

When going outside, wish that all sentient beings be freed from samsara. When opening a door, imagine that you are opening the door to realization for all sentient beings.

When closing a door, imagine that you are closing the door to the lower realms.

When walking down a road, wish that all sentient beings enter the noble path of the Bodhisattvas.

When climbing a mountain, imagine that all sentient beings are climbing to the pure lands.

When meeting someone, imagine that this meeting is like the meeting between ordinary beings and a Buddha.

When walking, imagine that each step you take is the steady work of benefiting others.

When encountering someone adorned with necklaces and jewels, wish that all beings attain the major and minor marks of a Buddha.

When encountering someone living in poverty, wish that all sentient beings become like yogis who care nothing for worldly life and devote themselves solely to the Dharma.

When seeing a cup or bowl that is full to the brim, imagine that it is the completion of all good qualities.

When seeing an empty cup or bowl, imagine that all faults have been abandoned.

When seeing a being who is rejoicing, imagine that it is the happiness of all beings who have received the precious Teachings.

When seeing a being who is grieving, wish that all beings
realize the nature of impermanence and renounce their
worldly lives.

When seeing a being suffering from an illness, wish that all
beings be freed from sickness.

When hearing someone speaking praises, imagine they are
praising the Buddhas and Bodhisattvas.

When seeing even the simplest representation of the body
of a Buddha, wish that all sentient beings may gaze
without obstruction upon the face of the Enlightened
Ones.

Finally, when seeing a merchant doing business, imagine
that all beings will attain the seven riches that adorn the
nature of ultimate reality.

These are only a few of the ways we can train vigilantly in pure perception. By combining Longchenpa's instructions with the three excellences, we can practice the transcendental Paramita of Ethical
Discipline. At the completion of our practice, we should dedicate the
merit, as in the *Prayer of Arya Maitreya*:

Endowed with flawless discipline that is guided by rules
And a discipline that is completely pure,
With discipline free of an arrogant mind
May I perfect the Paramita of Ethical Discipline.

The` result of the Paramita of Ethical Discipline is attaining happiness
in this and future lives, and it is also said to be the cause of attaining a
precious human rebirth.

The Paramita of Patience

The Paramita of Patience is divided into three types: the patience to
take on the suffering of others, the patience to undergo hardship in
order to practice Dharma, and the patience to endure pain and hard-

ship inflicted by others. From among these three, the most important one for us to practice at this stage is that of enduring pain inflicted by others. Most people would probably agree that is it extremely difficult to practice patience instead of allowing feelings of anger, victimization, or revenge to arise.

We can use two approaches in the practice of patience: a focused style that relies upon an object, or a style that is unfocused. To practice a focused style of patience, we begin with the generation of aspiration Bodhichitta. Next, we examine the nature of the situation that has been bothering us in conjunction with the Buddhist Teachings.

For example, if we believe in past and future lives, we could think of all of the faults and bad deeds we ourselves have committed in the past, which have led directly to the ripening of a painful situation in our lives right now. Even if we do not accept past and future lives, by applying logic we can still realize that any negative action that we do now will yield a negative experience in the future. Thus, we can be sure that retaliation will only bring us more problems and misery. If it is possible for us to make the situation better, then there is certainly no reason to get angry, which is what it means to lack patience. But if we cannot improve the situation, losing our patience will give us absolutely no relief. Finally, we should realize that the object of our contempt is a sentient being who is suffering just as we are, and is acting out of his or her own negative karma and delusional mindset. This kind of contemplation requires great effort. As the sublime Shantideva said,

> There is no negativity greater than anger,
> And no practice more difficult than patience.
> Thus, we must make great effort to practice patience.

When we practice an unfocused style of patience, we slowly examine the three spheres in relation to the situation that is bothering us to logically realize that they are all completely empty. For example, upon close examination, we find that our enemy's body, speech, and mind are all ultimately empty of existing independently of causes and conditions. Thus, even harsh words that may sting us are absolutely insubstantial. Likewise, our own body, speech, and mind, as well as our own mental afflictions, are only empty appearances. Once we have gained certainty in the emptiness of the three spheres, we should rest in the uncontrived view that is beyond all conceptual thought.

To complete the three excellences, we should dedicate the merit, as in the *Prayer of Arya Maitreya*:

> Just like the elements of earth, water, fire, and wind,
> [Bodhisattvas] do not remain trapped [by mental constructs].
> [By attaining] patience, anger never arises.
> May I attain the Paramita of Patience.

The Paramita of Heroic Effort

Without heroic effort, we would be unable to accomplish anything in this life, not even if it were for our own survival. If we were not even able act on our own behalf, we would have no hope of being able to benefit others. The sage Chandrakirti said,

> Without exception, the development of all good qualities
>   follows heroic effort,
> Which is the cause for the accumulation of merit and wisdom.

Thus, the relationship between progress in Dharma practice and effort is directly proportional. If we practice with constant diligence, our meditation is sure to develop steadily. On the other hand, if we hardly practice at all, we are unlikely to see any result in our meditation. It does not matter what path we choose to follow; our time will be wasted without the application of effort.

Since the Tibetan Buddhist Teachings have been removed from their traditional context, I feel that the idea of realization has come to be a bit misunderstood, and that this misunderstanding directly relates to the practice of effort. There seems to be a sense of confusion about the difference between intellectual understanding, which is the appearance of having realized something, and true realization, which is having practiced something until it becomes an integrated habit that sparks a true transformation. The West has a brilliant tradition of scholarship and a long-standing interest in the development of science and technology. While it is true that the skills of listening and contemplation taught in Tibetan Buddhism mirror the style of study that is pursued in the West, the practice of meditation, which leads to realization, is something completely different.

Realization is not something we can just glean from a text, nor is it the high we feel after receiving a teaching, or even the momentary experience of the nature of mind we might experience when we are with our Spiritual Friend. Realization comes from using all the good causes and conditions we have accumulated and training in the uncontrived view with enthusiastic effort. The measure of whether or not we have realized the meaning of the Teachings is not our intellectual understanding. Instead, realization can be measured on the basis of whether and to what degree we still experience mental afflictions, or have been able to truly abandon self-attachment. A one-time experience or merely using the technique of contemplation cannot cause us to abandon our mental afflictions and abide in the natural state. If these are the good qualities we wish to attain, we had better make effort our mantra and train with as much energy and courage as we can muster.

One way to practice the Paramita of Heroic Effort is to set aside time especially for this purpose, where we are making as much effort as we can to practice an instruction or technique that we have received from our Spiritual Friend. Another is to exert effort to the actions in our daily life, and accompany this with vigilant training in the generation of Bodhichitta, abiding in the uncontrived view, and dedicating the merit. But, no matter what action we engage in, we should constantly strive to dedicate even the smallest amount of virtue to the attainment of enlightenment for the benefit of all beings. Then we should dedicate the merit, as in the *Prayer of Arya Maitreya*:

Through the power of previous effort,
Having become stable, enthusiastic, and free of laziness,
And through a strong body and mind,
May I perfect the Paramita of Heroic Effort.

The Paramita of Meditative Concentration

It is said in the Teachings that without taking up the Paramita of Meditative Concentration, it would be impossible to realize the nature of mind. We should think of meditative concentration as the practice that brings stability to our minds, and creates the good conditions to practice unfocused meditation—in other words, resting in the uncontrived natural state.

If we make a quick examination of our own mind, we can see the reason this kind of stability is so crucial. Although physics has observed light to be the fastest traveling phenomenon known to man, actually the speed at which our minds travel is even faster. We can circle the globe in a matter of seconds, and our minds generate doubts, emotions, and conceptual thoughts at a speed that defies that of all other phenomena. Because we lack basic mental stability, conceptual thoughts arise endlessly. So, if our goal is to realize the nature of mind, we first have to learn to still our minds, and free ourselves from distraction. The method for quieting the mind is called "meditative concentration." Once we have gained some initial mind stability, it is even more important that we continue our training so that this stability will increase. Without such stability, it is impossible for us to successfully learn to abide in the uncontrived view.

The way to practice meditative concentration is to first assume the sevenfold posture: legs crossed in the vajra position, back straight, hands face up on lap with right on top of left and thumbs touching. It is fine if you wish to place the hands palm down resting on the knees. Eyes should be gently open with a relaxed gaze directed toward but not fixated on the nose, chin slightly tucked in, shoulders even and well apart, and the tip of the tongue touching the palate. Then, take up the Union of Dzogchen and Bodhichitta and practice whatever method you are using to train in meditative concentration. Begin your meditation again whenever you realize your concentration has been interrupted by inner or outer distractions.

There are a multitude of methods that can be used to practice meditative concentration that differ according to the lineage of Teachings being given by the Spiritual Friend. I have included several methods used in the "Longchen Nyingthig" in the "Meditation" section of Chapter 7, and the explanations of these methods should be enough to allow beginning practice. However, students who truly wish to develop meditative concentration should seek out and rely directly upon a qualified Spiritual Friend, who can make sure that their meditation is progressing properly.

After we finish, we should dedicate the merit, as in the *Prayer of Arya Maitreya*:

> Through the samadhi where all is illusionlike,
> Through the samadhi of the hero's stride,
> Through the samadhi that is diamond hard,
> May I perfect the Paramita of Meditative Concentration.

The Paramita of Wisdom

Although we cannot truly say that one Paramita is more important than another in absolute terms, the Paramita of Wisdom is said to be the most important for one reason. Without the Paramita of Wisdom, the other five remain worldly Paramitas, and we are denied the means to transcend samsara. On the other hand, it would be impossible to practice the Paramita of Wisdom without relying upon the other five. As it is said in the the sage Tog-me Sangpo's *Thirty-seven Practices of a Bodhisattva (rGyal sras lag len so bdun ma)*,

> Without wisdom, the other five Paramitas
> Cannot [lead us] to the attainment of perfect Buddhahood.
> Cultivate the wisdom that does not conceive of three spheres
>   together with skillful means;
> This is the practice of a Bodhisattva.

The first step in practicing the Paramita of Wisdom is to meditate on the fact that samsara is like eight types of illusionlike phenomena: dreams, lightning, mirages, hallucinations, echoes, the reflection of the moon on water, magic display, and rainbows. This is because at first we are unable to meditate directly on the nature of ultimate reality. Next, we take the appearances of the natural world around us, as well as our own bodies, and examine them analytically. For example, if we examine the mind, we will find that it changes from moment to moment, and that it is completely impermanent. The outer phenomenal world has this same nature of impermanence. Based on this examination, we come to feel a sense of certainty about the emptiness of inherent existence of both the self and phenomena.

Once we experience this certainty, we should then contemplate the idea that all phenomena have the indivisible nature of appearance and emptiness. Although they appear before us, they are completely devoid of self-existence. And although they are empty of inherent existence, they still appear. Once we have gained certainty that all appearing phenomena are empty, we should then rest in the vast, skylike nature of mind, which is the union of appearance and emptiness. This is the perfect view, which is the expression of the Union of Dzogchen and Bodhichitta.

After we have rested in the view, we should dedicate the merit, as in the *Prayer of Arya Maitreya*:

> Through actualizing the three gates of full liberation,
> The equal nature of the three times,
> And the three types of knowing as well,
> May I perfect the Paramita of Wisdom.

CHAPTER 5

From Confusion to Wisdom

T HE DISCUSSION about the nature of mind that follows will be
divided into two parts: the first describing the nature of
appearances, and the second describing the nature of mind. By understanding these two, we can gain insight into the view of the indivisibility of appearances and emptiness. However, to avoid any confusion
on the part of the reader, I would like to give a short explanation before
I begin.

When we discuss the two aspects of appearance and emptiness, it
may not seem that we are actually talking about the Union of Dzogchen and Bodhichitta. In other words, it may not seem that the view of
the indivisibility of appearances and emptiness and the Union of
Dzogchen and Bodhichitta are actually the same thing. But if we think
that, we must think again. True realization, in which we realize that all
phenomena are empty appearances, relies upon both method and wisdom—which is none other than the Union of Dzogchen and Bodhichitta. Not only that, but the nature of mind itself, in which nothing
can be described as either "this" or "that," is the completely nondual
expression of the Union.

From here on out, we are going to see a lot of references to "the
union," which may seem to be describing a multitude of different
things. But whenever we see or hear such a reference, we should understand it to be referring to the same union we have been talking about
all along: that of Dzogchen and Bodhichitta. These references are simply placing the Union of Dzogchen and Bodhichitta into a different
context, in order to help us deepen our understanding. In fact, as we
continue reading this text, we should make it our challenge to completely understand the Union of Dzogchen and Bodhichitta in relation to the Outer, Inner, and Secret Teachings.

BODHICHITTA AS THE METHOD

Dahenta, student of the great Dzogchen masters Garab Dorje and Mañjushrimitra, spoke of the importance of relying upon the method of Bodhichitta when he said,

> Bodhichitta is the Buddhas of the three times:
> The Buddhas of the past all arose from it;
> The Buddhas of the present all abide in it;
> And it is the cause for all the Buddhas still to come.

So, no matter how we think about it, it is crucial that we realize that without the method aspect of the path, realization of the nature of mind cannot arise. In other words, without the method we have nothing.

This is not true just in our practice of meditation. It does not matter what line of work we are in; we always need the proper method to accomplish our goals. In some types of work it may seem that we can get by without knowing a lot. For example, we might work in a shop where we can "go on instinct" and learn as we go without much training. But what if we are engineers or brain surgeons? If we did not know the precise methods involved in these types of work, we could never be successful. Could any of us imagine trying to perform a heart transplant without having first trained for years in order to learn how such a procedure should be done?

This is the kind of importance we should place on the method when we are working with the nature of mind. We should not let ourselves think that our not knowing is no big deal, and that we will just figure it out eventually. Wisdom eludes the conventional mind, and there is simply no way that we can figure it out on our own; nor is there any need to reinvent the wheel.

Regarding the realization of the nature of mind, Tibetans have always considered listening and contemplation to be of the utmost importance. This is because, as in the example I just gave, many people hear only a little bit about it and think they have understood it deeply. If we feel that we have understood the nature of mind when we really have not, we can become distracted by our confusion. But even worse, our misunderstanding can be a great obstacle to our practice in the long run. In Tibet, Lamas use a famous proverb to describe the kind of confusion that occurs when we misunderstand the nature of mind. The proverb says that some dogs bark when they see a thief, while other dogs bark when there is nothing there at all.

If we truly want to understand the nature of mind free of any confusion or doubts, the only possible method for doing so is to rely upon a Spiritual Friend who has the ability to introduce us to the nature of mind directly, and can gradually teach us the way to abide in it properly. However, we also need a basic understanding of the mind itself, and of the relationship between the mind and the world that appears to us.

In order to provide a holistic understanding of the mind, I will now present a discussion of it in terms of appearance and emptiness, which we should now realize is the Union of Dzogchen and Bodhichitta. First, I will logically establish that all appearances arise out of the delusions and habitual tendencies of the mind, and are of the same nature as illusions. Then, I will establish that the nature of mind is actually uncontrived, and is primordially pure wisdom.

THE NATURE OF APPEARANCES

Whether we experience the suffering of samsara or the peace of nirvana completely depends on our state of mind. This is not to say that by simply perceiving the world around us to be free of suffering we will only experience happiness. Meditation is not denial. Actually, to say that samsara and nirvana rely on our state of mind means that our experiences are based on the extent to which the mind is obscured by confusion.

Ordinary beings who are born in samsara are deluded by ignorance; they do not realize that the nature of mind is wisdom. Based on this ignorance, their minds produce all kinds of mental afflictions. As a result of that, they accumulate karma and undergo the three kinds of

suffering that we discussed earlier. However, by purifying their delusions and the root of ignorance, all sentient beings have the potential
to realize the nature of mind, and thus to abide in the state of nirvana.
In fact, this is the true meaning of the word "wisdom"—being completely free of ignorance.

The Teachings say that all sentient beings have what is called the
"Buddha nature." Some people mistakenly take this to mean that we
are "already a Buddha if we could just keep that idea in mind." But the
fact that we have the Buddha nature does not mean that we are perfect
Buddhas in the relative sphere. What it means is that each and every
sentient being has the potential to become a Buddha, and that this
potential can be actualized with sustained effort. We do not have to do
anything special to earn this potential; it is already ours to develop if we
wish. So this is an uplifting point. We all have the basis for realization
within us. It is said in the Tantras,

> All sentient beings have the Buddha nature,
> But it is veiled by the obscurations.
> By removing the obscurations, we become a Buddha.

However, when we say that we wish to gain liberation or attain the
state of nirvana, it is not actually ourselves as individuals, but the mind
that must be liberated. If we wish to be free of confusion, it is the
mind that must be purified. In other words, the mind must recognize
its own ultimate nature.

CONVENTIONAL AND ULTIMATE REALITY

In Buddhist logic, it is important to begin any discussion on the nature
of mind by carefully distinguishing conventional and ultimate reality.
When speaking in terms of appearances and emptiness, conventional
reality is the aspect of appearances—the way in which things appear to
ordinary samsaric beings. More specifically, Mipham Rinpoche said
that conventional reality is that which can be expressed through

"thoughts, words, and images." For example, when someone talks about a car, we know what is being talked about because we have seen a car before. It is possible that an actual image of a car comes to mind, and that we can analyze it; to think about its color and shape, how fast it goes, and what it can be used for.

If our perception of conventional reality is flawless, we call it unmistaken conventional reality. Unmistaken conventional reality has three defining characteristics: the entities that appear to us have an appearance that all beings in a particular realm agree upon, a function that can be described, and an empty nature that can be understood through analysis. However, it is also possible to have a flawed perception of conventional reality. An example of such flawed perception is the way in which the eye perceives the ignited red end of a rope that is being twirled round and round above the head as a ring of light, rather than a single, glowing light that is moving through time and space. Regarding conventional reality the master Patrul Rinpoche also said,

> The confused mind [of the perceiver]
>   and the objects [of its perception]
> Are conventional reality.
> Ultimate reality is the nature of suchness,
>   or in other words, reality itself.

Mipham Rinpoche described ultimate reality as that which is beyond "thoughts, words, and images." It is easy for us to see how true this is. No matter how hard we try to imagine the nature of suchness ourselves, or describe it to someone else, it simply cannot be done with any great degree of accuracy. Although words can be used to point out the nature of ultimate reality, the actual experience cannot be conveyed in the same way that the image of a car, or any other ordinary object, can simply be brought to mind by seeing a car, an image of a car, or the label "car." In this way, ultimate reality is inexpressible. Ultimate reality can only be realized by relying upon the mind's self-arising wisdom awareness, which we call *rikpa* in Tibetan.

If we want to gain an understanding of ultimate reality, we must begin with a discussion from the point of view of the appearances of conventional reality. Again, we are using appearances to gain a penetrating understanding of the empty nature of all phenomena and the nature of suchness. So on that note, let us turn again to the way in which things appear.

How Appearances Arise from the Mind

To begin, let us return for a moment to the idea that desire realm beings born into one of six classes experience samsara's suffering based on ignorance and the mental afflictions. While it might be easy to accept that mental afflictions arise out of ignorance and habitual tendencies, it might seem harder to accept that the way in which beings and the world appear to us manifests for the very same reason. The logic behind this is explained at length in the *Sutra Requested by Padma Nampar Rolwa (mDo padma rnam par rol ba)*, in which Padma Nampar Rolwa discussed the nature of appearances with the Bodhisattva Mañjushri:

> First, Padma Nampar Rolwa asked Mañjushri, "How is it that outer appearances appear to us? Were they created by someone or something?"
>
> Mañjushri answered, "No, they were not made by anyone. Rather, they arise from the conceptual thoughts, confusion, and habitual tendencies of the mind."
>
> Padma Nampar Rolwa thought about this for a moment, and then asked, "But how could things like the ocean, the sun, the moon, and the earth have arisen from mind? Each of these things has its own defining characteristics, like heat, coldness, and hardness. That is why I cannot understand how such things could have come from the mind."
>
> Mañjushri answered, "I assure you it is possible. Let me give you a few things to consider so you can decide for yourself whether or not it is true. First of all, in Varanasi there

once lived a man named Dramse Mishin. Dramse Mishin had dedicated himself to meditating on the idea, and visualizing, that he was a tiger. One day the people living in the city around him actually perceived him as a tiger and they fled in fear, so that from that day on the city was empty."

Mañjushri continued, "But if this is not enough to convince you, I will give you another example. Did you know that the Teachings on meditative concentration give various methods by which practitioners train in the way to perceive appearances? For example, some train in the method to perceive all appearances as earth, others train in the method to perceive all appearances as water. In fact, when a practitioner's meditation becomes stable, they really do perceive the appearances that they have trained themselves in, and nothing else. Also, when Hinayana monks meditate on all samsaric appearances as being ugly and impure as part of their monastic conduct, they actually do come to perceive all of samsara as a wasteland littered with carcasses and bones. If such practitioners can alter their perceptions in only one lifetime, then why could it not be that sentient beings, who have been developing their habitual tendencies of mind since beginningless time, would perceive appearances based on their own confusion and habitual tendencies?"

Padma Nampar Rolwa answered, "If this is true, then please explain to me how we can tell that appearances really do arise out of the habitual tendencies of the mind."

[Mañjushri replied,] "We know that appearances arise out of the tendencies of the mind because appearances are indeterminate. Let me explain to you the meaning of *indeterminate*. For example, some beings perceive the earth as land, while others perceive it as their home. Yet other beings see the earth as food and eat it. As for water, some perceive it as something to drink. Others perceive it as their environment or home, and yet other beings breathe it in like air. As for trees, some beings perceive them as plants that give shade and wood, while others perceive them as food or shelter. And not only that, but some perceive rocks as the building blocks for houses or roads. Others hide or live under the same rocks, and yet others perceive the rocks as precious stones that bring them wealth if they hoard them. Now you can understand what I mean by *indeterminate*. The way we perceive a particular appearance definitely depends on the habitual tendencies of the mind."

Mañjushri gave one final example: "Perhaps this example is even more clear. Have you ever thought about the fact that one single being can appear in countless ways depending on who it is that perceives that being? For example, the same man could be perceived as a Lama, a husband, a son, a father, an uncle, a brother, a friend, or an enemy, just to name a few. Though the appearance seems definite to the one who perceives it, it is only definite when looked at from their point of view. If this is true, then we must logically accept that the appearances of all phenomena arise from the habitual tendencies of each individual's mind."

Based on these argument, some might then assume that the objects we perceive are actually equivalent to mind itself. But if we think this, we have misunderstood Buddhist logic. If outer objects were the same as mind, then our mind would have to be identical with a mountain, a tree, an ocean, and any of the other myriad things we perceive. But even our own common sense tells us this cannot be the case. Rather, in Buddhist logic, we distinguish between the *appearance* of an object to the perceiver and *the object itself* when we discuss the way objects are perceived.

The Buddhist Teachings give us the example of the reflection of a face in a mirror as a way to understand the way in which things appear to our perception. We should understand that the clear surface of the mirror acts as the condition for the appearance reflected by it, and that the face has the ability or potential to appear reflected in the mirror. Thus, when the face and the mirror come together, based on the coming together of causes and conditions, a reflected image of the face can be seen upon the surface of the mirror. But if we ask whether the reflection in the mirror is the face itself, we could not reasonably say it is. And if we ask whether the reflection of the face is something other than the very face being reflected, we could not say that is exactly the case either.

One way to understand this metaphor is by taking the face to be the outer object, the mirror to be the mind, and the reflection to be a perceived appearance. Unlike the clear mirror in the above example, however, the samsaric mind, obscured by previous karma and the veils of mental afflictions, is like a mirror with dirt, cracks, or scratches on it, and is therefore far from clear. Because of that, it can distort the objects that appear to it, and actually believe that those objects exist the way in which they appear.

The traditional way of interpreting this metaphor is that the mirror is simply an expression of dependent arising itself. As it is said in the *King of Samadhi Sutra (Samadhirajasutra, Ting nge 'dzin rgyal po'i mdo)*,

> Like a woman with a beautiful face who gazes
> Into a mirror or a vessel into which she pours butter,
> Although the mandala of her face appears,
> It is neither [her face] nor is it not [her face].
> All phenomena should be understood in this way.

The teaching of dependent arising is used to establish the fact that all phenomena are free of a truly established nature, and are completely empty. For, if appearances arise out of the coming together of causes and conditions as well as the habitual tendencies of the mind, then it logically follows that they have no permanent qualities whatsoever. The simplest way of saying this is that the nature of dependent arising is empty. Thus, to say that the nature of phenomena is dependently arisen and free of a truly established nature is like seeing two sides of the same coin. But even this metaphor falls short of the actual relationship between emptiness and dependent arising, which is that they are completely indivisible. Thus, we could say that the Union is also that of emptiness and dependent arising. A more detailed description of the nature of dependent arising will follow in Chapter 6.

As I will discuss later in this chapter, the mind itself is also empty of inherent existence, and thus has no truly established nature. But how are we to understand our world if both our minds and the objects we perceive have no truly established natures? Because phenomena that appear to us or that we perceive are not established as existing inherently, or from their own side, and do not permanently abide "out there" or "in the mind," or anywhere in between, *we should understand them to be just like the eight types of illusions.*

To summarize, we are obstructed from realizing the nature of mind because, based on our grasping at the mind and objects as truly existent, we fall into the extreme of permanence. As a logical consequence of falling into this extreme, we also grasp at the self. Based on this grasping, we generate mental afflictions, which cause us to accumulate karma. Based on the accumulation of karma, we are bound to samsara. So we can see that the root of this was the initial grasping at the mind and objects as having some kind of permanent quality.

Even though phenomena are not established as existing objectively, they are perceived as outer objects and grasped at as being real. There is a subtle point to be understood here. The Teachings say that we apprehend appearances in two stages. The first apprehension of an appearance is free of grasping and analysis. After this initial apprehension, we grasp at, interpret, or analyze the appearance.

As it is said in the Avalokitavrata's *Commentary (Avalokitavrata, sPyan ras gzigs brtul zhugs),*

> *That which embraces* is the mind that apprehends
> And *grasping* is the analysis that arises from the mind.

Another way to explain this same point is to examine the difference between the "mind" and "that which arises from mind." For example, when we look at an object, the perception that we have in the very first moment is what is called the "mind." We may look at a cup and see a cup. But any details or analysis of the cup and its attributes after that point, for example what color the cup is, how large it is, or that it is painted gold on the inside, is "that which arises from mind."

MAKING IT RELEVANT

So, to make all this relevant to the discussion of how appearances manifest, let us take the example of arriving at a park on a summer day. Our first glance at the park, which is free of grasping, is the appearance that we call "the mind." In the very next moment, we begin to examine what the park looks like, the beautiful sunny day, and the vibrant colors that surround us. We think to ourselves, "what a wonderful day, I'm so glad I came, how great the sun feels on my back." These thoughts and images are the grasping of the mind. But if the object of the appearance, meaning the park itself, were identical to the appearance, we would have to take it with us when we left in order to remember what it looked like.

By using this example, we can see two logical flaws in the idea that appearances and objects are one and the same. First, if appearances that we perceived and the objects of those appearances were one and the same, then the mind that apprehended the appearance would have to have the characteristics found in the park—literally, its colors, textures, and shapes. If this is not true, then the only other alternative is to say that the park has none of these characteristics. But if the park has none of these characteristics, then how could we perceive it? After all, we were there. We saw it directly. So we absolutely must distinguish between the objects that exist and their appearances. The appearances that we see, hear, smell, taste, touch, or think about are not objects themselves. Appearances arise from the mind, and like the reflection of a face in a mirror, are of the nature of dependent arising and emptiness.

THE NATURE OF MIND

When we are merely looking at the myriad appearances that manifest in the world around us, they seem to be real and abiding. But after we have examined them with impeccable logic, we realize that not even one of them has a truly established nature. Not only do they not have an objectively established nature, but if our logic and examination become extremely precise, we realize that they are actually beyond the "thoughts, words, and images" that characterize conventional reality.

But just as outer appearances are of the empty nature of dependent arising, so the mind is not truly established or ultimately findable. The mind has no form, color, or shape. No matter how much we may search, we cannot locate the mind. The only words we have to describe the mind are that it is completely uncontrived, and vast as the sky. In the *Heap of Jewels Sutra (Ratnakutasutra, dKon mchog brtsegs pa mdo)*, Buddha Shakyamuni gave the following instruction:

> What is the medicine that enables us to transcend worldly life? It is the diligence by which we are able to completely understand the nature of mind. When we begin to examine a mental affliction that arises in the mind, we should examine where it came from. Was it generated in the past, the present, or the future? We cannot say it was generated in the past, for the past is over. The future has not yet come, so we cannot say it came from the future either. If it was produced by the mind, it must have been made by this present mind. But how could this be so? The mind is momentary and does not abide for even an instant. The mind is not within the body or outside of it, it does not abide in the skeleton, the circulatory system, or the nervous system. In fact, we cannot find the mind no matter how hard we may search. It would be quite impossible for us to show it to someone if they asked us.

Because the mind does not abide within us or outside, or anywhere in between, the great sage Nagarjuna declared in the *Fundamental Treatise on the Middle Way* (*Mulamadhyamakakarika, dBu ma rtsa ba shes rab*),

> The mind is beyond verbal description.
> It cannot be understood as a mental object.
> It was not born and does not cease.
> The nature of mind is one with nirvana.

Based on this quote, we may then wonder what the nature of mind actually is. The nature of mind is the clear light wisdom that has not been spoiled by the delusion of ignorance. In fact, the only difference between the confusion experienced by ordinary beings and the wisdom experienced by enlightened beings is the obscurations that obstruct us from seeing the mind's true nature. As it is said in Maitreyanatha's *Ornament of Clear Realization* (*Abhisamayalamkara, mNgon par rtogs pa'i rgyan*),

> As for the mind, it does not abide.
> The nature of the mind is clear light.

THE UNION OF CONVENTIONAL AND ULTIMATE REALITY

From the point of view of ultimate reality, inner and outer phenomena are not truly established. However, from the point of view of conventional reality, they are born, abide, and cease. The union of conventional and ultimate reality, or appearance and emptiness, is explained in the *Secret Essence Tantra*:

> Emaho! It's the amazing and magnificent
> Secret teaching of all the perfect Buddhas.
> There is no birth, but all things are born [in
>   conventional reality].

Though birth appears, there is no birth [in ultimate reality].
Emaho! It's the amazing and magnificent
Secret teaching of all the perfect Buddhas.
There is no cessation, but all things cease.
Though cessation appears, there is no cessation.
Emaho! It's the amazing and magnificent
Secret teaching of all the perfect Buddhas.
There is no abiding, but all things abide.
Though abiding appears, there is no abiding.
Emaho! It's the amazing and magnificent
Secret teaching of all the perfect Buddhas.
There is no perception, but all things are [dichotomously]
    perceived.
Though [dichotomous] perception appears, there is no
    perception.
Emaho! It's the amazing and magnificent
Secret teaching of all the perfect Buddhas.
There is no coming or going, but things come and go.
Though things appear to come and go, there is no coming
    or going.

From the point of view of ultimate reality, both the mind and all
phenomena are free of birth, abiding, and cessation. However, ordinary beings who do not realize this grasp inner and outer objects as
being real based on their ignorance. Thus, they perceive all phenomena
as having a truly established existence. The Teachings liken this to an
individual who has glaucoma and cannot see objects accurately. When
they look far into the distance, they sometimes see things that are not
there at all. Or at other times, they mistake a tree or a rock for the form
of a human being. In this same way, ordinary beings bound by ignorance mistakenly perceive phenomena as being truly established even
though their nature is completely empty. Based on their mistaken perception, beings form attachments and grasp at them. This grasping
results in their taking birth in samsara. The master Longchenpa said,

The appearances of entities are not beneficial or harmful,
But by grasping at them, [beings] are shackled to [samsaric]
    existence.
It is not necessary to examine the myriad appearances that
    manifest;
Rather, cut through the root of the mind's grasping!

Thus, we should realize that ignorance, which results in grasping at subject and object, as well as birth, abiding, and cessation, is what we must purify through our Dharma practice. And if we wish to purify this ignorance that is like an illness that has impaired our eyes, the only antidote is self-arising wisdom awareness. In other words, we must realize that samsara is completely empty of inherent existence, and this emptiness that is samsara is inseparable from its appearance.

If we wonder how to realize rikpa during this very lifetime, the answer is not that we must get it from somewhere or something outside of us. Actually, this self-arising rikpa is part of the Buddha nature, and the seed for it is already within the continuum of the mind. But to bring it out and experience it so that we can use it, we need to rely on the compassionate method of Bodhichitta, and the uncontrived view, or "that which arises from the method" established by the great Middle Way. By taking up these two in union, we can be sure not to fall into the two extremes of grasping at nirvanic peace and grasping at existence, and relax the mind in the vast expanse of the Dharmadhatu.

Falling into either of these two extremes is a serious obstacle to the attainment of enlightenment. In order to cut through the extreme of grasping at nirvanic peace, the quality of Bodhichitta absolutely must be present in the view and meditation. If it is not, we will become like the Arhats who have attained liberation from samsara but do not realize that they have not yet attained Buddhahood, which renders them unable to progress on the path. At the other extreme, in order to cut through grasping at existence, it is imperative that we meditate on the nature of emptiness. Otherwise, we will perceive both the mind and outer objects as being objectively real or truly established, which will spoil the correct view. It is only when we rely upon the Union, in which we take up both elements of appearance and emptiness, that we are able to free ourselves of the two extremes. This is the proper way to take up the Union of Dzogchen and Bodhichitta, which is the essence of all phenomena and the true nature of the Great Perfection.

We should note that each of the four schools of Tibetan Buddhism has a unique name for the method of realizing the nature of mind. In the Nyingmapa School, we call it Dzogchen, or the Great Perfection. The Kagyupa School calls it the Mahamudra. The Sakyapa School calls it the Union of Samsara and Nirvana. Finally, the Gelugpa School calls it the Great Middle Way. But despite the different names each school has for the method, we should recognize that the Teachings of all four schools rely upon the Union of Dzogchen and Bodhichitta, which acts as the underlying principle of all the profound methods.

CHAPTER 6

*Dispelling the Obstacles to the
Practice of Dzogchen*

I F WE LIVE IN A COUNTRY where Buddhism is being taught for
the first time, with no historical precedent to fall back on, it
may be difficult to understand the benefit of practicing the Teachings
on the Paramitas and the Middle Way. But practicing these Teachings
is truly of great value. For if we wish to recognize the uncontrived
view of Dzogchen free of mistakes and doubts, then a deep understanding of the Teachings on the Middle Way and the Paramitas (which
I have already shown to be twofold Bodhichitta) is necessary. Without
being well versed and established in these Teachings, we will not be
able to dispel the obstacles to the practice of Dzogchen.

The great yogis and scholars of the past who attained complete mastery over the Dzogchen Teachings—such as Longchenpa, Jigme
Lingpa, Patrul Rinpoche, and Mipham Rinpoche, to name only a
few—placed extreme importance on the Teachings of the Middle Way
and the Paramitas. It was based on these Teachings that they taught the
method to realize the uncontrived view of Dzogchen. When they gave
Teachings, they focused on the three aspects of Dharma practice: the
foundation, the path, and the result, which are said to contain the root
of all the Teachings.

When they gave Teachings on the Middle Way, they taught that the
foundation is the inseparable two truths: relative and absolute truth
or, in other words, conventional and ultimate reality. The path is the
inseparable two accumulations of merit and wisdom. And finally, by
taking up the inseparable two accumulations, we attain the result of
the inseparable two kayas: the Rupakaya and the Dharmakaya. We can
see through the presentation of these three aspects just how essential

Mipham Rinpoche

it is for us to have a clear understanding of conventional and ultimate reality, which creates the conditions for us to realize the inseparable nature of appearance and emptiness—which is suchness itself.

Actually, when such yogis gave Teachings on the Paramitas, the foundation, path, and result were taught to be exactly the same as when they taught the Middle Way. So, based on this, we may come to the conclusion that the two truths are only important in terms of studying Sutra. However, this is not the case. If we examine the Teachings that were given on Tantra, we will find that the way these three aspects were taught was exactly as in Sutra.

I will back up for a moment in order to explain what I mean by "Tantra." Although most students normally think of Tantra as a group of texts, in Tibetan the word "Tantra" actually means "continuum." It refers to the continuum of mind. The continuum of mind refers to the Buddha nature that is present in each and every sentient being. This, in turn, brings us to the method for realizing the nature of ultimate reality—which is why such texts are known as Tantra.

In the Teachings given on the foundation, path, and result of Tantra, or the continuum of mind, we also use the inseparable two truths as the basis. So, what we should take away from this explanation is that in all of the Teachings of both Sutra and Tantra there is not even one teaching that does not rely upon an understanding of the union of conventional and ultimate reality. Usually in the Sutras we refer to the nature of reality as the union of appearance and emptiness. However, in the Tantric Teachings we refer to this same idea as "clarity and emptiness."

In considering conventional and ultimate reality and the Tantric Teachings as a whole, we may begin to wonder which of the Teachings, Dzogchen or Bodhichitta, is the most important or the most essential in terms of our practice and realization. Our answer would depend on what kind of examination we have made of the Teachings, the mind, and outer phenomena. Those who have not understood the nature of appearances to be empty would probably choose Dzogchen. Such students might come to the conclusion that relative and absolute truth are like fire and water. In other words, that which is experienced in conventional reality is mere confusion and has to be done away with, and the absolute truth of ultimate reality is the thing to be focused upon, and realized. But this is a grave mistake. As the master Mipham Rinpoche said,

> If the conventional is thrown to the other shore,
> Then there is no ultimate.
> These two are the method and that which arises from the
>   method.

If we do not take up the truths in union, but rather associate ultimate reality with wisdom and conventional reality with delusion, then the inseparable view of appearance and emptiness will also be divided. If we separate the nature of appearance and emptiness, we have already strayed far from the realization of the nature of mind. That is why the Teachings say that there is no realization of ultimate reality without relying upon the Union, which is the uncontrived view.

THE NATURE OF DEPENDENT ARISING

As I began to explain in Chapter 5, all phenomena that appear in samsara arise from the coming together of causes and conditions. This coming together is called "dependent arising," or maybe an easier word to help understand this might be "interdependence." A simple way to think about dependent arising is to examine something small in our daily lives, like the act of buying a loaf of bread in the store. If we just look at the appearance of the loaf of bread, we may want to say that it is just a loaf of bread and that's all. But actually, if we examine it closely, we will realize that many, many causes and conditions had to come together for us to be able to behold and enjoy a loaf of bread.

For example, the loaf of bread was made up of all kinds of ingredients that had to be mixed by the employees who worked at the place it was baked. The ingredients used to make the bread also arose from causes and conditions. The seeds that would yield the grain had to be planted by farmers tending fields; the mature crops had to be harvested, processed, and packaged in factories, where more people worked. The people who worked for the shipping companies were also necessary in ensuring that the ingredients were sent to the right places.

We are also a factor in the situation. We are the ones who decide to buy the bread, and that decision is based on other causes and conditions in our life. For some reason, we choose to go to a particular store and buy a particular loaf of bread. When we think in this way, we realize that all of the many countless objects that we neatly perceive as being just this or that, or as being only what appears concretely before us, actually become immensely complicated. Each one of them, each action we take, and even each moment arise from a plethora of causes and conditions that had to come together to create what appears before us. After we have examined the bread and realized how it is not actually a truly established loaf of bread with some kind of essential "breadness," we can see how precise the nature of dependent arising actually is. If just one of the causes or conditions that were needed to make this loaf of bread appear were missing, it could not have appeared at all.

Because the appearances that manifest before us are actually the momentary expression of causes and conditions coming together, not one among them can exist independently or without changing. That is why we say that dependent arising, like appearances, is empty. The view of the Middle Way is based on the perfect logic that establishes the emptiness of all phenomena: that all phenomena are ultimately free of birth, abiding, and cessation. In the *Fundamental Treatise on the Middle Way,* the master Nagarjuna said,

> There is not even a single phenomenon
> That does not arise in dependence [on something else].
> And, [given that,] there is not even a single phenomenon
> That is not of the nature of emptiness.

For a student who has not trained in this style of logic, it can actually be quite difficult to understand. In this text, I will present the basic logic used to establish the view of the Middle Way, which is free of all extremes. Of course, it would be impossible to include all of the logical arguments in the Middle Way canon, which would take years of study and contemplation to master. For students who really want to gain insight into the Middle Way, further study of treatises such as Nagarjuna's *Fundamental Treatise on the Middle Way*, Chandrakirti's *Entering the Middle Way*, and Shantarakshita's *Ornament of the Middle Way* (*Madhyamakalamkara, dBu ma rgyan*) is necessary. Such texts present the four or five major styles of logic used in establishing the view of the great Middle Way.

To begin a discussion of the Middle Way, we should start with this assertion by the sage Nagarjuna about the nature of all phenomena:

There is no birth from the self or other.
It is not from the self and other.
Nothing is without cause.
No matter what entity [is examined],
There is no birth.

We have said that all phenomena arise based on causes and conditions. And because we have examined the nature of dependent arising, we also know that all things dependently arisen are empty. That is why it is said in the Teachings that all phenomena that arise from causes and conditions have no birth or origin. The Secret Teachings refer to this as being "unborn." This does not mean that birth does not appear, but that birth is not truly established.

The masterful Middle Way scholar Chandrakirti said,

Besides a wagon, which is made of parts, nothing else can
    be called a wagon.
Though there is no other [wagon], it is not truly established.
As such, it is made of parts, but the parts [that make up
    the wagon] are not [the wagon itself];
Neither is the sum of the parts, or the [wagon's] form.

This metaphor illustrates the way in which we should understand phenomena as having no truly established nature. If we apply this metaphor to an analysis of the self, we find that by the power of dependent arising the self appears based on the support of the five aggregates of the body. However, neither the parts, the sum of the parts, nor the form of the body actually comprise a real, abiding self. From these examples we can see why it is said that the self, as well as all phenomena, is not truly established.

Actually, when we use the word "suchness," we are translating a term in Tibetan which means "reality as it is." The word "suchness" has been coined in English to point out the same meaning that is illustrated by Chandrakirti's metaphor. Because there is no essential or established quality of the self or phenomena, the suffix "ness" has been added to the word "such" to give the meaning that reality is "just as such," and that it is free of concepts or established characteristics.

DEVELOPING CERTAINTY

In Buddhist philosophy it is said that all phenomena that can be apprehended can be described as falling into either conventional or ultimate reality. When examining these two, we are aiming to understand the relationship between the impure phenomena of conventional reality and the perfectly pure phenomena of ultimate reality. The degree of certainty with which we understand this relationship also acts as the basis for certainty to develop in our practice of meditation. This is because through our certainty we become convinced that the only possible way to attain realization of the Teachings is to take up the Union of Dzogchen and Bodhichitta, and to rely upon the path's inseparable aspects of method and wisdom. Thus, we can say that it is actually our certainty that ultimately gives rise to accomplishment. Not only that, but it also determines the length of the path we must follow to reach enlightenment. That is to say, a skillful understanding of conventional and ultimate reality shortens the path to enlightenment. So we could actually say that not only accomplishment, but also the short path that is one of the defining characteristics of the Vajrayana itself, relies upon our complete understanding of the conventional and the ultimate.

It is crucial that we gain certainty in the two truths in order for our meditation to progress. If we throw away the method and attempt to take up only meditation on emptiness and the uncontrived view of Dzogchen, we are in danger of falling into the extreme of nihilism. This is what has led me to believe that perhaps contemporary Buddhists do not properly understand the definition of Dzogchen. As I have said, Dzogchen is the "great perfection" because it is perfectly complete. It is not Dzogchen if it lacks the method. There is no Dzogchen if only half of the Teachings are present.

If we wish to take up the path based on the union of the two truths, we should understand conventional and ultimate reality to be as Mipham Rinpoche taught:

> All that appears is pervaded by emptiness,
> And emptiness is pervaded by appearance.
> No entity exists that appears but is not empty,
> And emptiness that does not appear cannot be established.

If appearances were not empty but were truly established, we could not call the appearances of samsara conventional reality. Based on logic, we have already realized that all phenomena that can be apprehended in samsara are empty. If appearances in conventional reality were truly established, they would be permanent and belong to something other than the reality we are talking about.

Because of this, we are unable to place any of the phenomena we apprehend into either extreme of appearance or emptiness. In other words, we cannot think of a single phenomenon that appears but is not empty, or that is empty but does not appear. Appearance is emptiness, and emptiness is uncontrived. From the point of view of the Middle Way, as well as the union of samsara and nirvana, it is impossible for us to give more importance to either appearance or emptiness. In other words, we absolutely must take them up in union.

In terms of the Union of Dzogchen and Bodhichitta, we may wonder what the Middle Way Teachings have to do with taking up the path, or our own realization of the Teachings. Actually, in order to take up meditation on the uncontrived view, we must be certain of what the view is, without a single doubt. This certainty is attained by gaining a deep understanding of the view presented by the Middle Way Teachings. Based on our deep certainty about the view presented by the Middle Way, it becomes possible to take up the uncontrived view presented by the Dzogchen Teachings without making a mistake. I am not suggesting that there is no difference between the uncontrived views that are presented by the Teachings of the Middle Way and Dzogchen. As we will see in the next chapter, they are similar in one respect and distinct in another. However, a thorough study of the Teachings of the Middle Way can help us to recognize what the view is, and point the way to abide in it properly. Mipham Rinpoche said,

> In order to polish and perfect primordial wisdom
> It is vital to master the Middle Way.

And the Dzogchen master Khenpo Shenga said,

> Without understanding the Middle Way view,
> [We will] not realize the union of appearance and emptiness.
> Without understanding the union of appearance and emptiness,
> [We will] not know [it is] the union of clarity and light.
> Without knowing [it is] the union of clarity and light,
> [We will] not realize the Great Perfection.
> If we do not realize the Great Perfection,
> [We will] not attain Buddhahood in this life.

That is to say, if we wish to realize the view of Dzogchen and attain the short path to enlightenment, a thorough understanding of the Middle Way is necessary.

When we are in the process of examining conventional and ultimate reality, as well as the remaining Middle Way Teachings, it is extremely important for us to proceed carefully. A mistaken understanding of the Middle Way is said to be a great obstacle for those who are still working towards realization. As I have already said, if we misunderstand the uncontrived view of the Middle Way Teachings, we are liable to fall into the extreme of nihilism, which is like a great void where nothing seems to matter. In such a void, we cease to believe that our actions in conventional reality are of any consequence at all, and lose our conviction in karma. In the Teachings, one who makes this mistake is likened to a person who grabs a poisonous snake without knowing the proper way to pick it up. The opposite extreme of nihilism is called eternalism. We fall into the extreme of eternalism when we grasp at phenomena or the self as being permanent.

Actually, it is the realization of the inseparable nature of clarity and emptiness of all phenomena that saves us from falling into either of these extremes. From the point of view of clarity, all phenomena appear, which keeps us from falling into the extreme of nihilism. And from the point of view of emptiness, all phenomena are empty and impermanent, which keeps us from falling into the extreme of eternalism.

THE REFUTATION OF THE FOUR EXTREMES

When we refer to the uncontrived view of Dzogchen, we may wonder why it is said to be uncontrived and how to understand what this view is. The word "uncontrived" comes from the Teachings on the Middle Way, which assert that all phenomena are free of four types of extremes. It was said by the great scholar Aryadeva in *The Compendium on the Essence of Wisdom (Jñanasarasamuchchaya, Ye shes snying po kun las btus pa)*:

> [All phenomena] do not exist, do not lack existence,
> [They do] not [both at once] exist and not exist,
> [Nor do they at once lack both] existence and nonexistence.
> The one of the Middle Way is free of the four extremes.

The Middle Way view is free of four extremes. The extreme of existence is equivalent to a phenomenon that is truly or permanently established, which has been refuted by all of the Buddhas. And, because we know the essence of all phenomena is empty of inherent nature, we know they do not exist inherently. The extreme of absolute nonexistence also cannot be true because by the power of dependent arising phenomena arise. The other two extremes, of both existing and not existing, or not both existing and not existing, are illogical. The extreme of both existing and nonexisting would be like seeing light and darkness at the same time. The extreme of not both existing and nonexisting would be exemplified as something that arises without cause. So when we talk about the uncontrived view, we are referring to that which does not fall into the four extremes refuted by the logic of the Middle Way.

The master Shantideva said that habituating ourselves to emptiness through our meditation practice would enable us to abandon our grasping at entities as being truly established. However, when we begin to meditate on emptiness, our meditation still relies upon a form of grasping, so it is not really uncontrived. This grasping, or trying to apprehend a negation, an absence of self existence or true establishment, is necessary when we are still learning how to meditate. But if we practice with diligence for a long period of time, we can slowly abandon that grasping too, which allows us to develop meditation that is truly uncontrived and free of extremes.

This apprehending or lack of apprehending a negation is referred to in the Teachings in the presentation of the two kinds of ultimate reality: nominal ultimate reality and actual ultimate reality. Nominal ultimate reality is the view of emptiness based on what is called a "nonaffirming negative." A nonaffirming negative negates an object without implying the existence or presence of something else. Thus, it is a concept that is used to imply nonduality. This concept of a nonaffirming negative must also be abandoned in order to take up the uncontrived view. Once this subtle type of grasping has been abandoned, we can abide in actual ultimate reality.

TAKING UP THE UNCONTRIVED VIEW

To summarize the way to practice the uncontrived view of the Middle Way, we must first understand all phenomena to be of the nature of appearance. Next, we contemplate and gain certainty in the fact that appearances are empty, and that emptiness is dependent arising. Finally, we gain certainty in the union of appearance and emptiness. The great scholar Je Tsongkhapa said,

Without a doubt, all appearances are dependent arising,
And emptiness is beyond description.
But, for however long ordinary beings separate these two,
They will not realize the Buddha's view.
One day, upon unifying these two,
The grasping at all objects as being real melts.
This is known as seeing the Dharmakaya.

However, there are many ways in which we can misunderstand the way to take up the uncontrived view. For however long we meditate on the uncontrived view while still holding fast to the idea that while we are meditating we must not grasp or abandon, we will be unable to recognize what is truly meant by the uncontrived view of the Middle Way, which is free of extremes. The great master Tilopa said to his student Naropa,

My son, mere appearances do not bind.
Grasping binds.
Naropa, cut through all grasping.

In addition, the pop culture version of the Buddhist term "the uncontrived view" has not captured the essence of what it means to be free of extremes. Rather than being free of the extremes of existence, nonexistence, both existence and nonexistence, and neither existence nor nonexistence, the pop culture version has come to be something that is more like "just close your eyes and think about nothing." To clear up this serious misunderstanding, we must understand the correct and mistaken ways to take up the uncontrived view.

THE PERFECT, UNCONTRIVED VIEW

The perfect, uncontrived view of Dzogchen can also be described as the Dharmakaya itself—the union of Dzogchen and Bodhichitta, the union of appearance and emptiness, the union of clarity and empti-

ness, the union of the two truths, or the union of awareness and emptiness. All of these descriptions of "the union" point to the same thing.
Based on faith and devotion, as well as the introduction to the nature
of mind by the Spiritual Friend, it is possible to experience rikpa, and
based on this experience as well as the proper instructions, meditation,
and conduct, we are able to realize the view. There is probably no need
to mention that we also need extensive training in the uncontrived view
of the Middle Way and the method provided by the Paramitas, since
that is the topic of this chapter.

A Bodhisattva who wishes to realize the view must take up uncontrived meditation and rest in rikpa. When resting in ripka, all concepts
and grasping at subject and object are self-liberated. This is called "the
setting of duality." The metaphor given for this in the Teachings is
"pouring water into water." In other words, it is the true expression of
nonduality. This state, which is the union of clarity and emptiness, is
beyond all thoughts and words and can only be described as being as
vast and open as the sky.

Obstacles to the Unmistaken, Uncontrived View

It is possible to make a mistake when meditating on the uncontrived
view of Dzogchen, and there are several conditions that would con-
tribute to such a mistake. In this section, I will try to clarify some of the
major obstacles to taking up the perfect, uncontrived view of the
Dzogchen Teachings.

The first obstacle would come to a practitioner who wanted to practice the uncontrived view but had no foundation in listening and contemplation. Such a practitioner would have no experience studying the
scriptures and the logic of the Middle Way, and would not have cultivated a strong relationship with a Spiritual Friend, and thus would not
have received perfect oral instructions. This would lead such a practitioner to have no basis on which to understand the terminology that
is generally associated with the view of Dzogchen—words like "effort-

less," "self-liberation," and "uncontrived." So, grasping at these words, the practitioner would think that the goal of meditation was to just relax and try to "empty the mind." The idea is that by not allowing any conceptual thoughts to arise, one can become free of contrivance and be able to rest in "that quiet place" which is "the view."

This kind of practitioner is like one who has fainted and become unconscious, which is to say that he has tried to place himself in a state in which sense perceptions are not feeding the mind a lot of information. But if we wish to equate this state with wisdom, we must first examine what good qualities or wisdom such a dissociated and unconscious state holds. In truth, it does not hold any. It is simply the wrong approach, and is not what the Teachings are referring to. This kind of meditation does not enable us to liberate the mental afflictions. It gives us neither the method to cultivate love and compassion, nor the opportunity to attain the good qualities that are gained when progressing along the path towards enlightenment.

The next obstacle might come when we hear the instruction that says that in our meditation we should be "free of grasping." We should always remember that the meaning we glean from the Teachings is based on our own training and experience. A practitioner who has had exposure to and training in the scriptures and the Middle Way, under the careful guidance of a Spiritual Friend, will have the ability to recognize what is meant by saying that meditation should be "free of grasping." But if we have not relied on any of these vital supports, we should see this as one of the greatest obstacles to the development of our meditation. If we do not know what is meant by this weighty phrase, we will almost certainly make a mistake when trying to put it into practice.

Yet another obstacle could come to our view if we think that simply taking up the sevenfold posture, widening our gaze, and using mantric syllables such as PHAT will lead us to liberation. The physical posture we take up in meditation will never be as important as our understanding of how to work with and liberate the mind. If we have not received and properly understood the oral instructions, such practice can in no way liberate us from samsara. We should always make sure that the posture we assume when we meditate has the strong support of certainty gained by listening to, studying, and contemplating the Teachings.

I would also like to stress how important it is in Vajrayana Buddhism to learn to meditate and visualize with open eyes. If we practice meditation with our eyes closed, another obstacle can come to the view. When we meditate, we are not aiming to cut off the appearances of conventional reality, even when we wish to take up the uncontrived view. If we meditate by closing our eyes and trying only to grasp at nothing, we will be abandoning the only method that we have to realize emptiness. As I have stressed, the realization of emptiness is based on appearance, so closing our eyes would actually deprive us of the method.

Another obstacle can come to the view if we take the fact that the self does not exist on mere faith, devoid of any careful and penetrating examination that would lead us to certainty. It is impossible to be liberated from self-attachment based on the mere feeling, flash, or intuition that there is no self. We could use the example of mistaking a piece of striped rope for a snake to understand why this is true. If we simply deny to ourselves that there is a snake before us, and hold fast to the idea that it is not there, we will not be able to eradicate our fear. However, if we make an examination of the snake that leads us to realize that it is not in fact a snake at all, but just a piece of rope, we will naturally and authentically lose our fear of the snake, rather than merely suppressing that fear. Like this, we should use the Teachings of the Middle Way and the two truths to become convinced that there is no self in order to gradually eradicate our self-attachment.

Most people like the idea of a style of meditation that is "effortless," but this in itself can be a heavy obstacle if we do not understand what aspect of our meditation should be effortless. If we think the true meaning of the word "effortless" is that we do not have to make any effort at understanding the view or our practice of meditation, we will find that we lack the diligence we need to progress along the path.

Instead, we should realize that we have made no effort thus far, which has caused us to take birth in samsara again and again from beginningless time. Actually, what comes effortlessly for samsaric beings is (if we are honest with ourselves) to act selfishly and in ways that are harmful to both self and others. It is up to us to rely upon a Spiritual Friend so that we can receive the Teachings that will give us insight into which particular aspect of the path this word actually refers to.

The next obstacle concerns the way we think of the conditions for realization like study, contemplation, training in logic and scriptures, and guidance by a Spiritual Friend. We should realize that these are truly the factors that determine whether or not we will progress along the path. In terms of taking up the uncontrived view of Dzogchen, it is said that relying upon these factors creates a difference that is as great as the distance between a valley and the top of a high mountain peak. There are several notions we might have that could cause us to abandon reliance upon such supports.

We could think, for example, that we have special karma with the Teachings, or an uncommonly good habitual tendency from past lives upon which we can rely, and thus need no training. Alternately, we may underestimate the profundity of the view and have the idea that the view is something that is actually rather easy to realize. However, even the greatest *tulkus*—incarnate Lamas—in the Tibetan tradition seek out and receive extensive training, so the idea that our habitual tendency could be so great that we do not need education and training is a naïve one that could not be true. And, if we look back to the story of Milarepa, one of the greatest yogis in all of Tibetan history, we will see that it was precisely because he thought the ultimate view was an easy thing to realize that he did not gain liberation even after receiving the oral instructions the first time.

Another obstacle could arise when we are making an examination of the mind, for example what the color and shape of mind is, or where it originates and how it abides. When making such an examination, we are bound to come to an intellectual understanding of emptiness. But, this intellectual understanding should not be taken to mean that we have been "introduced" to the nature of mind. Why would thinking that we have recognized the nature of mind based on our analytical examination be a mistake?

It is true that the mind has no color, shape, or form, but we do not need to possess any great intellect or skill to arrive at this understanding. So, if we have examined the mind and realized that it is empty of self-existence, we should not make the mistake of believing that we have realized something profound. Indeed, in the Dzogchen Teachings there is much talk about the "introduction to the nature of mind," but this introduction must be given by the Spiritual Friend to the student. It cannot take place based on our own study or analytical examination, and it is certainly not something we can gain through something as simple as the logical deduction of the emptiness of the mind.

✦ CHAPTER 7
✦ ✦ *View, Meditation, and Conduct*
✦

As we have discussed up to this point, there is no view other than the uncontrived view, which the logic of the Middle Way establishes to be free of extremes. But in order to gain the result of the Teachings, we need more than just the unmistaken view. If we examine the lives of the great yogis of the past, we will find that it is essential to rely upon the unmistaken view, meditation, and conduct in order to attain realization. The master Jigme Lingpa said,

> View, meditation, conduct, and result:
> These four are the essence of [Buddhist] philosophy.

In this chapter, I will examine the life of Padmasambhava's consort Yeshe Tsogyal to show how she took up the first three elements to attain the supreme result.

THE VIEW

Regarding the view, the consort Yeshe Tsogyal said,

> The view is nothing more than the
>   defining characteristic of all phenomena.
> When it is experienced,
> It is not nonexistent, it is clear awareness.
> It is not permanently established, its nature is empty.
>
> The essence of these two is called the view.
> Its essence is free of eternalism and nihilism.

> The meaning [of these assertions] is understood
>   when the mind is examined,
> And [rikpa] is seen or not seen.
> Seeing [rikpa]
> Is called the view.

In this teaching, the view is said to be the "defining characteristic of all phenomena." In other words, it is the nature of suchness, the vast Dharmadhatu that is beyond all extremes. The view is first understood through listening and contemplation. But when we directly take up the view, it is experienced as the union of clear awareness and emptiness. As I have already said, the union of clear awareness and emptiness is free of the two extremes of eternalism and nihilism.

Next, Yeshe Tsogyal says that in order to realize the view, we must examine the mind. There is always some confusion around this instruction. It seems to mean that some kind of outer object must be seen in order to attain the view, or must manifest as a sign that we have attained it. However, we should not understand Yeshe Tsogyal's words to mean that "seeing" rikpa means that there is actually something to see. The uncontrived view is free of the three spheres, and thus completely nondual. It is the self-arising wisdom awareness that is the union of clarity and emptiness.

In regard to this same idea, the renowned yogi Milarepa said we must examine the mind both night and day. But he clarified this by saying that when we examine the mind, there is nothing to see. To rest in this "not seeing" is the view itself. It is actually because the view is beyond the duality of subject and object that it is so difficult to describe.

THE PRACTICE OF MEDITATION

Many people these days have the wrong idea about the practice of meditation. They think of it as a beautiful experience, like a movie, which will give them some kind of instantaneous realization. Often I have heard practitioners describe having visions of magical deities, Buddhas, and Bodhisattvas. But when we see Dharma and the practice of meditation as something that is out of the ordinary, we are in danger of using it for purposes other than our spiritual realization. When viewed as something magical or extraordinary, meditation is often motivated by the desire to attain something in exchange for taking up the practice. No matter what it is that we wish for, if it is not endowed with the perfect aspiration of Bodhichitta, it is bound to interfere with our spiritual realization. That is why it is so often said that the path is the goal. Any desire or attachment we generate towards our practice will spoil the view, and hinder the development of our meditation.

When we meditate on the view, we are not meditating on an object. There is nothing to assimilate or understand. The word "meditate" in Tibetan can be roughly translated as "to habituate," and the etymology is also related to the colloquial phrase "get used to." Meditation is working with the mind, and trying to change the fundamental habits that we have developed since beginningless time. When we meditate, we are meditating with the view—so we could say that meditation is actually the process of habituating ourselves to the view. The great Sakya Drakpa Gyaltsen said that if there is any grasping at all in our meditation, then it is not meditation.

The Four Attachments

When taking up meditation, our practice must be free of the four attachments. It is said that if we have attachment to this life, we are not a practitioner of the Dharma. If we have attachment to samsara, we lack the renunciation necessary to attain realization. If we have attachment to our own well-being, we lack the qualities of a Bodhisattva. And if we generate attachment during our meditation, we have lost the view. When we take up the path and practice free of these four factors, it is called meditation.

However, if we want to become skillful at the practice of meditation, we need to base our meditation on a foundation of listening and contemplation. The foundation of listening is gained by receiving Teachings on the Sutra and Tantra systems from a Spiritual Friend who is skillful in explaining their meaning, and whose own conduct shows signs of profound practice. As we listen to the Teachings, we should explore the meaning of the Teachings and cut through any doubts or confusion we might have about them. Next, we should contemplate what we have heard, in order to gain deep certainty in the meaning. In Tibet, we say a practitioner should aspire to a certainty that cannot be robbed by doubts or confrontations with others who may disagree or who have no faith. So, when we actually begin to meditate, we are beginning from a place of deep certainty regarding what it is that we are setting out to gain experience in.

I have heard from some of my students that meditation is hard. I always answer that if meditation were easy, either samsara would be empty or the world would be fully populated by yogis practicing in solitary retreat. However, meditation, which in Tibetan relates to the word "habituation," is something we can get used to doing. The great Shantideva declared that with habituation, there is not a single thing that does not become easy.

Actually, worldly work is quite difficult, as is taking on all of the financial and familial responsibilities that are part of the modern world. It is actually because people in the modern world have become habit-uated to these responsibilities that they seem manageable. We should have confidence that we can also get used to meditating if we put the same amount of energy and effort into it as we put into our worldly lives.

This is equally true for those people who think they do not have time to practice meditation because they are too busy or have too many responsibilities. I do not actually believe it is possible that someone could be too busy to meditate. We do not have to trick ourselves into believing that even five minutes is not enough to practice meditation if that is all the time we have in one day. We might have to make very simple changes in the way we live, and gradually increase how much time and energy we put into our Dharma practice over time. But we can do it, if we are determined.

The Practice of Meditative Concentration

Another reason why meditation is difficult is because students often lack a foundation in meditative concentration. As I have already said, meditative concentration is what enables us to take up the short path of meditating on the view. So if we are finding that our efforts at taking up the view are falling short, it may be a good time to start working with the techniques for developing shamatha.

Regarding the importance of meditative concentration, the master Shantideva said,

> Because we realize that the mental afflictions are completely
>   destroyed
> By meditation endowed with skillful meditative concentration,
> We first learn to develop meditative concentration.

Here, "meditative concentration" refers to shamatha, which is practiced to gain stability of mind. "Meditation" refers to meditation free from all reference points, and is the practice of taking up the uncontrived view of Dzogchen.

In Tibet, the practice of Guru Yoga has always been indispensable for developing the skills of meditative concentration. However, I am not sure that contemporary practitioners know its value in terms of taking up the uncontrived view. As we will see in the story of the consort Yeshe Tsogyal that comes later in this chapter, it was Guru Yoga that formed the foundation for her realization. By considering the example of one of the finest practitioners of Dzogchen that ever lived, it is easy to see just how essential Guru Yoga and the foundation of meditative concentration are.

The method for taking up the practice of Guru Yoga is described at length in the great Patrul Rinpoche's *The Words of My Perfect Teacher*, so I will not include it as part of this text. For students who are serious about wanting to develop meditative concentration and this practice, as well as doing the remaining foundational practices that are taught in Patrul Rinpoche's text, Guru Yoga is truly essential. In this text, I will present several other methods that can be used to develop meditative concentration. Although any student is free to work with these practices, traditionally they were intended for students who had already completed the foundational practices and who were experienced in the practice of Guru Yoga.

To take up the first method, we should adopt the sevenfold posture and then visualize the three channels in the body. The central channel should be visualized to be a rich indigo blue and as straight as a pillar that does not lean to either the left or the right. It has four characteristics. It is blue in color, which is symbolic of the Dharmakaya and the unborn nature of all phenomena. Its walls are as fine as a lotus petal, which is as thin as the veils of the habitual tendencies that obscure the true nature of mind. It is as bright as the flame that dispels ignorance. And it is completely straight, which symbolizes that it will never lead to the lower realms.

When we are visualizing, we should always understand the references to "right" and "left" to be from our own point of view, rather than someone looking at us. For males, the channel to the left of the central channel is red and the channel to the right is white. For females this is just the opposite: the channel to the right is red and the channel to the left is white. These two channels symbolize the inseparable nature of method and wisdom. The red channel is the aspect of wisdom, and the white, of method.

Next, we should visualize the wind energy, or the breath, as light that is the colors of the five Buddha families: white, yellow, red, green, and blue. Then, we should visualize the wind energy flowing through the left and right channels as we inhale and exhale. To gain some initial concentration, we should visualize the five-colored breath as it flows from deep in our belly until it leaves our nose when we exhale, and then as we take it back in when we inhale. Initially, we should do this five times. After we have counted the first five inhalations and exhalations, we should relax in the view before we continue. Then, using our mala, we should visualize the five-colored breath as we inhale and exhale just as we did before, while counting an entire round of our mala. Our breathing should be relaxed and slow. If we are diligent in taking up this practice, our coarse discursive thoughts will slowly begin to die away.

To develop the concentration of the mind further, we can use the technique of meditating upon an object. Although I have said that when we meditate upon the view we should always keep the eyes open, for this shamatha technique it is important to practice with the eyes closed. First, with our eyes open, we should focus on an object like a statue, the shape of a mantric syllable like OM or HUM, a thangka, or any other object we find suitable, without moving either our eyes or our mind. Any sound that comes into our ears, smell perceived by the nose, or any other kind of conceptual thought should be cut off and we should focus only on the object on which we are concentrating. If we find that our meditation becomes one-pointed, we should close our eyes and visualize the object as clearly as if our eyes were still open. When we are distracted by discursive thoughts or our visualization becomes unclear, we should open our eyes again and once again focus on the meditation object. In this style of meditation, we are actively trying to abandon anything that distracts us and to concentrate exclusively on the meditation object.

After we have progressed in this style of meditative concentration, we should then train in seeing all appearances as the bodies of the Buddhas and Bodhisattvas. Whatever sounds we hear, we should train in hearing them as mantric syllables and joyful prayers. By practicing in this way, gradually all of the objects perceived by the five sense faculties and by the mind can be used to train in one-pointed meditative concentration. Thus, it is said in the Teachings that if we become skilled at meditative concentration, no matter what appearances, sounds, tastes, smells, or tactile sensations are experienced, we will find that they are unable to disturb us or break our meditation.

It is important not only to transform what is perceived by the five sense faculties into pure appearances, but also what is perceived by the mind. In terms of taking up the uncontrived view of Dzogchen, gaining experience in this type of training is quite essential. In the Dzogchen Teachings, we are told to perceive all appearances as the mandala of the body, all sounds as the mandala of speech, and all thoughts and memories as the mandala of the mind. Here, "body, speech, and mind" refer to the body, speech, and mind of the Buddhas and Bodhisattvas. If we do not gain experience in this type of shamatha, and instead just try to take up the practice of pure perception as it is presented in the Dzogchen Teachings, it may sound good to say that we perceive "all as the mandala," but our practice may not amount to much more than these words.

The method for training the mind in pure perception can also be done through training in visualization. First, we should visualize ourselves as a deity in which we have particular faith, such as Padmasambhava, Tara, or Avalokiteshvara, and then meditate one-pointedly on its pure appearance. When we experience a moment when our visualization and concentration are especially clear, we should transform our meditation. To do this, we should visualize clear light coming from our heart center and flowing in the ten directions. We should offer this light to the Lama, Buddhas, Bodhisattvas, Dakinis, and Deities. Then, we should visualize that light being sent back to us, and imagine that as it washes through us, all of our negativities have been purified and we have attained all of the perfectly pure, good qualities of body, speech, and mind. Next, we should visualize the light emanating from our heart center once again, this time touching all sentient beings within samsara, whom we visualize as being situated beneath us. Then, we should imagine that by this generosity, all of their impurities of body, speech, and mind are made to completely vanish. Next, we should see all beings as the retinue of Bodhisattvas and all the appearances of the world as a pure land that is completely free of negativity. Finally, we should once again visualize light emanating from the retinue of enlightened beings and entering our chests, and think that we have attained the merit, spiritual radiance, and holy appearance that will enable us to benefit beings. We should continue to do this cycle of visualization as many times as we can in one session.

I guarantee that someone who trains in meditative concentration by taking up these methods will find that their practice gains stability.

Truthfully, meditative concentration is one of the most important skills we develop on the path. But if we do not have the patience to develop it, then our training in meditation and especially taking up the uncontrived view of Dzogchen will not yield the desired result. This is because shamatha is the basis for meditation that is free of reference points. In other words, our realization of the uncontrived view depends upon the stability of our meditative concentration. If we have failed to take this to heart, we will find our practice full of unnecessary complications and hardships.

To Examine or Not?

When practicing the profound, uncontrived view of Dzogchen, we might wonder if the proper way to take up the view is to rely upon examination and analysis, or to practice without any examination whatsoever. Traditionally, there have been two kinds of practitioners who take up the view. Some practitioners feel that in order to practice perfect meditation, it is not necessary to rely upon any examination whatsoever. They do not examine what emptiness is, nor do they try to come to an understanding of the four extremes of existence, nonexistence, both, or neither. Despite the fact that they have not examined any of these things, they still feel that they will be able to practice uncontrived meditation. Such practitioners think that making an intellectual examination of the view could actually keep them from recognizing the natural state. Instead, they believe that practicing meditation that is not based on such examination is what is taught in the most profound and secret of all the oral instructions of Dzogchen.

The other type of practitioner believes that emptiness is something that must be mentally examined over and over again in order to understand it properly. However, they only trust careful intellectual analysis and rely solely upon their mental faculties, to the rejection of cultivating the understanding of that analysis in meditation. They do not believe that uncontrived meditation holds any value at all. In fact, if they are not relying upon analysis, they feel that meditation is no different from sleeping. However, if we want to practice meditation in a way that is completely unmistaken, we need to avoid both of these extremes. Rather, it is important to combine them and use both as good and necessary conditions for our practice.

If we do not study the logic of the Middle Way or examine the profound, natural state in order to develop certainty as the basis for our meditation, it is actually still possible to develop meditative concentration and formless meditative absorption. However, these types of meditation would only be developed based on cutting off our conceptual thoughts. In other words, they would not be developed based on the uncontrived view, which is free of extremes.

The problem is that gaining stability in this type of meditative concentration would not enable us to liberate our mental afflictions. Not only that, but also it would not enable us to gain certainty about emptiness, now or in the future, which robs us of the chance to have a first-hand experience of the profound, natural state. So if we wonder if it is possible for such a practitioner to truly take up meditation on the uncontrived view, I would have to answer that this is simply not possible. If we do not experience self-arising rikpa as a result of taking up the view, we will not realize the method to self-liberate the mental afflictions. If we fail to cut through our mental afflictions, we will not only be obstructed from attaining Buddhahood, but we will also not even be released from samsara. To make a long story short, if we do not examine what is meant by words like "emptiness" and "free of contrivance," then we will not know how we are to meditate.

When we listen to or read Teachings on the uncontrived view of Dzogchen, we often come into contact with the instruction that we should "transform our doubts, conceptual thoughts, and mental afflictions to wisdom." But if we have never even considered, much less gained certainty about how and why this is possible, then trying to do it in the course of our meditation will prove to be quite impossible. On the other hand, if we have devoted a lot of time and energy to examining the Teachings on the union of appearance and emptiness, and the nature of dependent arising, then after some time the fact that wisdom and worldly appearances are of the same root will seem quite natural and obvious to us. When we have this certainty and experience to rely upon, it becomes much easier for us to put the Teachings into practice.

In Tibet, we use the example of a practitioner who has died and is wandering in the bardo state to show why such examination and certainty in the meaning of the Teachings are so important. It is widely known that it is possible to attain some kind of realization or positive rebirth by recognizing and resting in the natural state after death. However, let us consider the example of a Lama who is sitting next to a practitioner who has died, and is calling out the instructions on how to self-liberate the mind. If the practitioner never gained certainty in the two truths, the union of appearance and emptiness, and the nature of dependent arising during their lifetime, then how could such instructions be meaningful to them after death? We can only realize what we have become habituated to. In other words, even if the opportunity for liberation is upon us, it is all too easy to fail to use such precious circumstances.

The reason for making such an extensive examination of emptiness is that since beginningless time we have been strongly attached to entities and the self as being real and permanent. However, if we do not rely upon our examination of the logic and Teachings of the Middle Way, it is extremely difficult to realize emptiness. I cannot honestly say that it would be impossible to realize the uncontrived view without such study; for there have been examples in history of great yogis who, as a result of their uncommon and supreme devotion to their root Lama, did attain realization of the Teachings. But such yogis are rare, and most beings do not have the ability to realize the uncontrived view based solely on devotion. That is why I say that the easiest way to gain realization is to rely upon the Teachings of the Middle Way in order to gain certainty in the fact that all phenomena are primordially free of extremes.

However, while the logic of the Middle Way is used as a basis for establishing the uncontrived view, there are differences between the uncontrived view of the Middle Way and the uncontrived view of

Dzogchen. While in the Middle Way Teachings the uncontrived view can largely be equated to emptiness, this is not completely correct from the point of view of the Secret Teachings. We should understand this to be one of the striking differences between the Inner and the Secret Teachings.

From the point of view that Dharmadhatu is empty and free of extremes, the understanding of the primordially pure natural state as presented in the Dzogchen Teachings and the uncontrived view of the Middle Way Teachings are one and the same. However, in order not to fall into the extreme view that this emptiness is in fact nothingness, the Secret Teachings assert that emptiness is in union with the wisdom of great bliss (this union is synonymous with words like "clear light wisdom" or "rikpa"). This complementary aspect is only given in the Secret Teachings. That is why the direct experience of the union of the wisdom of great bliss and the great expanse of emptiness, in which the grasping at subject and object has been completely liberated, is the superior and unsurpassable defining characteristic of the Vajrayana Teachings.

The union of great bliss and emptiness, which is completely uncreated, can be described from three different points of view. However, these three are distinguished only by their names, and their essence should be understood to be one and the same. The three aspects of the wisdom of great bliss and emptiness can be most easily understood by allying them with the three kayas. From the point of view of its essence, which is completely empty, it is the Dharmakaya. From the point of view of its clear light nature, it is the Sambhogakaya. And from the point of view of its complete pervasiveness, it is the Nirmanakaya.

Often, when we discuss the three defining characteristics of the nature of mind in English, the true etymology as it is expressed in Tibetan cannot be precisely translated. As a result, I am afraid that the understanding of the Union of Dzogchen and Bodhichitta *as the nature of mind itself* is sometimes lost. I think this is one reason that the perfect result of the Teachings of the Great Perfection is often seen to rely mainly on the aspect of Dzogchen rather than the Union. After much examination, it is now easy for us to associate clarity and emptiness with the uncontrived view. But what about the third aspect of the nature of mind? I believe it is in the translation of the term "complete pervasiveness" that we can enhance our understanding of the Union as the nature of mind.

In Tibetan, "complete pervasiveness" means *tuk je*, which can be translated in several different ways. In the Secret Teachings, it is usually translated as "capacity," referring to the fact that it is all-pervasive. But in other contexts, this same word can be translated as "compassion," "noble purpose," and is sometimes used as the name for Avalokiteshvara. It most definitely refers to Bodhichitta. When viewed from the point of view of Tibetan etymology, there is no doubt that the Union of Dzogchen and Bodhichitta is the nature of mind itself.

Because the union of great bliss and emptiness contains all three of the characteristics of the nature of mind, we will fall into neither the extreme of existence nor peace if we properly take up the uncontrived view of Dzogchen. The reason for this is simple. Because its essence is completely empty, we will not fall into the extreme of existence. And because it is completely pervasive and of the nature of clear light, we will not fall into the extreme of peace. But in order to attain the result of the three kayas, we must rely on the methods of the compassionate Bodhichitta and the wisdom that is the union of great bliss and emptiness. When we do not take up the Union as the foundation and the path, it is simply impossible for us to experience the rikpa that is the essence of the three kayas.

I have used the phrase "in union" over and over again in this text. Let me clarify for a moment what I mean by practicing two things in union. Metaphorically speaking, we could imagine this to mean coiling together two separate strands of cord, one white and one black, so that they make one rope. But this metaphor does not describe a perfect union. Again, I come back to the metaphor that is used in the Dzogchen Teachings: "the union" is like pouring water into water.

When we are practicing meditation, we should also be free of grasping at what the Union is. We must rely upon as many different methods as necessary to examine and gain certainty in the uncontrived natural state. Once we have gained deep certainty, so unshakable that it cannot be destroyed by any doubt whatsoever, we should rest one-pointedly in it. By doing this, our certainty will continually increase. And, based on this certainty, our coarse and subtle mental afflictions, as well as mistaken conceptions, will begin to decrease. That is why it is crucial that once we gain certainty in the view, we practice it with as much diligence as we can. There has never been, nor will there ever be, a practitioner who realized the Dzogchen Teachings without making diligent effort. But if a practitioner does gain certainty in the view and practices diligently in both this and future lives, such a practitioner has never failed, nor ever will fail, to attain liberation as a result of their practice.

The Way to Meditate

Regarding the practice of meditation, the consort Yeshe Tsogyal said,

> The [essence] of phenomena is the foundation of meditation.
>
> To summarize the way to take it up,
> See the essence of the view,
> And meditate without being distracted or shackled by
>   grasping.
> This is called meditation.
>
> By practicing meditation in this way,
> No matter if [we] are practicing the generation or the
>   perfection stages,
> We will experience "that which cannot be expressed."
>
> Most importantly, the practice of the generation and perfection
>   stages
> Must be free of the three conditions of wildness, mental fog,
>   and darkness,

And colored by a lack of distraction and a lack of forgetting.
Resting in this way is called meditation.

We should understand Yeshe Tsogyal's words to mean that meditation is based on the certainty that the uncontrived view is the union of
clarity and emptiness. Based on this unwavering certainty, we should
abide in a state in which we are neither grasping nor abandoning.
Remaining within the natural state of clarity and emptiness is what is
called meditation. Next, no matter what type of meditation we take
up in the generation and the perfection stages, our meditation should
be free of the three obstacles of wildness, mental fog, and darkness.
"Wildness" refers to being caught up in or overwhelmed by conceptual
thoughts. "Mental fog and darkness" refer to a lack of clarity or feelings of sleepiness—either metaphorically or literally. Also, our meditation should be free of distraction and we should not forget that we
are meditating. So, when we practice in a way that is free of the first
three and endowed with the last two, our meditation is the kind of
meditation that Yeshe Tsogyal herself practiced.

There are two factors that influence whether or not we will able to
meditate unmistakenly on the view. The first is whether or not we have
received the perfect oral instructions from the qualified Spiritual
Friend, and the second is whether or not we have gained deep certainty in the nature of suchness. This deep certainty cannot come from
relying upon what someone else tells us. The kind of deep certainty I
am talking about is the certainty that arises from wisdom awareness and
is not reliant upon outside influences. It arises within the mind and is
so strong that it cannot be dispelled by the contrary words and opin-
ions of another.

However, the fact that our certainty should not rely upon another
should not be taken to mean that we do not need to rely upon a Spiritual Friend. For, if we wish to attain this kind of uncommon, deep
confidence in the natural state, we absolutely need the good conditions
provided by relying upon a Spiritual Friend, the development of faith
and devotion, pure perception, and the compassionate wish to benefit

others while we gather the two accumulations. Based on these perfect conditions, and the introduction to the nature of mind, we will experience rikpa. This, in turn, will lead us to develop confidence and certainty in the way to practice meditation and abide in the natural state.

By gaining certainty in the unmistaken, perfectly pure, uncontrived view, it becomes possible to practice meditation that is also unmistaken. However, if we have not gained a proper understanding of the view, we will fail to take up meditation correctly. We might wonder how we would know if we had properly understood the view and taken up the practice of meditation correctly. In truth, even if we looked for one, there is no outer sign that appears to tell us that we are doing things right. But just as the appearance of rising smoke tells us that a fire is burning, we can see signs of abandonment and realization in our body, speech, and mind. That is to say, as a result of our meditation, we should see signs like slowness to anger, less self-attachment, less suffering in our daily lives, and greater stability in the mind. As long as we continue to make an effort at meditation, these good qualities should continue to increase in the same way that the moon waxes until it is full.

However, if we gain deep certainty in the emptiness of all phenomena, an inner sign does appear. At this stage, we will begin to perceive all phenomena as being of the nature of dependent arising. Because we perceive all phenomena as being of the nature of dependent arising—and thus emptiness, we begin to feel a deep certainty in cause and effect. This certainty actually enables us to change our conduct so that it is completely and subtly in accord with the law of karma.

Actually, a practitioner who has gained certainty in the unmistaken, uncontrived view becomes more and more skillful at acting in line with karma because they understand the proper way to take up virtue and abandon nonvirtue in any situation. Thus, their actions embody the virtuous conduct of conventional reality to a very high degree. Then, by further training in Bodhichitta, their virtuous conduct becomes even greater and nonvirtuous conduct all but disappears. In the Teachings, this is the kind of practitioner we would say has truly taken up the

Union of Dzogchen and Bodhichitta, and this is the kind of practitioner we call a Dzogchen yogi.

However, if we have made a mistake in the way we have understood and practiced the view, this is also easy to discern. Our good qualities will not increase, and we will notice no transformation in the conduct of our body, speech, and mind. Not only that, but we will also encounter obstacles on our path, and we will find that we are not progressing towards enlightenment at all. The way in which the good qualities can be lost through a mistaken understanding and practice of the view can be seen by using the example of a tea strainer. When water is poured through it, the freshly brewed tea—which is the very thing we want—flows out of the holes. Only the tea grounds are left, and they have been used up and robbed of their flavor.

Even worse than simply not developing the good qualities is that one who practices meditation in this way comes to think that cause and effect are of no real consequence. This causes their self-attachment to become even stronger than before. The danger of this happening in itself is a good reason to be careful. Once we have begun to strengthen our self-attachment, the obstacles to progressing on the path seem to snowball.

Conduct

Regarding conduct, the consort Yeshe Tsogyal said,

> To summarize the way…to take up conduct,
> Meditate within the confidence of the view,
> Essentially free of distraction, and loose.
> But no matter what various kinds of conduct are taken up,
> Conduct should not oppose [the view]; abide in suchness.
> [By doing this], meditation [on the Union] will increase.
>
> In short, when traveling, walking, sleeping,
> Eating, or resting, as well as in all other conduct,

> When meditating on the generation stage, perfection stage,
>   or Dzogchen,
> Always remain within the view.
> This is the proper way to practice conduct.

We should take the first lines to mean that there is no meditation other than abiding in the view itself. We should rest in the view in a way that is relaxed and without distraction. No matter what situation we come across or what action is taken, we should remain undistracted within our meditation. Thus, action endowed with meditation on the view is called conduct.

Thinking in this way, it is easy to see that there is no meditation other than the view, and no conduct other than meditation. Even within our daily lives, the proper way to take up any action is endowed with meditation on the view. However, even though I say that all conduct within our daily life should be endowed with the view, we should understand this instruction to be made from the point of view of a fully realized being like Yeshe Tsogyal. From the point of view of an ordinary being who is just taking up the path, this is not possible. Instead, practitioners should aim to develop the good qualities of realized beings so that they are able to properly take up conduct in the future. In short, such a being has two good qualities that are necessary to attain. First, such a being has developed an uncommonly deep certainty and awareness of the uncontrived view. Then, with their extraordinary diligence, they have taken up the practice of meditation to such a degree that their conduct would never oppose it.

However, when considering the highly realized yogis of the past, we should also realize that yogis like Milarepa, Yeshe Tsogyal, and Longchenpa were not always the highly realized beings that they later became. They, too, had to train in Bodhichitta and gather the two accumulations. As we will see in the next section, Yeshe Tsogyal underwent extreme hardship to perfect her practice of the Dharma.

We should think of the work we are doing now, in taking up our daily practice, or applying the Teachings and techniques of meditation we have learned thus far, as setting the stage for what will come later. In this stage of Dharma practice, the most important thing is to make a continual effort to keep our conduct in line with the Dharma, and endow any action with the aspiration to realize the nature of suchness for the benefit of ourselves and others.

THE EIGHT HARDSHIPS UNDERGONE BY YESHE TSOGYAL

To give an example of the way to take up the unmistaken, uncontrived view and engage in unmistaken meditation and conduct, I would like to turn now to the life of the Dakini Yeshe Tsogyal. After Padmasambhava had given the majority of the Outer, Inner, and Secret Teachings to Yeshe Tsogyal, he instructed her to undertake eight hardships so that she would be able to completely develop all of the good qualities of a practitioner of Dzogchen:

> Ehma! Listen to me without distraction, Dakini Tsogyal,
> You who steal my heart with one glance.
> When you attain the golden trunk of the precious [human] life,
> Knowing the way to use it, you can attain the ultimate [result].
> Not knowing, you will not even be able to fill your stomach.
> That is why you should follow the instructions I have given.

The eight were (1) to undergo the hardship of eating by extracting the essences from rocks and stalked plants, and consuming wind energy as food; (2) to undergo the hardship of clothing by wearing only ornaments made of bones and then taking up the practice of tummo, or the yoga of internal heat; (3) to undergo the hardship of speech by uttering only mantra or prayer and no other kinds of speech; (4) to undergo the hardship of body by practicing prostrations, circumambulations, and meditation; (5) to undergo the hardship of mind by training in meditative concentration, taking up the generation and perfection stages, and training in the union of bliss and

The Dakini Yeshe Tsogyal

emptiness; (6) to undergo the hardship of taking on the Teachings and activities of the Dharma by teaching, debating, and composing texts; (7) to undergo the hardship of benefiting others by praying in the way taught in the Mahayana, and offering one's own life in the service of others; and (8) to undergo the hardship of compassion by seeing no difference between enemies and kin, and exchanging self for others.

Padmasambhava emphasized that by taking up these hardships it would be possible to attain the supreme accomplishment of Buddhahood in only one life if Yeshe Tsogyal developed a foundation of Bodhichitta, practiced the union of the generation and perfection stages, and took up the path of the inseparability of method and wisdom. However, he also said that if she were to separate the aspects of method and wisdom, she would fall into the extreme of nihilism and the chance to attain Buddhahood would be lost.

After Padmasambhava had given these instructions, Yeshe Tsogyal vowed to take up each of the eight hardships in turn, even if she died trying. Although I will not go through each of the eight hardships in detail, I think reading about Yeshe Tsogyal's life is an easy way to become inspired in one's own practice. It is helpful to have a vision of how a supreme practitioner of the Vajrayana has practiced. Specifically, we should notice the skillful way in which Yeshe Tsogyal took up the view, meditation, and conduct.

The first hardship Yeshe Tsogyal undertook was that of generating internal heat by practicing tummo. Before she began, she went high into the mountains near the border of Tibet and India to a place called Tuldro, where it was sure to be unbearably cold. She climbed past the timberline until she had reached the rocky peaks, where she began to practice clad only in garments made of thin cloth. At first, Yeshe Tsogyal could not generate internal heat, so she was unable to keep warm. The cold winter air was bitter against her bare skin, and the frosty snow and ice were almost too much to bear. Her skin became blistered from the cold and her stomach became full of bleeding sores.

Finally, one day when she was close to death, Yeshe Tsogyal re-affirmed that she would never break the vow she had made to her Lama, not even if it brought on her death. She began to pray one-pointedly with reverent devotion to Padmasambhava. By the power of her devotion, prayers, and pure perception, she felt some initial warmth, and gained experience in the way to work with the wind energy in order to generate heat.

After experiencing this initial warmth, she began to practice even more diligently than before. She practiced until she finally began to experience the bliss of heat. Then, as is instructed in the practice of tummo, she recognized the essence to be the nature of mind itself. The uncontrived view arose from the play of her mind, and she experienced it as being inseparable from the wisdom realized by Padma-sambhava. At that moment, all appearances manifested as is described in the practice of Guru Yoga and the four chakras of her body burned with the blissful heat of the four joys. After this burning commenced, Yeshe Tsogyal's own appearance was transformed and she experienced all to be the wisdom of great bliss and emptiness that is the union of method and wisdom. From that time on, the feelings of cold and pain that she had experienced were shed like skin from a snake. Yeshe Tsogyal remained high in the snowy mountains of Tibet for one year, practicing in this way.

Next, Yeshe Tsogyal took up the hardship of the body. First, she practiced by circumambulating many stupas, temples, and monasteries. Next, she began to prostrate day and night without resting. After some time, her hands, knees, and forehead split open and began to bleed and fester, but she persevered. Finally, she took up various meditative postures and gazes that she adhered to strictly while she practiced. Based on the purification of the body, the knots in her channels were untied and she gained mastery over the practices of tsa lung.

Then, Yeshe Tsogyal undertook the second aspect of the hardship of clothing. She took off even the thin cloth she had worn while practicing tummo and adorned herself only with the six types of ornaments made from bones: necklaces, bracelets, earrings, a crown, a bone wheel at the heart held in place by sashes, and dabs of crematory ashes. She had already attained mastery over the channels, energies, and essences, so now she took up the uncontrived view, meditation, and conduct.

During this phase of her practice, she did not even have a single grain of barley to eat. She ate only the essences taken from rocks and drank water as she continued to deepen her meditation. After a while, her body began to lose its strength and she was finally unable to support her own weight when standing. Once again, Yeshe Tsogyal found herself near death, with little strength in either her body or mind. She began to pray deeply to the three roots of the Lama, Meditational Deity, and Dakini, determined that she would never break the vow she had made to Padmasambhava.

When she had finished praying and began to meditate once more, a brilliant red woman who was completely naked appeared before her. The illuminated woman approached Yeshe Tsogyal and caused a supremely holy nectar to flow as though inexhaustibly into her mouth.

Upon imbibing this nectar Yeshe Tsogyal was filled with the wisdom of great bliss and emptiness and she attained strength that was as great as a lion. She realized the primordially pure nature of mind that is described in the Secret Teachings by synonyms like clarity and emptiness, awareness and emptiness, or great bliss and emptiness.

Next, Yeshe Tsogyal undertook the hardship of food. Continuing to practice unclothed, she ate only wind energy as food. At this stage, she decided to take up the hardships of the body, speech, and mind simultaneously. Practicing while naked was the hardship of the body. Eating only the wind element, upon which all sound and speech arise, was the hardship of speech. Meditating on the union of clarity of emptiness was the hardship of mind. At first, working with the channels, energies, and essences and meditating on the Union came easily, and for a time the expression of rikpa seemed to accelerate. However, at one point Yeshe Tsogyal felt a slight doubt about the idea of eating only wind energy as food, which caused it to become like a poison that made her sick. She was unable to breathe and her throat became dry and constricted. Her stomach heaved until she was once again on the verge of death.

In this state, Yeshe Tsogyal began to practice Guru Yoga and prayed one-pointedly to Padmasambhava. Suddenly, Padmasambhava's body of clear light appeared before her and he blessed her. Then, he gave her several new instructions. He told her to again extract the essences of rocks and stalked plants as food, and then further develop rikpa by recognizing these essences as well as all phenomena as expressions of the mind. He also gave a prophecy that said that in the future Yeshe Tsogyal would become the keeper of all of his Teachings and treasures. Then, he blessed her with the empowerments, transmissions, and oral instructions of an even more profound nature than before.

After receiving the empowerments, transmissions, and oral instructions from Padmasambhava, Yeshe Tsogyal traveled with several of her attendants and students to a place called Monsengezon in central Tibet. There, in accordance with Padmasambhava's instructions, she extracted the essences from rocks and stalked plants. After she had consumed them and had once again begun to practice meditation, the nature of her body became indestructible like a diamond; so hard that it could not be penetrated or harmed by even the sharpest of weapons. Her voice became like the melodious voice of Brahma: so soothing that it could pacify even the strongest arrogance or aggression in another. Her mind was completely purified and she attained Diamond Hard Meditative Concentration.

After gaining these attainments, Yeshe Tsogyal undertook the hardship of speech by ceaselessly praying mantras day and night. She began by praying the one-hundred-syllable mantra of Vajrasattva, and then visualized the mandalas of the Action, Performance, and Yoga Tantras while praying their mantras. Finally, she read many volumes of the Teachings given by Buddha Shakyamuni aloud. By undergoing these hardships, not only did she purify her speech, but she also attained the good quality of not forgetting anything, no matter how long or complex it was. This prepared her to fulfill Padmasambhava's prophecy that she would become the keeper of his Teachings and treasures.

After Yeshe Tsogyal had taken up the three Outer Tantras, she took up the three Inner Tantras one by one. First, she generated the mandala of the Eight Kagyed deities of the Mahayoga Tantra and then took up the four ways of approaching retreat: through visualizing a symbolic being, the near achievement of a wisdom being, actual achievement, and great achievement. She continued this practice and prayed the mantra of the Mahayoga Tantra ceaselessly until she directly saw the faces of the Kagyed deities. Based on this vision, she attained the common and supreme accomplishments. Finally, she received a prophecy that said that she would dissolve into the Dharmakaya Samantabhadri and attain enlightenment.

Next, she took up the Anuyoga Tantra, relying on a tantric deity that is described as having the essential good qualities of all the Lamas. Although usually the mandala of the deity and the Buddha field are practiced as an outer visualization, Yeshe Tsogyal practiced them as the chakras and channels of her own body. Then, based on her mastery of the channels, energies, and essences, she cut the four great rivers of birth, sickness, old age, and death. At that moment, she embodied the true meaning of the word "accomplishment." As a result, she gained a boundless gratitude for the kindness of her Lama, Padmasambhava, and developed even greater respect for the law of cause and effect, Bodhichitta, and pure perception.

When Yeshe Tsogyal finally took up the practices of the highest Tantra, called Atiyoga Dzogchen, she traveled to a cavernous land called Senge Nerang, which is in the pristine wilderness and high in the mountains. There in her cave, she vowed to undertake the Teachings of Atiyoga while keeping three types of discipline: that of remaining in the sevenfold posture with her eyes in the proper gaze, abiding without speaking, and resting her mind in unwavering meditative concentration. Then, she took up the view of Trekchod and the practice of Todgyal, which are the supreme view and secret practice within the Dzogchen Tantras.

However, the form and formless gods, as well as the maras and nagas, gathered near the cave where she was practicing. They had gathered there out of jealousy of Yeshe Tsogyal's accomplishments. Because of their burning resentment, they decided to try to distract her and cause her to generate attachment to worldly life. First, they conjured the appearances of beautiful clothes, delicious food, riches and gems, elegant horses, and anything else the heart could possibly desire. However, by the power of Yeshe Tsogyal's meditative concentration, she cut through the root of attachment and she saw all appearances as none other than illusions and mere reflections. Next, they conjured the appearances of a retinue of young boys as beautiful as the sons of the gods, with glowing skin and sweet smiles. In an attempt to draw Yeshe Tsogyal out of her meditation, they called her "Mother Tsogyal" in hopes that she would believe they were her children. However, Yeshe Tsogyal remained undistracted. When this ploy failed, they appeared as handsome young men who called out "Lady Tsogyal" as they danced alluringly and tried to seduce her. And when their mere sweet talking failed, they began to touch her naked body all over in an attempt to arouse her. But even their physical presence could not distract Yeshe Tsogyal from her meditation. She began to generate Bodhi-chitta and to practice Tonglen in order to subdue them. By the power of her practice of Tonglen, a few of the appearances disappeared, while the others manifested again in ways that were not pleasing to the eye at all: several as wrinkled old men, and others as lepers or beings with other disfiguring diseases.

When they were unable to distract her with peaceful appearances, they attempted to terrorize her with wrathful, violent appearances. First, they sent earthquakes and thunderstorms rumbling throughout the land. Flashing bright lights and deafening sounds filled the cave. But even these appearances were no match for Yeshe Tsogyal's medi-tative concentration. She continued to meditate until the land became peaceful once again. Next, they sent sharp, pointed weapons like arrows, phurbas, knives, and spears into the cave towards Yeshe Tso-gyal's heart . However, once again, based on the strength of her med-itative concentration, the weapons disappeared. Finally, they sent fierce carnivorous animals like lions, tigers, cobras, leopards, and wolves to the mouth of the cave. They crouched and sprang to attack her. Yeshe Tsogyal began to generate Bodhichitta once again, meditating on love and compassion, and then practiced Tonglen. The terrifying animals relaxed and went back to where they had come from.

Finally, when the gods, demonic interferers (or maras), and nagas realized that they would be unable to distract Yeshe Tsogyal by caus-ing her some kind of physical harm, they wreaked havoc on the lands surrounding the cave. The people who lived in the villages throughout Senge Nerang were struck by sickness and famine. After this unfortu-nate circumstance befell them, they gathered together to discuss the terrible state of the land. They all agreed that this misfortune had been caused by the "foolish" woman who was staying in a cave in the moun-tains high above them, whom they believed must be saying a black mantra. They were, of course, referring to Yeshe Tsogyal. So the vil-lages mobilized an army, which marched up to Yeshe Tsogyal's cave and demanded that she take back the black mantra she had been say-ing, or else they would kill her.

Yeshe Tsogyal realized at once that this obstacle, too, had been created by the gods and other evil spirits. She realized, too, that there was no essential difference between this obstacle and all the others. And, unwilling to break her vow to remain in unwavering meditative concentration in her cave, she remained in the sevenfold posture in undistracted meditation. When they realized that Yeshe Tsogyal was not going to do as they had demanded, the army assailed her. They threw dust in her eyes, pierced her ears with swords and spears, struck her over the head with large rocks, and did whatever else they could think of. But not even these tortures could break Yeshe Tsogyal's meditation. After they realized that there was absolutely nothing they could do to disturb or injure her in any way, they gave her the name "Liberated from Fear" and were forced to leave in peace.

At this point, the obstacle makers, too, realized that they could not defeat Yeshe Tsogyal. So the gods, maras, and nagas became Yeshe Tsogyal's retinue of protectors, vowing that they would do whatever was necessary to keep any other being from harming the good qualities and activities of her body, speech, mind. Not only that, but the king, army, and villagers of the land also repented, and became her devoted followers. The health of the land was restored, along with its rainfall and fine harvests. Yeshe Tsogyal herself, having perfected the view, meditation, and conduct, became like a Heruka warrior. She was even more beautiful than before, with skin that shone as if with sunlight. Finally, the Long-Life Buddha blessed her and she attained the indestructible body. He then prophesied that she would remain in Tibet for the next two hundred years as the keeper of the Dharma and the treasures.

+ CHAPTER 8
+
+ *The Passage of the Secret Teachings*

From *The Garland of Sound Tantra (rNa rgyan lung gi phreng ba)*:

When the Buddhas came to the worldly sphere,
They gave the supreme [Secret] Teachings.
But because some lack faith and acceptance,
The history of the Teachings should be given first.

O F ALL THE DIFFERENT PATHS and vehicles that were taught by the Buddhas as the method to reach liberation, the Secret Teachings are paramount. They are the essence of the wisdom of the Buddhas of the three times, the heart of all Dharmas, the highest of all vehicles, the king of all Teachings, and the root of all oral instructions. The Secret Teachings are made up of the Inner and Outer Tantra, which together contain six different styles of Tantric Teachings. Of these six, the Tantras of Mahayana, Anuyoga, and Atiyoga (which is synonymous with Dzogchen) are the most esoteric. But, as the verse quoted above states, it is important that we know where these Teachings came from, and how and why yogis have followed them for over a thousand years. Knowing the history of these Teachings inspires a feeling of faith in us, and helps us to accept the Teachings with a genuine sense that when we take them up, we are part of a living lineage that continues to this day.

THE REQUEST FOR TEACHINGS

The Buddhas who had gone to bliss and whose minds were resting in the inseparable Dharmakaya knew that all phenomena were primor-

dially the Buddha. The Dharmakaya Samantabhadri, the consort of all
of the Enlightened Ones, beseeched them to give Teachings on the
Indestructible Secret Mantrayana (which should be understood to have
the same meaning as "Secret Teachings," "Vajrayana," "Tantra," and
"Tantric vehicle") to those who had superior faculties, and would be
capable of understanding them. She beseeched the Buddhas to give the
Teachings of the Mahayana to those who were of middle or lesser faculties, and thus would not be able to understand or practice the Secret
Teachings.

Usually, when we hear about the Secret Teachings, we hear about
them in relation to three Buddhas: Samantabhadra (and the consort
Samantabhadri), Vajrasattva, and Vajradhara. We should think of
Samantabhadra as the very first enlightened being. He embodies primordial enlightenment, and is the Dharmakaya Buddha who never
experienced confusion about his true nature. So when we speak of
Samantabhadra in the Secret Teachings, we should think of him as the
Dharmakaya aspect. We should think of Vajrasattva as the Sambhogakaya aspect. When the Secret Teachings were passed to the Buddhas
of the five families, Vajrasattva was the aspect that arose directly from
the heart and mind of the Dharmakaya Samantabhadra. For this reason, Vajrasattva also reigns supreme over the Secret Teachings. Finally,
Vajradhara is known as the collector of the Secret Teachings because
he gathered together all of the Teachings given by Samantabhadra in
the vast expanse of his mind. So, we say his mind is the wisdom
essence of all of the Buddhas of the three times.

THE TEACHINGS INDIVISIBLE WITH
THE MIND OF SAMANTABHADRA

The wisdom of the Secret Mantrayana called "the Teachings on the
essence body" (or Svabhavakaya) was given based on five conditions
that were described as being excellent and abundant: the place, the
giver of the Teachings, the recipient, the time, and the Dharma that
was taught. The place where they were given was in the perfect palace

of the uncontrived Dharmadhatu. We cannot understand this palace to be like a normal place we might visit; rather, we should understand it to be completely nondual. It has no inner or outer, no this side or that side, and is completely unobstructed. "Palace" is a name that has been given to the spontaneous presence of the primordially pure natural state.

There, the five Buddhas who embody the nature of suchness itself, called the Svabhavakaya Buddhas of the five families, were resting in perfect union with the retinue of Buddhas, Vidyadharas, and Arya Bodhisattvas. Since they were resting in union, it is difficult for us to separate them into categories like teacher and student; however, from the point of view of appearance, this was the actual situation. So we should understand this teaching to have been given directly, communicated through the resting in the natural state that is beyond the duality of subject and object. The time the Teachings were given is said to be completely incomprehensible, which means that it is beyond linear time in which past, present, and future are experienced. Finally, the perfect Dharma taught refers to the ultimate Teachings lacking birth: the unborn Dharmakaya itself.

To summarize, we should understand that this teaching was given in a sphere that was completely nondual, in a time that was beyond the relative, and communicated in a way that was beyond subject and object. As a result, the King of Dharma, the Dharmakaya Buddha Samantabhadra, gathered together the complete meaning of the Teachings of Atiyoga in the vast expanse of his mind.

THE TEACHINGS INDIVISIBLE WITH THE MIND OF VAJRASATTVA

The wisdom of the Secret Mantrayana called "the Teachings on the body of truth" (Dharmakaya) was also given in the presence of five things that were excellent and abundant. The place the Teachings were given was in the celestial mansion of self-arising wisdom, which is the nature of suchness itself free of arising and cessation. The transmitter

Vajrasattva

of the Teachings was the Dharmakaya Samantabhadra, who was continuously resting in the wisdom of great bliss and emptiness. The Teachings were given to a retinue of inconceivable Dharmakaya Buddhas
and Vidyadharas who shared Samantabhadra's perfect qualities of
abandonment and realization. In this way, we can again think of the situation as being completely nondual. The time was beyond the relative
experiences of past, present, and future, so the Teachings are said to
have taken place in the "time of suchness." As for the Teachings,
Samantabhadra passed on the blessing of the unborn Dharmakaya in
a way that is beyond words and symbols.

Based on this blessing, the retinue of Dharmakaya Buddhas and
Vidyadharas realized the ultimate nature of the unborn Dharmakaya,
and became one with the mind of Samantabhadra. Vajrasattva then
gathered the Teachings of the generation stage, perfection stage, and
especially the Teachings of Atiyoga Dzogchen, and they became indi-

Vajradhara

visible with the vast expanse of his mind.

In the transmission of both the Svabhavakaya and the Dharmakaya, the Teachings were expressed between a giver and recipient who were completely indivisible. These two situations illustrate the meaning of the word "mandala," which is often used in the context of the Secret Teachings. As in these examples, a mandala is a pure appearance that arises as the expression of wisdom. More about the mandala will be included in Chapter 10.

THE TEACHINGS INDIVISIBLE WITH THE MIND OF VAJRADHARA

Finally, the wisdom of the Secret Mantrayana called "the Teachings on the perfect enjoyment body" (Sambhogakaya) was given in the presence of five things that were excellent and abundant. The place was in the heaven of Akanishtha, and in the palace of the Dharmadhatu. This palace was made of all sorts of gems and precious jewels, which glimmered like the unobstructed nature of a rainbow, with no inside or outside. The givers of the Teachings were the Sambhogakaya Buddhas of the five families, to whom nothing in the universe is a mystery. The retinue who received the Teachings was composed of Arya Bodhisattvas abiding in the ten Bhumis, that is to say, Bodhisattvas who had already achieved a direct realization of emptiness. The time when the Teachings were passed was called "the time of meditation" because there was not one single moment when the beings in this realm were distracted from meditation. The Teachings that were passed on were of the nature of sounds, signs, and symbols that prompted realization based on the power of dependent arising. The retinue of Bodhisattvas, upon seeing the signs and symbols and hearing the sounds, attained the supreme state of Buddhahood. Based on this, Vajradhara gathered together the Teachings of the Mahayana, Anuyoga, and Atiyoga, which became indivisible with the vast expanse of his mind.

THE THREE LINEAGES

In considering the Secret Teachings, there is also what we call the lineage of the teaching, meaning the way it was communicated when it was passed on. From the *Ocean Tantra* (*rGya mtsho'i rgyud*):

> The Buddhas, Bodhisattvas, and yogis
> [pass the lineages] directly, symbolically, and orally.

In other words, the three lineages are: the direct (or intention) lineage of the Buddhas, the symbolic lineage of the Vidyadharas, and the oral (or whispered) lineage of the disciples. The direct lineage of the Buddhas was the expression of wisdom and the blessings given by the Dharmakaya Samantabhadra to the Sambhogakaya Buddhas of the five families. The Teachings could be described as the direct transmission of unobstructed clear light, and took place based upon the union of the transmitter and receiver of the Teachings.

The symbolic lineage of the Vidyadharas was transmitted by the Buddhas of the five families to the Bodhisattvas using signs and symbols. By the power of dependent arising, the retinue of Bodhisattvas was able to completely realize the meaning of what was communicated. Finally, the Teachings of the oral lineage were transmitted by the Bodhisattvas to their own retinues of disciples, who had uncommon devotion and supreme faculties.

The Passage of the Secret Teachings to the God Realms

Up until now we have been recounting the way the Secret Teachings were passed from the Svabhavakaya, Dharmakaya, and Sambhogakaya aspects to the Buddhas, Vidyadharas, and Bodhisattvas. But before the Secret Teachings were actually passed to the human realm (Nirmanakaya), they were first passed to the realm of the gods.

From the point of view of ordinary individuals, Buddha Shakyamuni took birth in the human realm and gave Teachings on the ordinary vehicles. However, in the heavenly realms of Akanishtha, Tushita, as well as the Heaven of the Thirty-Three, he gave Teachings on the Indestructible Secret Mantrayana to those with superior faculties. Buddha Shakyamuni gave the complete instructions to perfectly take up the Tantric vehicle to a group of five practitioners, called "the five Dama," which we could loosely translate as "the five with rikpa." These five beings did not seem like a likely group, as they were different types of beings not of the same realm. They were: a God named Trakden Chokkyong; Jyopo, who was the king of nagas; a demon named Skar Dadong; a cannibal named Lodro Tapden; and a human named Lhutsampo Drimedtakpa.

At that time, the Tantric Teachings were practiced only in secret; they did not gain popularity and probably nobody had even heard of them. We might wonder why these Teachings, which have the power to liberate so many, were not given to many beings right from the beginning. The answer is that Buddha Shakyamuni prophesied that the time for the widespread practice of the Vajrayana had not yet ripened, for beings still had to be subdued by various methods before such practice would be effective. However, after Buddha Shakyamuni gave the Teachings to his five disciples in Akanishtha, he also gave a prophecy that in the future the time would come when the Teachings of the Indestructible Secret Mantrayana would be practiced throughout the human realm.

THE PASSAGE OF THE SECRET TEACHINGS TO THE HUMAN REALM

As recorded in the Tantras, Buddha Shakyamuni said,

> When I no longer appear here,
> After eight and twenty years,
> King Za will be born
> In the eastern lands of the world.
> [He will be] a sacred one, holder of the essence of the
>   doctrine,
> [and] renowned in the three abodes of the Gods.
> By his ability [to gather] great merit,
> The face of the secret Master will appear to him.

Twenty-eight years after Buddha Shakyamuni passed into the state of nirvana, the five endowed with rikpa were resting in meditation when they realized that the time of the Buddha's prophecy had arrived. As soon as they realized it, they miraculously traveled to the peak of Mount Malaya in the south of India. Mount Malaya could be called the center of the Secret Teachings since it was the place where the wheel of the Secret Dharma was turned. It is said that this mountain appears differently to different individuals, based on their faith and disposition. To some, it appears as a mountain of precious jewels. To others, it appears as a jagged, rocky peak that scrapes the sky. To yet others, it looks like a mountain made of metal that would be impossible to ascend. The peak of Mount Malaya is shaped like an eight-spoked wheel. But no matter what appearance we ascribe to Mount Malaya, we should remember it as the place where the Secret Teachings were heard just before they were passed into the human realm.

When they reached the peak of Mount Malaya, the five endowed with rikpa began to pray "The Twenty-three Verses of Longing" (gDung tshig nyi shu rtsa gsum) to the innumerable Buddhas and Bodhisattvas who abide in all directions. These verses were declarations of faith and yearning for the Buddhas to return to samsara and relieve the suffering of ordinary beings. One verse said,

> Kyema! We are in the expanse of suffering,
> The light of the Guide's lantern has gone out.
> Who will dispel the darkness of the world?

Upon hearing their prayers, the Dharmakaya Samantabhadra appeared before them in the form of Vajrapani. Although the Teachings of the Secret Mantrayana had already been given in the god realms, he was prepared to give the Teachings as many times as necessary. He had vowed that from beginningless time until samsara was empty he would give the Secret Teachings to anyone who sought them, in accordance with that being's disposition and capabilities. So, it was based on his earlier vow that Samantabhadra gave the Secret Teachings to the five endowed with rikpa.

These Teachings, which were the direct expression of the wisdom of Samantabhadra's mind, were hidden as mind treasures to be found in the future, when the time had come to put them into practice. The recording and hiding of these mind treasures was based on the coming together of seven excellent conditions. First, the scribe of the Teachings was to be the disciple Lodro Tapden. Second, when he wrote them down, they were to be written on sheets of gold leaf paper. Third, the ink used to write the Teachings was to be made from precious gems. Fourth, the recorded Teachings were to be placed inside spheres made of precious metals and jewels. Fifth, the Teachings were to be protected by the Wisdom Dakinis. Sixth, the king named Za was to be the holder of the Teachings. Seventh, the treasures were to be hidden in the sky by the five endowed with rikpa.

Based on the blessing that was given when Samantabhadra gave the Secret Teachings at Mount Malaya, King Za had a miraculous dream with seven parts, which indicated that the Secret Teachings would be bestowed to the worldly sphere. In the first part of the dream, he dreamed that the Buddhas of all directions had gathered at the peak of Mount Malaya. Then, from the Buddhas, and especially Vajrapani, a bright light emanated, burning the surface of the earth and purifying it. The light was sent back to where it had come from. But before it reached the Buddhas, it formed the sun, which then changed into the syllable OM and rose up to the middle of the sky. From the letter OM came a light that dispelled all darkness. Then, the letter OM moved until it rested on King Za's head, and dissolved into his body.

From his throat light emanated and the sound of the Great Vehicle echoed like thunder. Then, the light reflected back to where it had come from, but before it reached his body, it formed the shape of the moon. The moon came to rest below his feet and dissolved into his body. Light emanated from his heart and dispelled all of the darkness in the world. When the light reflected back to him, it first formed a vajra, and then dissolved into his heart. Finally, he ate the external world and all sentient beings, indicating his complete omniscience and the fact that he was to become the holder of the Dharma.

In the second part of the dream, he envisioned that the sky was filled with jeweled boxes of sacred scriptures, which rained down on the roof of his palace. In the third part, he saw the Buddhas and Bodhisattvas astride the sun and the moon and holding the silver wheel of the Dharma, which symbolizes the passage of the Teachings. Then, King Za appeared on the roof of his palace, where he heard a discussion about the Secret Teachings held between the Buddhas and Bodhisattvas. In the fourth part, the Buddhas and Vidyadharas praised him for his excellent birth and for being the keeper of the Secret Teachings. In the fifth part, Vidyadharas, Arya Bodhisattvas, and Gods circumambulated the scriptures that had fallen from the sky and then made offerings. In the sixth part, a rain of precious jewels fell from the sky and flowers blossomed throughout the world. King Za and the other wisdom beings present ornamented themselves with flowers. In the last part of the dream, light emanated from the light of a lantern made of precious jewels and metals, dispelling all of the darkness in the world. Then, medicinal nectar fell from the sky and purified the suffering and sicknesses of all sentient beings.

The next morning, King Za recounted his miraculous dream to his most trusted followers. They decided to go up to the roof of the palace and see if anything similar to what he had seen in the dream had come to pass. When they arrived, it was just as King Za had foreseen. On the roof of the palace there were stacks of scriptures written on gilded paper by ink made of precious gems. Standing beside the scriptures was a golden statue of Vajrapani about a foot and a half tall. Delighted, King Za began to turn the pages of the scriptures in order to take a look at them, but he was unable to understand anything that was written there. He became filled with such sadness that he began to weep, and ordered his men to invite the greatest panditas in the land to investigate the meaning of the scriptures.

However, the panditas were not so sure that this was a good idea. "If we do not understand the meaning of these scriptures any better than the King himself, we will be extremely embarrassed," they thought, and so they asked that, instead, the scriptures be brought to them. King Za's men loaded the heavy stacks of golden scriptures onto the backs of elephants and delivered them to the panditas' quarters. However, the panditas could not understand a word that was written down either, and so they quickly gave up and sent the scriptures back to the King.

King Za was even sadder than before. However, he thought to himself, "It is my own fault, for I have not accumulated the merit to receive such Teachings." So, after he had made many different kinds of offerings to accumulate merit, he held the statue of Vajrapani and the Tantric texts of Vajrasattva as the supreme objects of his veneration, and began to pray reverently. After six months of relying upon this type of aspirational prayer, he was blessed by a vision in which he directly saw the face of Vajrasattva.

Vajrasattva asked King Za, "What is it you wish for?," and the King answered that his only wish was to obtain the method to realize the meaning of the scriptures before him. So it was that Vajrasattva gave King Za Teachings on the meaning of the Tantric scriptures. Then, he gave King Za the blessings and empowerments that would enable him to completely realize the meaning of these Teachings for himself. After Vajrasattva had gone, King Za turned to the scriptures once more. This time, he perfectly understood the meaning of what was written there, and realized it completely.

The tale I have just recounted is the way in which the Eighteen Great Tantras were passed by the Sambhogakaya Vajrasattva in Akanishtha to King Za in the human realm. In the same way that was foreseen in King Za's dream, the remainder of the Teachings of the Secret Mantra-yana fell from the sky in other parts of Southeast Asia. The Teachings known as the Kriya Tantra landed in an area of China near present-day Yunnan. The Teachings known as the Charya Tantra and Yoga Tantra both landed in India. These three make up the Outer Tantras.

The group of Teachings that landed on the roof of King Za's palace is known as the Mahayoga Tantra. The group of Teachings known as the Anuyoga Tantra landed in present-day Sri Lanka. However, the Teachings of Atiyoga Dzogchen, which is known as the Nondual Tantra, did not fall from the sky like the others, but was given directly by the Sambhogakaya Vajrasattva to the Vidyadhara Garab Dorje, who wrote them down as scriptures. These three make up the Inner Tantras.

THE LIFE OF GARAB DORJE

The version of Garab Dorje's life story that follows is taken from the Teachings compiled by the great translator Vairochana. However, other

The Nirmanakaya Garab Dorje

versions are sometimes told and these versions can be quite different, such as one by Jigme Lingpa in which young Garab Dorje is abandoned by his mother out of her shame at being without a husband. Personally, I trust Vairochana's version because he himself traveled from Tibet to India, where he met both the masters Mañjushrimitra and Shri Simha. It is also sometimes recounted that he met Garab Dorje. So, I feel that he had more direct contact with the events that happened there, and that is why I have chosen to include that particular version in this text.

In the Heaven of the Thirty-Three, Vajrasattva directly gave the blessings, empowerments, and oral instructions to a son of the Gods named Sem Lakchen. Sem Lakchen realized the complete meaning of the Teachings and turned the wheel of the Dharma throughout the god realms, giving widespread Teachings on the Indestructible Secret Mantrayana.

Far away, in the human realm and in a land called Oddiyana, located somewhere in the region of present-day Pakistan and Afghanistan, there was a lake called Lake Kuda. Near the lake there lived a king named Dahenadalo, who had a daughter named Dahararnu, who was said to be completely free of faults, having perfected all of the good qualities, and especially to be of the compassionate lineage of the Bodhisattvas. Based on her wish to practice the Dharma, she took full monastic vows and lived with a retinue of five hundred fully ordained nuns. Around this same time, Sem Lakchen had completed giving Teachings in the god realms and realized that he could benefit no more beings through his Dharma activity. Thus, he decided that it was time to pass the Teachings of Dzogchen on to the human realm.

On what was said to be the auspicious eighth night of a summer month, Dahararnu had a miraculous dream. In the dream, the Buddhas and Bodhisattvas gathered above her in the sky and light emanated from them. The light split in two and formed the two bodies of the sun and the moon. The sun appeared above Dahararnu's head and dissolved into her body and moved down into her heart center. The moon appeared below her feet and dissolved into her body and moved up into her heart center. The next morning, when she went to the lake to bathe, Vajrapani emanated as a golden goose, and Sem Lakchen turned himself into the seed syllable HUM, gold in color, which flew into the goose's mouth. The goose flew down to the lake where Dahararnu was bathing and struck her chest three times with its beak. The third time, the golden HUM dissolved into her chest.

When Dahararnu told her father the King about her dream and the appearance of the golden goose, he was overjoyed. He told the members of the court to prepare, for the emanation of a Buddha would soon be born, and gave his daughter every possible comfort during her pregnancy. When it was time to give birth to the child, first a golden vajra came from Dahararnu's chest, and then the vajra turned into a beautiful child. In his right hand the baby boy grasped a vajra and in his left, a jeweled scepter.

From the time that the child was born, he prayed continuously to

Manjushrimitra

Vajrasattva. Because everyone who heard about his birth was over-whelmed with delight, he was named Garab, meaning "great joy." And because he was spontaneously born from a vajra, he was named Dorje, which is the Tibetan translation of this same word.

When Garab Dorje grew older, he met Vajrasattva directly, and Vajrasattva gave him the transmissions, empowerments, oral instructions, and blessings, which enabled him to completely realize the meaning of the Teachings. Based on this, the perfect meaning of the entire Sutra and Tantra dawned in his mind. But of all these countless scriptures, he gained perfect mastery over the most supreme, the 6,400,000 Tantras of Dzogchen, after which his mind became indivisible with the Buddhas of the three times.

After he realized the meaning of the Teachings, Garab Dorje began to teach Atiyoga to a few uncommon practitioners who became his students. Around that time, an emanation of Mañjushri named

Mañjushrimitra was living in India as the greatest scholar among a group of five hundred panditas. Mañjushrimitra received a prophecy directly from Mañjushri that said that in Oddiyana a Vidyadhara named Garab Dorje was giving Teachings on the king of all vehicles, which would enable him to attain Buddhahood in one lifetime. Mañjushri instructed him to go there, receive the Teachings, and take up the practices of Atiyoga.

The panditas living with Mañjushrimitra could not accept a type of liberation that was described as effortless, and so six of them accompanied Mañjushrimitra to Oddiyana with the plan of taking on and defeating Garab Dorje in a debate. Mañjushrimitra knew very well the meaning of the prophecy he had received, but he pretended to know nothing even when they met Garab Dorje for the first time. However, when engaged in debate on Sutra, the Paramitas, and Madhyamaka logic, Garab Dorje could not be defeated. But when examining the view, Mañjushrimitra realized that by taking up only emptiness, as was ascribed by the Middle Way Teachings, the view was not perfect. It was only through taking up the union of clarity and emptiness that the view could be totally uncontrived and free of extremes. Thus, Mañjushrimitra came to a direct understanding of the difference between the uncontrived view presented in the Inner Teachings, and the uncontrived view presented by the Dzogchen Teachings—which we call the view of Trekchod.

Based on the debate held by the panditas and Garab Dorje, Mañjushrimitra gained deep certainty in the uncontrived view of Dzogchen. For the next twenty-five years he remained with Garab Dorje and received the entirety of the Secret Teachings and the most secret of the oral instructions. Notably, he received Teachings on the 6,400,000 Tantras of Dzogchen and realized them as if the wisdom of his master's mind had been poured into his own like water from a vase. Mañjushrimitra remained in a human body until around the age of 125.

Mañjushrimitra's primary student was called Shri Simha. Shri Simha took birth in China, and was also a well-known pandita. However, one

Shri Simha

day he received a prophecy from Avalokiteshvara that said that he should go and seek out Mañjushrimitra and receive the oral instructions of Atiyoga from him. Following the instructions laid out by the prophecy exactly, he served Mañjushrimitra for twenty-five years, and attained all of the Teachings his master had ever received. As a result, he attained great realization, and his wisdom became indivisible from his master's. Shri Simha also remained in a human body until around the age of 125.

✦ CHAPTER 9
✦ *Dzogchen and Tantra*

WHY ARE THE SECRET TEACHINGS SAID TO BE SECRET?

THERE ARE THREE WAYS in which we could call the Secret Teachings secret. These three are: naturally secret, self-secret, and concealed. "Naturally secret" refers to the Buddha nature and the wisdom awareness that we all possess, but do not realize. We have had this nature from beginningless time, but we have never been able to see it. In the scriptures, this is likened to a poor family that lives in a shack built atop a golden treasure that could relieve all of their poverty and hunger, if they only realized it was there. From the Tantras:

> Like a poor family, beneath whose house
> Lies an inexhaustible treasure
> That they do not know is there;
> The treasure cannot declare, "I am here."
> In this same way, if one does not realize the precious
>   treasure within the mind,
> The stainless clear light nature that was not put there by anyone,
> This poverty of the mind
> Will always be the cause for experiencing the suffering of
>   rebirth [in samsara].

Next, "self-secret" refers to the way that, even though the clear light nature of mind and the fact that all beings have the Buddha nature are taught extensively in the Sutras and Tantras, we always dismiss the idea that the Buddha is within and look for it in an outer object. From the *Secret Essence Tantra*:

> Even by looking throughout the ten directions and the
>   four times,
> You will never find the perfect Buddha.
> The perfect Buddha is the nature of mind.
> Do not search for the Buddha elsewhere!

Finally, "concealed" refers to the fact that the Secret Teachings have been concealed from beings who do not have the proper disposition or ability to put them into practice and realize them. It is said in the Tantras,

> When one has not realized that which is self-secret,
> They cannot realize that which is concealed.

Ordinary beings grasp at the ego and objects as being permanent through their ignorance of the nature of mind. Even if they intellectually tell themselves that the Buddha is within, they do not truly believe it. That is why it is said that we must first realize what is self-secret before we can realize the meaning of the Secret Teachings.

However, there are other reasons for concealing the Teachings. For example, there are some beings who, through their misunderstanding of the Teachings, take them up improperly and cause harm to themselves and others in the process. In the history of India and Tibet there was a period of time when it was thought that liberation could be attained simply through sexual union with a consort. However, the conduct of these "yogis" lacked the mindfulness, motivation, and proper understanding of the oral instructions that are the supports of authentic consort practice. Without the foundation of Bodhichitta and certainty in the uncontrived view, it is impossible to gain any realization whatsoever from such a practice. Furthermore, engaging in sexual union thinking one is doing consort practice or engaging in consort practice without the necessary qualifications has caused many beings to hurl themselves into the lower realms.

I know that I have already said many times that it is imperative that we take up Dzogchen and Bodhichitta in union. But I want to assure you that I say this from experience. In the countryside around the village where I was born, thousands of yogis have attained the rainbow body as a result of taking up the Teachings of Dzogchen. But of all of these, there was not even one who neglected to take up Dzogchen and Bodhichitta in union. If we fail to take up the practice of Bodhichitta when we begin to meditate on the view, there is very real danger. Such practitioners have been known to take rebirth as dark-hearted beings, who are no longer in a favorable situation to practice the Dharma. I have heard many such stories in my lifetime, but now I will tell only one story, which occurred very near the place I was born.

About two hundred years ago, there lived a monk who was overlooked by many in his village and generally not very well thought of. As a result, this monk decided to stay in solitary retreat for his whole life practicing Dharma. He had never had much training, much less gained any certainty in the view, nor did he know how to take up the aspect of Bodhichitta in his practice. So, he spent his lifetime taking up the practice called "generation stage," which is taught as part of the Inner Tantra. His practice was devoid of any particular aspiration, and in addition to his meditation, he said millions of mantras while he stayed in retreat. Needless to say, this monk did not lack diligence! So what happened to him occurred only as a result of how he chose to practice.

After many years, the monk's meditation became very stable, and he had accumulated the recitation of a great many mantras. However, as we saw earlier in the story of Yeshe Tsogyal's life, there comes a time when a practitioner is tempted and tested in the stages before true realization is attained. When this monk reached this precarious stage, he had little to fall back on because he had never worked with the Teachings of Bodhichitta. He was unable to withstand the tests he was given, and he died while undergoing them. Based on his disturbed state of mind at the time of death and the style of meditation he had practiced during his life, he took rebirth as a dark-hearted being—in English we might call such a being a demon or an evil spirit. Although many people may think such beings are just fiction, I assure you that Tibet has a long history of being inhabited by such beings. From that time until the present, he has spent his time and energy creating obstacles for the people in my homeland, appearing here and there as a ghost, causing homes and crops to burn, and people and livestock to die.

Chupur Lama and Tsara Dharmakirti Rinpoche both encountered and were known to be successful at quieting this evildoer. From the time I was a young boy, Lama Chupur told me that when such tests came, the key to passing them was to rely on both the peaceful and wrathful natures when necessary. However, he also said that it was especially important to develop uncommonly deep compassion and to focus on the practices that develop Bodhichitta.

Likewise, Tsara Dharmakirti Rinpoche told me that there were many times when he received signs that he had been able to benefit this distraught being through using the methods to generate Bodhichitta and by practicing the Union of Dzogchen and Bodhichitta. My Lama told me that no matter what type of common or uncommon practice I took up, and no matter whether I was in a place as serene as a heavenly pure land or as terrifying as a hell realm, that I must always rely upon aspiration Bodhichitta and the Union in my meditation. Only in this way could I be sure that an obstacle would not come to me. My Lama said that even the most terrifying appearances in dreams can be pacified by taking up the union of Clear Light and Bodhichitta in the dream bardo.

Because I have been given this kind of advice since I was a small child and have seen the results for myself, I have devoted myself to teaching the proper way to take up the Union. The Vidyadhara Jigme Lingpa said that meditation taken up without the aspiration and conduct of Bodhichitta is a mere "reflection" of what is meant by the word "meditation." Likewise, Jigme Lingpa said that the situation I have just described, that of practicing solely the aspect of Dzogchen while neglecting Bodhichitta, has happened countless times in the history of the Secret Teachings—always with the same, unfortunate result. This is all the more reason to conceal the Teachings from beings who do not have the capacity to practice them properly.

THE ETYMOLOGY OF THE "INDESTRUCTIBLE SECRET MANTRAYANA"

In Tibetan, the Secret Teachings are called *sang ngak dorje tekpa* (*gsangs sngags rdo rje theg pa*), which means "Indestructible Secret Mantrayana." Of course, each individual word, or syllable as is the case in Tibetan, has its own particular meaning. The first syllable, *sang*, means "secret," which I have already explained. The next syllable, *ngak*, means "mantra." Mantra has three classifications: secret mantras, vidya (or knowledge) mantras, and dharani (or retention) mantras. "Secret mantra" refers to when we take up the method of compassionate Bodhichitta and the wisdom of emptiness in union. When we are free of all grasping and conceptual thoughts and the union of great bliss and emptiness arises, the written syllables of mantras appear as a mandala before us. Then, we rest in the Union and work with uttered mantra, and this acts as the antidote to all conceptual thought.

The other reason this type of mantra is called "secret" is that it becomes easier to establish the practice that we are taking up when we keep it a secret. In fact, in my homeland we believe in this so firmly that we never mention what practices we are taking up when we stay in retreat, nor do we let anyone see the mandala offerings on our altars once they have been made.

"Knowledge mantras" also rely upon taking up the Union of Dzogchen and Bodhichitta. They are described as the development of wisdom awareness and the good quality of activity through taking up the practices of the female deities. This is done by visualizing their forms and taking up their mudras and mantras. Finally, "retention mantras" are said in order to increase one's memory and enable one to remember a vast array of texts and oral instructions. Again, the consort Yeshe Tsogyal attained the fruit of such mantras when she attained the ability of not forgetting, and fulfilled the prophecy of becoming the keeper of the Teachings and treasures of Padmasambhava.

Next, the meaning of *dorje*, which means *vajra* in Sanskrit and "indestructible" in English. It was said in the *Mirror of Explanatory Tantras* (*bShad rgyud me long*),

> The nature of indivisibility
> Is known as indestructible.

As we established in Chapter 5, the appearances of all phenomena arise from the mind. And the nature of mind, which is the union of clarity and emptiness, is indestructible. It is like a diamond that is so hard that it can cut through any other surface or object, but which itself cannot be damaged or scratched. In this way, the union of clarity and emptiness can cut through any afflictive emotion, conceptual thought, or obscuration. And because there is nothing in the entire universe that can destroy or damage the nature of mind, we call it indestructible.

Finally, the syllable *tekpa* means *yana* in Sanskrit and "vehicle" in English. The word "vehicle" suggests being able to carry a great many things. In fact, the traditional metaphor for this type of vehicle is an elephant, a massive animal strong enough to move through even the most difficult conditions. In this same way, the Teachings of the Indestructible Secret Mantrayana have the ability to transform the phenomenon of samsara into nirvana, so it is the greatest vehicle of all. The vehicle is also referred to as the "vehicle of wisdom awareness" in the scriptures.

The Tantric Series

As I have already mentioned, the Tantric Series contains the Outer and Inner Tantra, both of which are made up of three groups of Teachings. In this text, I will give an explanation of only the three that make up the Inner Tantra. In the Inner Tantra, the Teachings of the Mahayoga are called "the Father Tantra." The Teachings of Anuyoga are called "the Mother Tantra." And the Teachings of Atiyoga are called "the Nondual Tantra."

The master Jigme Lingpa said,

[Within] the unsurpassable Inner Tantras of the Secret
    Mantrayana
Are the generation stage, perfection stage, and the union of both.
These are known as the Father Tantra, Mother Tantra, and
    the Nondual Tantra.

First, an explanation of the Father and Mother Tantras. As we saw
in the history of King Za, there are eighteen great Tantras, which can
be described as holding the meanings of the teachings of both the
Mahayoga and the Anuyoga Teachings. Although it is usually taught
that the Eighteen Great Tantras hold only the meaning of the
Mahayoga, this is not pervasive. This is because the Tantra that we call
the king of all the others, the *Secret Essence Tantra*, holds the condensed
meaning of all Eighteen Great Tantras. There are a wide variety of
commentaries on the *Secret Essence Tantra* written from both the
Mahayoga and Anuyoga points of view, so it is impossible to limit the
scope of these great Tantras to only the Mahayoga. In general, it is
said that the meaning of these eighteen Tantras can be condensed into
the Tantras of the body, speech, mind, good qualities, and activity of
the Buddhas.

The *Secret Essence Tantra* is considered paramount among Tantras for
the reason I just described. Because it holds the root of the Tantras,
Teachings on the *Secret Essence Tantra* have been passed carefully from
master to disciple through the years without breaking the lineage or
distorting the meaning. I received such a perfect lineage of Teachings
myself when I studied the *Secret Essence Tantra* with my root Lama in
Tibet. If the *Secret Essence Tantra* is studied in detail, we find that it contains the root meanings of the series of eight Tantras of Illusion *(sGyu
'phrul sde brgyad)* and the series of four Explanatory Tantras *(bShad rgyud
sde bzhi)*. The four Explanatory Tantras hold the explanations for the
two paths taught in the Secret Teachings, which are called *taplam*, or
path of skillful means, and *drolam*, or path of release.

When taking up the Inner Tantra, the practices of the Father Tantra
are practices that primarily work with the masculine aspect and energy

as expressed by the appearances of conventional reality. To do this, we work with the mandala and visualize mostly male deities adorned with jewels and colorful streamers. Within the Father Tantra, the generation stage is the most essential practice, but we should not take this to mean that the Father Tantra is restricted only to the aspect of appearance. We should always understand that it is necessary to take up both the generation and perfection stages in union. However, in the Father Tantra the primary practice is the generation stage, which is complemented by the practice of the perfection stage.

Regarding the Father Tantra, Jigme Lingpa said,

> By focusing on the generation stage,
> A great yogi who takes up the method of the Father Tantra
> Purifies the wind energy of the five elements.

Taking up the practice of the generation stage is the method for perceiving all appearances as the mandala, and the result of this practice is the purification of the wind energy. As the wind energy of the five elements is purified, so is the delusion that is the cause for impure perception. Then, by relying upon the inseparable path of clarity and emptiness, we are able to attain the common and uncommon accomplishments.

When taking up the practices of the Mother Tantra, we primarily work with the feminine aspect and energy. In this case, we visualize the mandala of mostly female deities and Dakinis who are naked, and adorned by only bone ornaments. In the Mother Tantra, we focus on the practices of the perfection stage, which work with the essences, which can also be translated as "wisdom drops." However, we should not take this explanation to mean that the Mother Tantra relies only on the perfection stage. As I have already mentioned, both the Father and Mother Tantra combine the methods of generation and perfection stages. But in the case of the Mother Tantra, the perfection stage is taken up as the primary practice, and the generation stage as the complement.

Regarding the Mother Tantra, Jigme Lingpa said,

> By focusing on the wisdom of the perfection stage,
> A great yogi who takes up the Mother Tantra
> Generates bliss and emptiness from the wisdom drops.

When we take up the perfection stage, we meditate on the inner mandala. First, we use our own body as the method to gain experience in the practices of tsa lung. Then, we rely upon a practice that enables us to attain the wisdom of the four joys, which leads us towards enlightenment.

The Teachings of the Nondual Tantra, which is synonymous with Atiyoga and Dzogchen, are usually explained from two points of view. From the common point of view, they are made up of sixty-four Tantras. And from the uncommon point of view, they contain 6,400,000 Tantras. But if we condense the meaning of all of these, they fall into the series of three that make up the Atiyoga Teachings: Sem-de, Long-de, and Mengak-de.

The Nondual Tantra of Atiyoga takes up the methods of the Father Tantra and the Mother Tantra in union. Jigme Lingpa said,

> By taking up the inseparable path of wisdom,
> The supreme yogi abides in the union of clarity and emptiness.

When practicing Atiyoga, we take up the view of Trekchod and the practice of Todgyal in order to attain the supreme results of the rainbow body and the "great transfer."

Dzogchen and Tantra

Because of the emphasis placed on Dzogchen in the West, I think that at times the relationship between Dzogchen and Tantra, as well as the Buddhist Teachings as a whole, might seem unclear. I, as well as the lineage holders of the Teachings that have been passed on to me,

consider Dzogchen a part of the Tantra and of the Buddhist Teachings as a whole. This is consistent with my belief that it contains the
complete meaning of both. After Vajrasattva gave the Teachings on the
sixty-four million Tantras of Dzogchen to Garab Dorje, Garab Dorje
then passed these Teachings on to Mañjushrimitra, Shri Simha, and
Padmasambhava. These unbroken lineages, which have been passed
from master to disciple up until the present day, are still what make up
the Dzogchen Teachings. So, it would be impossible for us to say that
the Teachings of Dzogchen that we know are separate from the Nondual Tantra that was passed from the Sambhogakaya Buddhas to Garab
Dorje in the human realm.

Also, if we look at the Inner Tantras from the point of view of the
Nyingmapa Teachings as a whole, we refer to Mahayoga as the Father
and Anuyoga as the Mother. The union of these two is the Nondual
Tantra of Dzogchen. Thus, the Nondual Tantra of Atiyoga inherently
contains the meaning of all the others.

Moreover, as we have already seen in looking at the history of the
Secret Teachings, the Teachings of Dzogchen have been passed to
other realms besides the human realm, such as the god realm and the
naga realm. However, even these Teachings were based on the emanations of Dakinis and other enlightened beings, who also passed on
the complete meaning of the Tantric Teachings when they gave the
Teachings on the 6,400,000 Tantras of Atiyoga. So I would have to say
that any text that contains the methods for the generation stage, perfection stage, Trekchod, or Todgyal is part of the Tantra—no matter
what realm it is practiced in.

Buddha Shakyamuni said that whatever texts contained the meaning
of the natural state and gave the methods for liberation without contradiction must be viewed as being a part of the Buddhas' speech. So,
we could actually say that Buddhism is practiced in many realms and
systems outside our own. In fact, Nagarjuna brought many texts with
him from the realm of the nagas and many contemporary Buddhists
still study and rely upon these texts today.

THE SERIES OF THREE IN ATIYOGA

Moving now to the series of three within the Teachings of Atiyoga, how are we to understand Sem-de, Long-de, and Mengak-de? The series called Sem-de is based on the fact that rikpa pervades the entirety of samsara and nirvana and does not fall into any of three possible extremes. First, it does not fall into the extreme of eternalism, in which entities are regarded as being truly established. Second, it does not fall into the extreme of nihilism, in which all phenomena are merely empty, without the necessary complement of appearance. And third, it does not fall into the extreme of grasping at the union of appearance and emptiness, for grasping is just another kind of extreme. Resting in the union that is completely beyond extremes and all grasping is how we describe the essential meaning of the Teachings of Sem-de. The Teachings of Sem-de were perfectly passed from Mañjushrimitra and Shri Simha to Vairochana, who passed them to Spang Mipham Gompo in Tibet. Spang Mipham Gompo passed them to thousands of students, and each and every one of them attained the supreme, uncommon accomplishment of the rainbow body.

The series of Long-de was also passed from Mañjushrimitra and Shri Simha to Vairochana, who brought the Teachings to Tibet. Two factors make up the essential meaning of this series. The first is that rikpa is indivisible from the heart center of the Dharmakaya Samantabhadra. The second is that all appearances are perceived as mere ornaments that are completely beyond the extremes of binding and liberation. In other words, they are beyond the three spheres of actor, object, and receiver, and are completely uncontrived. So, abiding in the primordially pure vast expanse is the way the Teachings of Long-de are put into practice.

Finally, the series of Mengak-de was passed from the great master Padmasambhava to the consort Yeshe Tsogyal. After the Teachings had perfectly passed, including Teachings called "The Heart Essence of the Dakinis" and "The Heart Essence of Vimalamitra," they were hidden as mind treasures. Later, these mind treasures were found by

Vimalamitra

Longchenpa, who passed them to Jigme Lingpa. So, we call the Teachings passed in this way the "Longchen Nyingthig," which means "The Heart Essence of the Vast Expanse." This is the lineage of Mengak-de, as well as Sem-de and Long-de, that I received from my root Lamas. However, because I have specifically cited Padmasambhava and Longchenpa in the context of Mengak-de, this should not be taken to mean that both of these masters did not attain and perfectly realize the Teachings within all three of the series of Atiyoga as well as all of the lineages passed in the Nyingmapa School. Both of these masters attained complete realization of the entire Nyingmapa canon. A more detailed description of both their lives will follow in Chapter 12.

The essential practice of the Mengak-de is to take up the view of Trekchod and the practice of Todgyal, and this results in seeing the four appearances that arise to a practitioner of Dzogchen. The practice of Todgyal is truly secret, so I will not give an explanation of it in this text. The first of the four appearances is a vision of the Dhar-mata, or the true nature of reality. The second is a further cultivation of this vision, the third its maturation, and the fourth goes beyond it. Taking up the view of Trekchod and the practice of Todgyal requires a very deep commitment to the practice of Dharma, as well as the proper preparation, an uncommon relationship with a Spiritual Friend, and various other good qualities that I have already mentioned. After having gone beyond the four appearances, it is possible to practice the subtle and deep meditation that enables one to attain the result of the rainbow body, as well as the other supremely profound accom-plishments.

The accomplishment series is part of the series of three within Atiyoga because it contains much of the Sem-de and Long-de Teach-ings. The accomplishment series is divided into two branches: "gama" and "terma." First, for an explanation of gama. Generally speaking, *gama (bka' ma)* is the word used to describe any of the Buddhas' speech. However, as practitioners of the Secret Teachings, a group of texts called "the Seventeen Tantras" as well as the Teachings on the Eight Kagyed Deities are the gama we most often hear about. The Eight Kagyed Deities are the instructions on the way to rely upon the eight "yidam," or Tantric deities, of the Nyingmapa School when taking up the generation stage of the Mahayoga Tantra. Although I will not go through all eight in detail, I think you will easily be able to get an idea of what these Teachings are like from the explanation that follows.

The first of the Kagyed Deities, called Jamphel Sku, was first trans-mitted by Mañjushrimitra. When Mañjushrimitra accomplished the practice of Mañjushri, he directly saw the face of Mañjushri's wrath-ful aspect, called Mañjushri Yamantaka. He received the empower-ments, transmissions, and oral instructions from the wrathful deity itself. These Teachings on the yidam deity were then passed on to Shri Simha, Hunkara, and Padmasambhava, who spread them throughout Tibet.

In the context of the Secret Teachings, there is much talk about both peaceful and wrathful deities. The reason for this is that not all beings can be subdued through peaceful methods, and the Secret Teachings utilize all possible methods to tame the minds of ordinary beings. In such a case, we could take up the practice of a wrathful deity, which would give us an entirely new range of energy to work with.

However, even after hearing this explanation, there is still sometimes confusion about the nature of wrathful aspects. It is sometimes perceived that the appearances of wrathful deities, when depicted in traditional paintings called "thangkas," condone violence and go against the compassionate nature of Buddhism. This is not the case. The foundation of all appearances, whether they are of a peaceful or wrathful nature, is the enlightened mind of Bodhichitta—which once again points to the pivotal role that Bodhichitta takes in our practice.

Some of the other lineages of the Kagyed Deities include the yidam deity of Hayagriva, which was passed from Nagarjuna to Padmasambhava and then spread throughout Tibet. Also, the yidam called Yangdak Tuk was passed from the Vidyadhara Hunkara to Padmasambhava and then spread throughout Tibet. And the yidam called Dutsi Yonten was spread by Vimalamitra throughout Tibet.

One of the most important lineages among the Kagyed Deities for us to know about is the yidam deity called Phurba Thinley, more commonly known by its Sanskrit equivalent "Vajrakilaya," which was accomplished by Padmasambhava before he spread it throughout Tibet. This particular lineage has a beautiful story behind it, in which Yeshe Tsogyal revealed the depth of her faith and the pure way in which she perceived her master Padmasambhava.

When Padmasambhava was staying in what is now Parphing, Nepal, he took up the practice of Vajrakilaya. In one month's time, he saw the face of Vajrakilaya directly, as well as the face of the Dakini Dewa Wangmo and the Vidyadhara Drabahathu, who had also received the empowerments directly from Vajrakilaya. From them, Padmasambhava received the empowerments, transmissions, and oral instructions on establishing the yidam deity Vajrakilaya eighteen times.

After Padmasambhava had received the Teachings, he went to Samye, Tibet. There, as he gave the Teachings on Vajrakilaya to Yeshe

Tsogyal, the mandala of Vajrakilaya appeared in the sky above them. This caused Padmasambhava to ask Yeshe Tsogyal, "Do you wish to receive the empowerments, transmissions, and oral instructions from me, or directly from Vajrakilaya?"

Yeshe Tsogyal replied, "The root of all accomplishment is the Lama, so I wish to receive the lineage directly from you." Because Yeshe Tsogyal's reply and deep faith created the perfect conditions for receiving the lineage, by the power of dependent arising Yeshe Tsogyal received the Teachings and became their primary holder. Although Yeshe Tsogyal is the holder of all of Padmasambhava's Teachings, the yidam practice of Vajrakilaya is one for which she is exceptionally well-known. In considering all eight of the Kagyed Deities, we could not say that one is of primary importance. However, the deep faith of Tibetan yogis in this practice has led thousands of practitioners who rely upon it to accomplishment, so in that way it does hold a prominence among them.

When I was nineteen years old, I stayed in retreat on Vajrakilaya with Tsara Dharmakirti Rinpoche. During the time that we stayed in retreat, Rinpoche spent hours conferring the instructions of the practice on me, so that I learned the proper way to practice it. Not only that, but Vajrakilaya was the primary yidam practiced by Lama Chupur, who gained all of the signs of accomplishment by relying upon it. He was so accomplished, in fact, that Tsara Dharmakirti Rinpoche told me that it was imperative that I receive the empowerments, transmissions, and oral instructions directly from him, which I did. Such was the respect and pure perception these two Lamas had for each other!

Later, I also received the empowerments and instructions on Vajrakilaya from a third Lama who has been of primary importance to my study and meditation, a ngakpa named Dorlo Rinpoche. Until his passing in 2003, Dorlo Rinpoche was the greatest practitioner and holder of the Teachings of tsa lung in all of Tibet, as well as being a Dzogchen yogi in the truest sense of the word. His uncommon and lucid realization set him apart from other Lamas, and he was regarded by Tibetans with great devotion—and I even heard of his being praised by the Siddha Chatral Rinpoche! More about the life of Dorlo Rinpoche will be included later in this chapter.

Terma (*gter ma*) means "treasure" in Tibetan and refers to Teachings that are hidden until the time to put them into use has ripened. After Samantabhadra had manifested the peaceful and wrathful mandalas and given the Teachings on the Eight Kagyed Deities, Vajradhara gathered the Teachings together. He gave them to the principal Dakini, who was named Lekyi Wangmoche. She placed the Teachings on each of the Kagyed Deities in eight different spheres made of precious metals and gems and hid them. The time to reveal was sensed by the Eight Vidyadharas. They went to the place where the treasures were hidden and remained there in meditation for seven days. On the last day, the Dakini Lekyi Wangmoche appeared directly before them and gave each of the Vidyadharas one of the eight treasures. After opening them and taking up the instructions that were contained within them, every one of the Vidyadharas perfectly accomplished them and earned the title of drubtob, which means "saint," "great yogi," or "realized being."

Padmasambhava studied the way to practice and realize each of the Kagyed Deities, one by one, with each of the Eight Vidyadharas. Because he received the instructions directly from them, he is actually both a holder and a drubtob of all eight lineages. There was one final treasure that was not opened at that time, but put aside until later because it had not yet ripened. This treasure was made of a combination of all eight precious metals and gems, and held within it the essential instructions of all eight yidam practices combined. As the time to practice the texts contained by this treasure had not yet ripened, the Dakini Lekyi Wangmoche kept this treasure and later gave it to Padmasambhava. As practitioners of the Secret Teachings, we should recognize Padmasambhava as the supreme master of the Vajrayana, who perfectly holds and has accomplished the wisdom of every single lineage of Teachings.

In Tibet, after Padmasambhava had given the profound oral instructions to Yeshe Tsogyal, she hid them as treasures to be found later. This accounts for the 108 treasures that were discovered by the "tertons," or treasure revealers, of Tibet. In particular, the treasure that is said to be like the "heart essence" of the Teachings was discovered by the pure wisdom of the great master Longchenpa's mind. So, this treasure is called a "mind treasure," since it exists only in the sphere of primordially pure wisdom. This mind treasure was revealed by Long-chenpa and passed directly to Jigme Lingpa, who passed it to his own heart student and then finally it was passed down to Patrul Rinpoche. From Patrul Rinpoche, it was passed down in the shortest manner from heart son to heart son until it reached my own root Lama, who is the fourth in a succession of heart sons who received their Teach-ings directly from Patrul Rinpoche. I became the fifth in the lineage of heart sons after Tsara Dharmakirti Rinpoche passed down these Teachings to me.

The Foundation, Path, and Result of Tantra

In the Inner Teachings, we looked at the foundation, path, and result from the point of view of the Middle Way. Because all types of med-itation can be condensed into these three, let us take another look at the foundation, path, and result, this time from the point of view of Tantra. It was said in the Tantras that,

> Tantra should be known as a continuum of cause, method, and result.

Along with the reasons I have already given, Tantra is said to be a continuum because there is no difference between the nature of mind of an ordinary being and that of a Buddha. The natural state, which is rikpa, is the nature of both. Although there are differences in appear-ance, which creates a kind of continuum, we should understand the essence of the nature of mind in both cases to be the same.

In the foundation (cause) of Tantra, rikpa is still hidden from us, because we have not met with the proper conditions to realize it. So the thing we must realize, that will act as the foundation of Tantra, is that rikpa is the natural expression of the mind. Another way to express the foundation of Tantra is that it is the time when we have not yet begun to purify the obscurations. Once we have recognized wisdom awareness, and begun to purify the two classes of obscurations, we have taken up the path (method) of Tantra. Based on practicing the path of Tantra, we attain the result of Tantra, which is continually abiding in rikpa, and is completely free of obscurations.

However, when considering the essence of mind (which we could also call rikpa, wisdom awareness, or the Buddha nature) we might wonder if there is any true difference between samsara and nirvana. In other words, is there truly something binding within samsara, and something liberating within nirvana? I would have to say that neither of these things is true. The nature of mind is primordially pure, and is beyond duality. So although the appearances of samsara and nirvana are different, the nature of mind is exactly the same when considered from either point of view.

If there is no actual difference between the nature of mind of sentient beings and Buddhas, we might wonder why their appearances are so different. We might even think that if this is true, human beings are actually enlightened! Again, the difference between sentient beings and Buddhas is not in the nature of mind. It is in whether or not they recognize and are able to rest continuously in rikpa and experience nirvana, or instead fall into the delusional realm of samsara.

This situation is easily examined by taking the example of the sun shining in the sky. At times the sun is shining brightly in a clear sky, and at other times it is covered by clouds. But the sun is exactly the same in both cases, although it appears quite different to us here on earth. In this same way, the clear light nature of mind either radiates without obstruction, or is obscured by clouds of ignorance.

The nature of mind can be described as being completely perfect, having the spontaneous presence of the qualities known as the "seven riches of ultimate reality." To understand these seven, let us again use the example of a mirror to examine the nature of mind. First, the clear surface of the mirror is like the vast expanse of ultimate reality. Second, from the point of view that the mirror is unstained and uncovered, it is like the ultimate nature of wisdom. The final five riches can be described by looking at what is called the "ultimate result." The ultimate result is the enlightened body, speech, mind, activity, and good qualities of the Buddhas. Just as a mirror has the ability to reflect whatever appears before it, so the vast nature of mind is completely unobstructed and has the potential to fully express these five riches. However, in ordinary beings these five qualities have not yet appeared, even though the nature of mind has the capacity to express them.

THE SUPERIOR TWO TRUTHS

In the Secret Teachings, we develop an even deeper understanding of the two truths than was presented in the Inner Teachings. When we understand the nature of mind to have the spontaneous presence of the seven riches of ultimate reality, this is called "superior ultimate reality." And the expression of superior ultimate reality as the wisdom mandala (of beings and the world they abide in) is called "superior conventional reality." Again, these two truths are not distinct; they are essentially indivisible. We should understand them to be inseparable in three ways: as gold cannot be separated from its golden color, as turquoise cannot be separated from its blue hue, and as a flame cannot be divided from its luminosity. Although we speak of conventional reality, ultimate reality, and the union of the two as though they were easy to conceptualize and understand, the actual state of union is beyond the capacity of mind to understand, and beyond the power of words to describe.

THE PATH OF TANTRA

The path of Tantra is the method by which we remove the stains that obscure the mind's true nature. No matter what Tantric practice we take up, our meditation develops along a continuum, and there are five distinct stages that can be recognized on the path that leads us towards the attainment of the perfect result. In his *Commentary on Mahamudra Shamatha (Bi ma la'i phyag rgya bsam gtan gyi 'grel pa)*, Vimalamitra said,

> Movement, progress, experience, stability, and mastery;
> These five [show] the development of meditative
>   concentration.

"Movement" refers to the mind in the beginning stages of meditation. Like a waterfall spilling over the edge of a steep, rocky mountain, the mind is not free of distraction for even a moment. It moves here and there like leaves blown by the wind. Often, when we first begin to meditate, we feel that our mind is even more restless than before. This is not really the case. But because we have never attempted to meditate before, we have never fully realized the extent to which our minds are constantly bombarded by conceptual thoughts, mental afflictions, and ideas. Once we have begun to practice meditation, the feeling that we actually have more conceptual thoughts than before could be seen as a sort of benchmark that shows we have made a very little bit of progress.

"Progress" refers to the fact that in the second stage, we have made a bit of headway in our practice of meditation. At this stage, we could use the metaphor of a creek that is falling down over a rocky mountain while trapped within a narrow crevice. In this case, the water is still spilling over the rocks at a great rate, but the flow of water is sometimes suspended and every so often there are moments when the flow of water stops and then starts again. So we could understand the flow of our conceptual thoughts at this stage, still moving quickly but with occasional momentary quietness. We could also describe this stage of meditation as "rest" for the mind.

"Experience" refers to the way an old man who is watching a child play does not follow the child. Although the child darts around here and there and never seems to tire of play, the old man is tired of playing. Like the example of the old man, our mind at this stage has become weary of following the endless cycle of conceptual thoughts.

We experience mostly stable meditation, interrupted only occasionally by conceptual thoughts, and we are not easily distracted. We could also describe this stage of meditation as the "exhaustion" of the mind.

We are said to have "stability" if we are able to abide easily in the view, mostly without distraction. We could liken this stage to hailstones striking the surface of a pond. The hailstones are hard and solid, and their impact causes small ripples to flow over the surface of the water. The ripples slowly fade away with no effort at all on the part of the pond. Just so, at this stage there is little that can shake our stability. However, it can still be shaken, so we should not understand it to be the perfect result. We could also describe stability as being the stage where conceptual thoughts can still move us.

"Mastery" is like a mountain that cannot be moved, or the vast expanse of the ocean. In this stage, there is no talk of pushing away, suppressing, grasping, or holding. We could also describe this stage as the attainment of freedom in our meditation.

A yogi who has experienced the signs of all five stages along this continuum and abides in the stage of mastery could truly be said to be able to use any experience or appearance they come across as the condition for meditation. However, until we reach this stage, I would have to say that it is crucial to our development to set aside a time to meditate every day. Based on the foundation we build through our daily practice, we will slowly, and only if we practice with extreme diligence, become able to meditate on all of the conditions that we come into contact with on a daily basis.

This does not mean that we should not practice Tonglen when we are feeling the weight of someone's suffering, or meditate on impermanence when we are feeling unhappy. Naturally, it is an essential part of the path to use all of the techniques we have received to reduce our mental afflictions in our daily life. However, it is unwise to think that we are habituated to the view and have attained the stage of mastery before this has actually happened. In truth, though, I have never heard of a Lama who attained the stage of mastery and subsequently quit their daily practice of meditation because they thought it was no longer necessary. Rather, once their capacity to practice was perfected, there never seemed to be a moment when they were not abiding in the view.

As we saw in Chapter 3, the path presented by the Indestructible Secret Mantrayana is called the "short path" because we are able to bypass the gradual paths presented by other vehicles. By applying intelligence, faith, insight, and diligence to the Teachings we are given, it is possible to attain the perfect result. Let us take a moment to examine the way in which the short path of the Vajrayana differs from the Hinayana and Mahayana vehicles. For example, on the gradual paths, the three poisons are presented as things to be abandoned. However, in the Indestructible Secret Mantrayana, this is not the case. Rather, it is taught that if the poisons arise while we are resting in the confidence of the view, the poisons are liberated into the Union. Specifically, desire is liberated into bliss and emptiness, anger is liberated into clarity and emptiness, and ignorance is liberated into awareness and emptiness. By taking up the path on which the poisons are transformed into wisdom, we are able to attain the perfect result of Buddhahood in the quickest possible manner.

Taplam and Drolam

As I have already mentioned, the path of Tantra has two main components called "taplam" and "drolam." In taplam, we work with the view of Trekchod; however, we are relying upon our mastery of the practices of tsa lung to do so. A metaphor for the way the poisons are self-liberated while taking up the path of taplam is given in the Tantras:

> If water flows into the ear,
> Water must release itself.

The meaning of this verse is that once water has flowed into the ear, if we actually pour more water into the ear, it will flow out on its own. A yogi who is working with the poisons while abiding in the uncontrived view applies this same method. Although the yogi does not abandon the poisons, they are no longer causes for remaining within samsara. And not only that, but this is the perfect method for quickly releasing the poisons. This is just like the work of an alchemist, who can turn ordinary metals into gold.

However, I would have to say that taking up this kind of practice has both an incredible benefit and a very real danger. If the yogi is truly an alchemist, he will really be able to transform the nature of whatever he encounters into gold, to speak metaphorically. But if he is not, not only will he be unable to turn ordinary metal into gold, but he will also destroy the ordinary metal itself in the process. In this same way, one who does not rest in the confidence of the view and attempts to take up the practice of not abandoning the poisons will not only fail to transform those poisons into wisdom, but will also descend into the lower realms or take an otherwise unfavorable rebirth.

Within the taplam, there are two types of meditation that can be practiced, which are called the "upper door" and the "lower door." As I already mentioned, both of these practices are based fundamentally on the mastery of tsa lung. The upper door is a style of meditation that relies upon the six chakras, which burn with heat. Then nectar melts and drips to fill the chakras completely. From the *Ocean Tantra*:

> The two sets of three chakras, and the three pillars of the
>   life force;
> By fire and wind, [heat] rises to the cow in the sky;
> [Like] milking, this is called the upper door.

The "two sets of three chakras" are the six chakras. The "three pillars" are the central, left, and right channels. On the top of the head is a sacred syllable, and this is the "cow in the sky." "Milking" refers to the nectar that drips from the chakras.

As we saw in the Chapter 7, the three main channels of the body run as straight as pillars through the body. The chakra of great bliss at the crown of the head is a wheel with thirty-two spokes. The chakra of perfect enjoyment at the throat has sixteen spokes. The chakra of phenomena at the heart center has eight spokes. The chakra of emanation at the navel has sixty-four spokes. The chakra of burning fire, which is the chakra located beneath the navel, is shaped like a triangle. Below this is the chakra of blowing wind, which is in the shape of a bow.

One who understands the proper way to work with tsa lung is able to push the upper breath down and hold it in the abdomen. Likewise, they push the lower breath up into the abdomen and hold it. This acts as the condition for the wind energy to move upwards from the chakra of blowing wind, and fan the flames of the chakra of fire. The combination of wind and fire causes heat to rise, which moves up the central channel, causing nectar to drip from above until it fills the chakra at the crown of the head. When the first chakra fills, joyful wisdom is attained. In this same way, when the chakras at the throat, heart center, and navel fill, the remainder of the four joyful wisdoms are attained: supreme joy, exalted joy, and innate joy. This is a very brief explanation of the way to take the taplam practice of upper door. However, if one has not already attained mastery over the practice of tsa lung, it would be very difficult to do this practice. However, of the two practices that make up taplam, the practice of the upper door is the easier one to put into practice.

These days, while I could say that quite a few masters have gained mastery over the view of Dzogchen, it is much harder to find a teacher who has completely mastered tsa lung. In Tibet, Dorlo Rinpoche is one of the only contemporary Lamas who was said to have completely mastered tsa lung. Not only that, he was also able to practice it in the traditional way, and pass the traditional style of Teaching on it to his close students. This is a great rarity indeed, for this style of introduction has mostly been lost.

When I was twenty-five years old, my root Lama sent me to stay in retreat with Dorlo Rinpoche to learn the way to practice tsa lung, and especially to generate inner heat. So, because of Dorlo Rinpoche's great kindness, I attained the uncommon lineage of the tsa lung Teachings of the "Longchen Nyingthig" during that time. As we saw in the story of Yeshe Tsogyal, the traditional way to study tsa lung in Tibet is to stay in retreat at the coldest time of year while wearing only scant clothing. Thus I, too, began my retreat during the bitter cold winter high in the mountains of Tibet. I can honestly say that I do not believe there is any colder weather to be faced on the planet. To tell the truth, even though I knew all about the history of the Teachings, at first I did not completely trust the blessings and power of tsa lung because I had never experienced them for myself. So it is easy for me to understand that there are people who have trouble believing that such practice is possible. I think this kind of skepticism can be a good thing, because it causes us to examine and really delve into a practice before we accept it.

When I arrived high in the mountains, there were no houses or warm shelters. There was nothing but rock, ice, and snow. There was not even any drinking water, and we had to melt blocks of ice over a fire when we needed a drink. During my retreat, I was only allowed to wear a very short traditional "skirt" and a yogi's cord across my chest.

However, after Dorlo Rinpoche gave me the instructions on the proper way to meditate and what posture to assume, my doubts quickly vanished. With a little bit of effort, I learned the way to work with wind energy, and I found that I really could generate heat and that I was not cold at all. At that time, Dorlo Rinpoche was seventy years old, and as I said, I was in my twenties. However, it seemed that he was the younger of the two of us because his body was so strong and virile as a result of his practice. Even though it was winter, the snow melted and grass and flowers began to sprout in a ring around the place where we were practicing as if spring had come!

After I had finished my retreat, I was tested by Dorlo Rinpoche and his consort. I was made to demonstrate each asana I had learned. Then finally, they draped an icy, wet shawl over me while I generated heat to see if I could make it dry. Along with perfectly passing the test given by Dorlo Rinpoche and his consort, I came away with unshakable faith in the practice of tsa lung, which continues to benefit me to this day. I believe that it was because of my deep faith in Dorlo Rinpoche that I was never ill during this time, and did not get injured despite the strenuous asanas I practiced. Because of this experience, I have truly come to believe that there is no Lama who could match Dorlo Rin-poche's skill and mastery in this area of the Secret Teachings.

When many people think of tsa lung, they think it is like what hatha or ashthanga yoga has come to be understood in the West: a physical practice meant to make the body strong. However, this definitely does not capture the essence of the practice of tsa lung. Tsa lung has three components: the physical action or position, the visualization and understanding of the channels, and the element of the view. Only when all three of these are present can we truly call an asana "tsa lung."

The second practice in taplam, called "the practice of the lower door," is the practice of sexual union—it requires an even more extraordinary mastery of tsa lung. In order to practice the lower door, the male and female consorts must have developed four skills in working with the channels, energies, and essences in order to be able to practice it properly: 1) pulling the essences down from the head to the secret door, 2) holding the essences, 3) causing the essences to rise through the channels, and 4) causing the essences to spread throughout the channels and chakras. If a consort has these four skills, as well as the numerous other good qualities laid out by the scriptures, he or she may be able to do the practice of the lower door successfully.

However, if the consort partners do not have these skills, it will do them no good to pretend that they are able to properly carry out the practice. In Tibetan, this is what we call "using the Dharma to hoard transgressions." A practitioner who does not have these skills but tries to carry out the practice anyway is in danger of injuring his or her body and internal organs, as well as mind, in a variety of ways. As I have already said, if we truly wish to attain the fruit of the Teachings, we must go beyond posturing as Dharma practitioners. It is only by fundamentally purifying the mind that we will gain liberation from samsara, so we must always make this our primary objective.

Drolam is a path that utilizes "the four great releases" in order to attain liberation. These four releases are the way we work with the view of Trekchod on the path of drolam. The Teachings on the four releases are taught directly by the Spiritual Friend when the introduction to the nature of mind and the oral instructions are given. While the practice of tsa lung acts as a good condition when taking up dro-lam, complete mastery over tsa lung is not necessary as it is in taplam.

Drolam requires the development of the three wisdom qualities of listening, contemplation, and meditation. First, the practice of drolam requires that we have the wisdom of listening, that we have heard an ocean of texts, and that we have understood the meaning of the entire Sutra and Tantra beyond any doubt. Not only that, but we have received the introduction to the nature of mind directly from the Spiritual Friend, and have no doubt as to what the uncontrived view is. With the wisdom of our contemplation, we have examined the Teachings and gleaned whatever wisdom and understanding we could from them, and then developed certainty in the way to take up the uncontrived view. With the wisdom of our meditation, we take up the view of Trek-chod and rest in rikpa. Then, when we are fully prepared, we take up the practice of Todgyal. As a result, we will be self-liberated from all bonds. "Drolam" is the name given to being released into the Dharmadhatu.

In my opinion, drolam is the best way for contemporary Buddhists to take up the Union of Dzogchen and Bodhichitta. As I said, the prac-tices of tsa lung are difficult to master, and this makes taplam especially challenging. Also, it is not difficult for us to develop a relationship with a qualified Spiritual Friend in this global day and age. When consider-ing which practices to take up during this lifetime, I think it is good to apply the old Tibetan proverb that says, "The minds of beings are not hidden from themselves." What this means is that we know our own minds, our own habits, our talents, capacities, and abilities. So if we want to make the most of the opportunities we have to attain libera-tion, we had better do it based on an honest self-assessment, and not on wishful thinking or what someone else does, or says they can do. Otherwise, we may lose a lot of time and fail to make the most of this precious human life.

Since I came to the West, I have heard it said that because this is a degenerate time, it is the proper time for people all over the world to learn and take up the practice of Dzogchen. While I would agree from the point of view that Dzogchen is the best method for dealing with extremely strong mental afflictions, on the other hand I also think that Dzogchen requires that a practitioner have numerous good qualities, such as a sincere love and concern for all beings, Bodhichitta, faith, intelligence, pure perception, and diligence. While our bodies require food to survive, if we do not eat the proper kind of food, or prepare it in the wrong way, or let it sit out too long, it will make us sick. This is to say that it is possible to use even the most perfect of methods badly, so I urge you to avoid this, and realize the true meaning of the Teachings for yourself by taking up the practices properly.

THE RESULT OF TANTRA

By practicing the three Inner Tantras, we attain the result of the Four Vidyadharas, which is attained on the Paths of Seing, Meditation, and No More Learning. The first two Vidyadharas, the Completely Ripened Vidyadhara and the Immortal Life Vidyadhara, are attained on the Path of Seeing. "Completely Ripened" refers to the fact that at this stage the mind has already ripened into the Body of Light, but is still held captive by the body. When both the body and mind have ripened into the Body of Light, this is called the Immortal Life Vidyadhara. The Mahamudra Vidyadhara is attained on the Path of Meditation. At this stage, the Vidyadhara works tirelessly for the benefit of both self and others. To benefit the self, the most subtle of the innate habitual tendencies are purified. To benefit others, the Vidyadhara emanates in innumerable ways in order to benefit ordinary beings. And finally, the Spontaneously Arisen Vidyadhara is attained on the Path of No More Learning. This is the state of Buddhahood.

There are other ways we can describe the result of the Teachings, such as through the three or five kayas, and also the two results of the unobstructed rainbow body and the rainbow body referred to as the "great transfer." The rainbow body is attained after the time of death, when the physical body dissolves completely into light and all that remains are the hair and fingernails. If we consider all of the hundreds of thousands of practitioners who have attained this sign of realization at the time of their death, the thing we should always keep in our heart is that their faith in and practice of the Teachings, as well as their Samaya with their Spiritual Friend, were like the blood in their veins and more dear to them than their own life.

About 150 years ago, there was an old woman who lived in my village. She seemed to be an ordinary woman, and as poor as they come. To earn her living, she spun wool that could be knitted into sweaters and other kinds of clothing. She was said to be quite an outlandish old woman, and although others were not unkind enough to scorn her, they certainly did not think she was anything special. At that time there lived a very accomplished yogi named Do Khyentse Yeshe Dorje, who was an emanation of Jigme Lingpa. Whenever this yogi came to my village, he always sought out this old woman and visited her. Everyone thought this was quite strange.

When the time came for her to die, the old woman left the village and went into an isolated area, where she climbed atop a large boulder. There, she took off her clothes and lay them beneath her like a carpet. Then, she sat down naked in the sevenfold posture and began to practice. Now, there was a lot of talk amongst the people back in the village. They referred to her as the "madwoman" who had gone away and was "pretending" to meditate. But when someone finally went to check on her, thinking that she might have been eaten by wild animals, they were astonished to find that her body had dissolved into light, and all that remained were her fingernails, hair, and necklace. That was the first time it had dawned on any of them that she was an accomplished Dzogchen yogini.

In 1998, one of my uncles, with whom I was very close, passed away. I had always thought his meditation was extraordinary and that he was a great yogi, but no one else I knew shared this belief. He was a very ordinary Lama who did ordinary things. He was ill for about seven days before he died. Then, on the morning he passed away, he first called his family in to have breakfast and tea with him. When he had said all that needed to be said, he assumed the sevenfold posture, and, meditating, passed away. Actually, it would be difficult for us to even sleep in the sevenfold posture, much less remain that way after we had died. But even after he passed away, his appearance was just like when he was still alive, right down to the gaze of his eyes. As the days passed, the signs of supreme realization manifested in him one by one, just as though we were reading it out of the scriptures. All around us, the only thing that could be heard was, "I didn't know he was like that...." I never did hear anyone say that they had ever suspected his meditation and realization were so profound.

✦ CHAPTER 10
✦
✦ *Empowerments, Transmissions,*
  and the Oral Instructions

IN THE SECRET TEACHINGS, there are three important parts of
transmitting a lineage of Teachings: empowerments, transmissions, and oral instructions. Empowerments are known as "that
which ripens," so they are like the fertile ground in which our practice
is sown. However, empowerments are given by relying upon the mandala. In order to convey a proper understanding of empowerments, I
will first give a brief introduction of the mandala as it is understood in
the Secret Teachings.

THE MANDALA

Relying upon a mandala enables us to receive a good quality. In
Tibetan, the word for mandala is *kyil kor (dkyil 'khor)*, which literally
describes a situation where one is surrounded by a retinue. In the
Nyingma Teachings, there are seven different types of mandalas that
are used in various contexts. From the *Tantra of Vast Illusion (sGyu 'phrul
rgyas pa)*:

> These seven are: natural,
> Reflection, superior reflection,
> Meditative absorption, superior meditative absorption,
> Bodhichitta, and supreme accumulation.

The natural mandala is, simply put, the expression of the primordially pure nature of all phenomena. Thus, the natural mandala is ultimate reality itself. The reflection mandala is the appearance of superior

conventional reality, which is a "reflection" of the natural state. The superior reflection mandala is all of the work that goes into creating and offering a mandala. For example, the place where the mandala will be offered must be chosen and blessed, permission must be gained from the guardian of the land, someone must decide how large the mandala will be, and all obstacles must be purified. These are only a few of the many tasks that go into making the offering.

The mandala of meditative absorption is the continuous appearance of the five wisdoms that manifest when we rest in the primordially pure uncontrived view. The superior mandala of meditative absorption refers to the effort that is made when using the focused practice of meditative absorption in order to work with the retinues of peaceful and wrathful deities. Primarily, we must make extra effort when sending and receiving light to the deities and enlightened beings of the mandala. The mandala of Bodhichitta is engaging in the practice of tsa lung, where outer Bodhichitta is the channels and wind energy, inner Bodhichitta is the essence, and secret Bodhichitta is the union of great bliss and emptiness. The supreme accumulation mandala refers to taking up meditation on what are referred to as either the first group, third group, or fifth group of deities who are both peaceful and wrathful in nature. For students who wish to learn about the mandala in more detail, as well as the practices of the generation and perfection stages, they are subtly explained in the *Secret Essence Tantra*. Of course, guidance by a Spiritual Friend is necessary to engage in any of these practices.

EMPOWERMENTS

Each enlightened being or yidam whose practice we take up has their own mandala, and these mandalas are visualized in accordance with whatever empowerment is bestowed. For example, if we receive an empowerment on the Medicine Buddha, then it is the mandala of the Medicine Buddha that will be used in the ritual. It is important to understand that these are not meaningless rituals. Rather, based on the faith one feels in the enlightened being whose empowerment is being given and the qualified Lama who is bestowing it, it is possible to truly receive the blessings of the lineage through such a ritual.

It is said that no matter what practice within the Indestructible Secret Mantrayana we take up, we will not be able to attain the common or uncommon accomplishments without receiving the proper empowerments. Jigme Lingpa said that one who does not receive the empowerments will not become established in the accomplishments just as one cannot get butter from sand. And it was also said in the *Secret Essence Tantra,*

> Those who do not rely on a Spiritual Friend
> Will not obtain the empowerments
> Or make diligent effort to listen to the Teachings.
> They will attain no result and will hinder their own progress.

Attaining the proper empowerments is dependent upon the coming together of two causes and four conditions. The result of receiving them is that the wisdom of Buddhahood enters the mind stream and becomes the basis for perfect realization. The first of the two causes is called the "concomitant cause," which is the belief that all sentient beings are of the Buddha nature. The second cause is called the "simultaneously arising cause," which means that the entire range of ritual items and offerings must be present in order for the Lama to give the empowerment.

Next, the first of the four conditions is the "causal condition." This means that the student who is to receive the empowerment is a proper vessel. For example, the student has good qualities such as faith, devotion, Bodhichitta, and intelligence. The second of the four conditions is the "fundamental condition," which means that the Lama giving the empowerment has abundant good qualities, holds an unbroken lineage of the empowerment they are bestowing, and is skilled at performing the ritual that will be used. The third condition is the "objective condition." This means that in order for the empowerment to be given successfully, the three elements of offerings, mantra, and meditative absorption must be present. The fourth condition is the "immediate condition," which is that the empowerments must be given in the proper sequence in order for them to ripen properly.

The Etymology of "Empowerment"

In Tibetan, the word that is used for empowerment is *wangkur* (Skt. *abhisheka*, Tib. *dbang skur*), which means both "to pour" and "to release." From the point of view that an empowerment washes clean the stains and impurities of the body, speech, and mind, it is said "to release." And from the point of view that based on an empowerment the capacity to develop perfect wisdom flows into the mind stream, it is said "to pour."

The Four Types of Empowerments

The Four Empowerments of the Indestructible Secret Mantrayana are bestowed by the Spiritual Friend and ripen into the blessings of the path. These four are: the vase empowerment, the secret empowerment, the primordial wisdom empowerment, and the precious word empowerment. The first three are given to ripen the good qualities of body, speech, and mind. The fourth, or the precious word empowerment, is a method by which the nature of mind is introduced by the Spiritual Friend. For students who wish to learn more about the Four Empowerments, they are described at length in the *Treasury of Precious Qualities* and the *Secret Essence Tantra*. However, for those who rely upon a Spiritual Friend and are able to receive the oral instructions, the Four Empowerments can be received by meditating upon the Union. The great Jigme Lingpa said,

> Rest in the union of *appearance and emptiness* to attain the vase empowerment! Meditate upon the union of *clarity and emptiness* to attain the secret empowerment! Meditate upon the union of *bliss and emptiness* to attain the primordial wisdom empowerment! Meditate upon the union of *awareness and emptiness* to attain the precious word empowerment!

The Good Qualities Attained

There are many good qualities we receive along with an empowerment. It is said in the *Secret Essence Tantra,*

> After receiving the empowerments, [one becomes] a child
>   of the Victors,
> Does not have to abide in the lower realms,
> Has a long life full of happiness and abundance,
> And [contains the seed] to become the king of the higher realms.

However, in order for all of the good qualities of an empowerment to manifest, it is also necessary to keep to the conduct that is required by a particular empowerment, and of course to take up the practices that will lead one to perfect realization. Not only that, but our Samaya must be stainless. For those students who wish to learn more about empowerments, they are discussed in detail in the *Secret Essence Tantra* and the *Treasury of Precious Qualities.*

TRANSMISSIONS

It is imperative that we receive not only the proper empowerments for a practice we wish to engage in, but also a transmission. It is said in the Secret Teachings that one who has not received a transmission of a Tantric text or practice is not even allowed to read it, and that even if they do, they will not be able to receive the benefits and good qualities that would otherwise arise from it. Followers of Vajrayana Buddhism believe that the blessings of the Teachings cannot be transmitted fully without the bestowing of both an empowerment and a transmission, so to attempt to practice or study a Tantra without them could ripen into a serious obstacle.

As I have already said of empowerments, it is important that we receive a transmission from an unbroken transmission lineage. Strictly speaking, it would be correct to say that a Lama who holds a lineage that has been broken does not actually "hold" that lineage. If they were to give an empowerment in spite of this, the student on whom they bestowed it could also not be said to have "obtained" the empowerment. However, obtaining a transmission from a qualified Spiritual Friend allows us to undertake a desired course of study or take up a practice and attain the proper results.

The idea of obtaining something that precedes our practice is not unique to Buddhism. Actually, the empowerments and transmissions are like the seal of a king or a diplomat. Without that seal, they are unable to do the work that they have set out to do. Even in our modern world, where compared to times past there is no longer as great a gap between the social classes, we still see that there are some people who are able to wield certain kinds of power that others cannot. And this ability could be likened to the blessings of the lineage we receive when we are granted the empowerments and transmissions from the qualified Spiritual Friend.

Another way we use the word "transmission" is when we quote the Dharma in texts, during Teachings, or in debate. This kind of transmission is used to inspire faith and gain another's trust, rather than to establish a foundation for practice.

THE ORAL INSTRUCTIONS

The oral instructions contain a wide variety of methods that are easily put into practice and realized. The oral instructions are described in the Tantras as,

> [Requiring] little effort, vast in meaning, innumerable
> [skillful] means, and clearly illustrating the difficult
> points.

Yogis or other Dharma practitioners usually receive Teachings from many different Lamas, whether they be an outer, inner, or secret Spiritual Friend. Although in each situation the Lama is viewed with extraordinary devotion, it is important to realize that differences do exist in the closeness felt between masters and students. Just as students may feel greater faith and trust in one Spiritual Friend than another, Spiritual Friends also view their students differently and convey different Teachings to them based on the students' capacities, faith, and other good qualities.

When we speak of oral instructions, we are not speaking about ordinary Teachings or empowerments that are given to a large group of people. Nor are the oral instructions what is meant by "pith instructions." This is not to say that these types of Teachings are not important as a catalyst for realization. What I am referring to in this context is a different sort of Teaching that is passed from a Spiritual Friend to his or her closest students.

The oral instructions can be understood through revisiting the lives of some of the Vidyadharas we have already discussed. For example, Mañjushrimitra studied with Garab Dorje for twenty-five years. Not only did he develop an uncommonly close relationship with his master over a long period of time, but he also had an unusual aptitude to put the Teachings into practice, and had pure perception of his master as an enlightened being. So a practitioner like Mañjushrimitra receives the oral instructions as a result of living a life of devotion with his master. However, it is important to understand that when we talk about the oral instructions, these are the most extraordinary of all the Teachings that a Lama passes on to a student, and there are probably very few students to whom they are willing to give such Teachings. Or in the case of many Lamas who stay in retreat for their whole lives, they often do not transmit these instructions to anyone at all.

In the best possible scenario, the oral instructions are granted during a one-on-one meeting between master and student. The second best scenario is that they be granted to a group of three or seven students. Finally, it is possible to give oral instructions to a group of up to twenty-one students, but if the group is any larger than this, we no longer consider the Teachings to be "oral instructions." The best possible situation in terms of receiving and realizing the oral instructions is to personally serve the master and remain with him or her closely for one's entire life. If that is not possible, then at least ten or fifteen years would be necessary to begin to attain the qualities that are embodied by the Spiritual Friend. What I mean to say is that merely receiving these instructions will not do. Coming back to the great Jigme Lingpa's metaphor of the sandalwood tree, it is only by spending many, many years in the constant presence of our Lama that their good qualities permeate us.

Perhaps it seems that, given the nature of the modern world, my advice would be difficult to follow. It is not just difficult in the modern world. Even in Tibet, it is relatively rare to find a student who is truly devoted to their master enough to stay with them for their whole life. However, to quote a Tibetan proverb that describes this situation, "Without bearing hard work, you can't enjoy a scrumptious meal." What could be more delicious than the taste of authentic realization? Rather than feeling that receiving Teachings in that way is something we are not capable of, it is better to use our wish to receive them as motivation to train in the Teachings we have already received to the very best of our ability.

Perhaps we could also use the simple rule that it is vital to get whatever instructions we can personally from our Spiritual Friend. Even if we are not in a situation where we can see our Spiritual Friend every day or meet them on a one-on-one basis very often, we should do whatever we can to cultivate the relationship we have with them in order that our meditation and good qualities continually increase. Not only is receiving instructions on meditation from our Lama beneficial, but simply serving or spending time with him or her is of tremendous benefit to our spiritual development. However, it should remain our goal to receive, practice, and realize the oral instructions in either this or future lives.

If we think about the oral instructions that passed from master to student throughout India and also Tibet, it is clear that receiving the oral instruction is no easy feat. Most Western Buddhists are probably familiar with the amazing life stories of the great Siddhas Naropa, Marpa, and Milarepa. So there is no need for me to recount what great difficulty yogis undertake in order to obtain these invaluable instructions. Instead, I will include a little bit about my own experience with the oral instructions, which I received primarily from my Root Lama, Tsara Dharmakirti Rinpoche.

It is my belief that there is no true difference in the blessings and abilities of all of the various masters throughout Tibet and, more recently, other parts of the world. However, from the point of view of karma and our own faith, there is a tremendous difference. It is based on these differences that we come to have a master who for us is uncommon and unsurpassable. Such a Lama is often a teacher whom we have relied upon for many lifetimes, and with whom we share a very deep bond. I have known since I was five years old, when I heard my Lama's name for the first time, that for me Tsara Dharmakirti Rinpoche was such a Lama—despite the fact that I had no understanding about such ideas or concepts.

One day not long after I had moved to my Lama's monastic university, he was giving Teachings to a group of students and he mentioned something about Dzogchen and the oral instructions. I was at that moment overwhelmed by the feeling that these were Teachings that I must receive. So after my Lama had finished teaching, I immediately approached him and asked him to please give them to me. At first my Lama said nothing. But then, to answer my question, he gazed at me in a way that absolutely terrified me and acted harshly towards me for several months, while at the same time putting me through rigorous practice. During those months I was filled with sadness, and I feared for some time that he would never give me the Teachings that I had asked for at all. But I vowed that even if I died trying, one day I would receive the Teachings.

Many months later, my Lama invited me to visit him early in the morning. It was a spontaneous invitation, for my Lama's appearance had been so wrathful over the preceding months that I had been unable to approach and ask him to give me the Teachings again. But on that morning, he gave me the first of the oral instructions. I was twenty years old at that time, and I remember the experience clearly because it was so unusual. Rather than being like something I was hearing for the first time, the feeling of recognition was astounding. It was the same feeling you have when you meet an old friend after a long time, and everything about them seems the same. As soon as I heard the Teachings, I was filled with a deep feeling of faith and certainty.

After the first time I received the oral instructions, I was given them privately by my Lama for several months each year. Whenever my Lama gave me Teachings, he told me to memorize them so that they would be with me always. This was not difficult for me, as I had always had the gift of memorization. Most students at my shedra had to work hard to learn the scriptures. However, during my studies I would look over a book once or twice and then just go to sleep. When I woke up, I would find that the words of the text were clearly imprinted in my mind. Sometimes the other students at my shedra teased me and called me a "tape recorder."

Depending on my Lama's wishes, whenever I was not receiving the oral instruction I either stayed in retreat, studied intensively, or gave Teachings. But I loved being with my Lama most of all. He, too, told me that giving me such Teachings filled him with great joy. He said the reason was that he had rarely met a student who was so easy to teach, and who required so little explanation before being able to master a teaching. And after he had finished giving me the entirety of the oral instructions, he told me that he always prayed that my meditation on the Secret Teachings would ripen to perfection and that I would be able to pass on the Teachings he had given me to others. I am filled with undying gratitude that I was able to be such a student for my Lama, and it is because he expressed such wishes for me that I especially want to pass on his unique style of teaching the Union of Dzogchen and Bodhichitta.

The most wonderful and uncommon thing that my Lama passed on to me in terms of the oral instructions was not only his lineage, but also his experience. When describing the oral instructions, the most common of the secret oral instructions are the Teachings themselves. These are very precious and wonderful to receive. The more secret of the secret oral instructions are the personal instructions that a Lama passes on to their very closest students, such as the way things appear to them, the postures they use, and the essentials of their own practice. And, the most secret of the secret oral instructions are the Lama's explanations on how they have taken up Trekchod and Todgyal. I was very fortunate, not only because I was born into a wonderful, religious country like Tibet, where I was raised from birth by a great yogi like Lama Chupur, but also because I received the entirety of my root Lama's oral instructions. Because of this, I feel like I have received an irreplaceable, priceless gift from my Lama, whose kindness I can begin to repay by putting the instructions I was given perfectly into practice.

When my Lama turned eighty, he became blind to the way ordinary beings perceive appearances. Since that time, I have acted as his eyes when we studied together. I would begin by reading a few lines of a text, and then my Lama would remember the rest and speak the words that were already inside his mind. I always remember the countless dear kindnesses he showed me, and how he always wanted to make sure I was turning out to be the practitioner he wanted me to be. However, I actually do not believe that my Lama could not see. Perhaps for the benefit of ordinary beings he had the appearance of being blind. But there were times when my Lama picked a hair off a cup, although he claimed his eyes could not see the words on the page he would give me to read. I do not believe my Lama was limited in any way at all. Such a being could not be.

Often when I went to give Teachings in other parts of Tibet, I would speak about my Lama to large gatherings of people. As soon as I spoke his name, I would begin to weep. This still happens to me, even today. Some people might be embarrassed if that happened to them. And indeed, my weeping was sometimes the cause of laughter for young Tibetans who did not understand the feelings of deep faith and devotion I have for my Lama. But I do believe that the blessings of the lineage are passed on through these currents of deep faith. So long as I weep out of longing for my Lama, I know his blessings are with me. Now that I am away from Tibet, not a night goes by that I do not dream of my Lama, and not a moment goes by that I do not miss him. But I also realize that my devotion is beyond the ordinary bounds of life and death.

＋ CHAPTER 11
＋
＋ *The Three Conditions for Realization*

W HEN I SAY that devotion, pure perception, and Samaya are
the three conditions for realization, what I mean is that it is
by cultivating these three that a yogi attains the supreme result, or by
failing to cultivate these three that he does not. A yogi who has developed deep devotion and unfailing pure perception will receive the
blessings of the teaching, the lineage, and the Lama in a way that is
unmatched by other practitioners. A yogi who has only developed
mediocre devotion and pure perception will receive the blessings only
partially. And of course, a yogi who has developed these only to a small
extent will receive the blessings in kind.

Based on what I have just said, it has probably become apparent
that the idea of receiving a blessing in the context of the Tantric Teachings is quite different from what many Westerners are used to. I have
heard that when put in the Judeo-Christian context, a blessing is something bestowed by some kind of benevolent God, without placing
much importance on the state of mind of the recipient of the blessing. It just shines down like rays of light, and touches the being for
whom it was intended. In Tantric Buddhism, rather, a blessing must be
received through the door of the individual's faith and devotion. It
depends not only on the altruistic aspiration of an enlightened being,
but also on what we, as beings on the path, feel in our hearts.

A metaphor that is commonly used to illustrate the way a blessing is
given is that of a hook and a gold ring. Even if the hook of the Buddhas' compassion reaches toward us, if we do not have a gold ring,
which represents our own faith, we cannot catch it. The Buddhas have
no feelings of attachment or aversion towards any sentient being. They
view all beings equally with love and compassion. The state of our

own mind depends on us. That is why, in the context of Tibetan Buddhism, it is actually possible for a being not to receive a blessing based on their state of mind. For example, beings who lacked devotion and pure perception might fail to receive a "direct introduction" to the nature of mind given by a Spiritual Friend simply because they were not open to it. Thus, as I have stated above, the extent to which we receive the blessings of the lineage is proportional to the depth of our devotion and pure perception.

Regarding a being that does not have strong devotion or pure perception while attempting to practice the profound path of the Vajrayana, it would be extremely difficult to receive the blessings that would enable such practice to mature. This type of person might become frustrated with his or her inability to progress along the path, and begin to proclaim that there is some fault in the Teacher, the Teachings, or the view that has hindered their practice. However, such speech stems from the fault of not perceiving even one's own self purely. For example, if we hold a piece of crystal in our hand in a room that has no light, it seems to be an ordinary clear stone. However, once we have held it up to the light, the entire spectrum of colors can be perceived emanating from it. In this same way, wisdom is able to radiate naturally from the mind, but it can only do so with the proper conditions.

Regarding a being that has developed deep devotion and pure perception, we might wonder exactly how this would enable wisdom to be expressed from the mind. Buddha Shakyamuni said,

> Whosoever has a mind of devotion,
> They will always be before me,
> And I will constantly bestow the blessings.

Also, it was said by Padmasambhava that he would never part from any practitioner who developed devotion and pure perception, but would always "sleep by their door." And he also said,

> I will never pass away from this life;
> There is a Padmasambhava in front of each being who has faith.

Thus, the power of dependent arising, our devotion, pure perception, and attainment of the blessings create the conditions for us to realize the view.

PURE PERCEPTION

A yogi who is truly realized sees all appearances of beings and the outer world as the perfect mandala of enlightened beings and the pure lands. In other words, all appearances manifest as the mandala of the body, or the enlightened bodies of Buddhas, Bodhisattvas, and wisdom beings. All sounds manifest as the mandala of speech, such as mantras and prayers. And all thoughts and memories manifest as the mandala of enlightened mind. Such yogis do not perceive things this way merely because they want to. It is not a contrived perception. Rather, from the point of view of ultimate reality, this is the actual situation, and these yogis recognize it as such. The great yogi Dodrupchen Kunsang Shenpen said that he perceived all things as "the three mandalas." Specifically, he perceived all appearances as Padmasambhava and Tara; he perceived all sounds as enlightened speech; and he perceived all thoughts as primordially pure wisdom. However, for the benefit of beings who could not relate to such appearances, he kept these perceptions completely to himself and related to others as though he was an ordinary practitioner.

In Tibetan, we describe the pure perception of the three mandalas as something we must "awaken to." For those who have awakened to them, it is said,

> Whether living in wealth or poverty,
> They will never experience the sadness of mental
>   afflictions and suffering.
> All of life is perceived as visiting a grand park.

Such a yogi would not feel the highs and lows that are brought about by attaining something seen as extraordinary, or the suffering of loss.

Ordinary beings perceive only the impurities of samsara, by which the daily interactions of sentient beings and the outer world ripen into suffering. And because they lack pure perception, not only do they perceive appearances impurely, but they also grasp at these appearances and assert that they truly exist. In order to change the habit of the mind that perceives things impurely, we should train in pure perception.

When training in pure perception, our practice must rely upon our examination of the difference between "situation" and "appearance." In other words, "situation" refers to the actual situation of ultimate reality, which is the expression of the three mandalas. "Appearance" of course refers to conventional reality, and is the way sentient beings and the outer world appear. So again, we can see how the Tantric path is fundamentally based on the two truths and the union of clarity and emptiness, which during our exploration of this text we have realized is just another way of saying the Union of Dzogchen and Bodhichitta. It is only through training in pure perception that situation and appearance become one and the same. If, by lack of careful training, this unity is not genuinely perceived, it is like wearing a mask or faking it, rather than attaining true realization. Other examples that describe this false vision are holding an ordinary stone while feeling convinced or declaring that it is gold, or mistaking the reflection of the moon in water for an actual celestial body.

The method for realizing the union of samsara and nirvana is also the development of pure perception. From Maitreyanatha's *Ornament of Mahayana Discourses* (*Mahayanasutralamkara, Theg pa chen po'i mdo sde rgyan*):

> For one who realizes the equality of all things,
> Even if they abide in the hell realms, they see the pure
>   lands of Tushita.
> For one who does not realize the equality of all things,
> Even if they abide in the pure lands of Tushita, they see
>   the hell realms.

The Benefits of Pure Perception

The benefits of developing pure perception are obvious when examining the lives of previous masters. To illustrate, I will now tell a story which occurred when Lama Chupur was about thirty years old. At that time, he was studying under the guidance of a great master named Gyage Drubtob. As his name suggests, Gyage Drubtob was truly a Siddha, an accomplished yogi. He lived in a hole dug beneath the ground, far away from any of the villages in the province of Kham. He had long, filthy hair and never wore clothes.

Lama Chupur told me that he liked beautiful things when he was young. He was an accomplished practitioner of Chod, and in his travels he had acquired a beautiful ritual drum called a "damaru," which was made of sandalwood. He always treated it very carefully. One day Lama Chupur went to see his master, but before he could even speak, Gyage Drubtob told him that he wanted to see the damaru. Lama Chupur was a little bit nervous at first. Although he had great faith in his Lama, he knew that his Lama cared nothing for worldly things, so he was not sure what his Lama would do with it. But Lama Chupur would never have failed to do anything that his Lama asked of him, so he gave his Lama the damaru. Gyage Drubtob examined it carefully, and then began to laugh. He took out his knife and slit the head of the damaru open and then threw it against the far wall of the cave, where it broke into pieces. Lama Chupur cringed inside, but there was nothing he could do. He genuinely viewed his master as none other than the Buddha himself, so he remained quietly in front of Gyage Drubtob without saying a word in protest.

A few days later, Lama Chupur visited Gyage Drubtob again, but this time he asked his Lama to give him the oral instructions. Gyage Drubtob shouted, "What Teachings do you want?," and suddenly unsheathed a long sword. He stabbed the sword into the back of Lama Chupur's thigh. Lama Chupur was terrified. He wanted to cry out, but he could not do so in the presence of his Lama. So instead, he pulled the sword out and covered the wound with his hand. But he soon realized that it did not hurt much. After a moment, he rubbed his fingers over the wound and found that it was gone. Next, he examined his hand and found that there was not even a single drop of blood on it.

Lama Chupur's meditation on the uncontrived view was already quite deep at that time. However, because of his devotion and unfailing pure perception, he received the blessings of his Lama and attained a direct introduction to the nature of mind that is known as a "wrathful introduction." Lama Chupur told me many such stories, in which Gyage Drubtob shot his students with guns or terrified them in other ways in order to heighten their pure perception and directly give them the oral instructions.

When Lama Chupur was prepared to leave, his Lama suddenly threw the sandalwood damaru back at him. The damaru was completely unharmed and looked exactly as it had before. Lama Chupur was overjoyed, and knew with certainty that his master was indeed a Buddha.

SAMAYA

Perhaps "Samaya" is a little known word among contemporary Buddhists. The Tibetan word for the Sanskrit *Samaya* is *dam tsik* (*dam tshig*), which means "bound to." We give the name "Samaya" to a vow or a promise that we never give up or stray from, whether awake or asleep. Usually, we describe Samaya in terms of five root and ten branch Samayas. The branch Samayas can also be classified more and more subtly until there are 360 in all. For someone who wishes to take up the Secret Teachings, it is essential to understand how to work with and keep Samaya. This is because, just as I said in the preceding sections on devotion and pure perception, whether or not we attain the common or uncommon result and the blessings of the Lama and the lineage depends on the purity of our Samaya. The supreme Padmasambhava said,

> For those who wish to attain enlightenment in this lifetime,
> Keeping the root and branch Samayas is of great importance.
> The root and branch Samayas, when not kept,
> Are like medicine improperly taken
> That becomes a poison.

By taking up the Secret Teachings, we are able to attain the supreme result very quickly. The very best practitioners attain enlightenment in this very lifetime, those with a lesser capacity at the time of death, and still others within the bardo. Other practitioners do not attain enlightenment until their next or even future lifetimes, but in comparison with the gradual path of the other vehicles, this is still very quick. If you are the kind of practitioner who does not want to put off realization until later, but rather want to take the short path that the Vajrayana Teachings promise, I urge you to learn more about the Tantric Samayas and how to abide by them properly.

The Teachings of the Indestructible Secret Mantrayana are without a doubt the most profound and excellent method for attaining liberation. If we practice these Teachings in the proper way, there is no possible reason that we would not attain the promised result. However, just because we realize this to be true does not imply that such profound methods are beyond being guided and sustained by rules or proper conduct. I believe that if a practitioner had real understanding of the Secret Teachings, they would agree with this position, since the Inner Tantras, including the Dzogchen Tantras, widely profess that devotion, pure perception, and Samaya are the three conditions absolutely necessary for realization.

Take the example of the supreme Longchenpa, who was one of the greatest Dzogchen yogis ever to take birth in the human realm. Longchenpa said that the longer he rested in the view, the more deeply he felt compassion and developed Bodhichitta. He also said that his Samaya was like the eyes he saw the world with, and more precious than his own life.

The Root Samayas

Although the explanation of Samaya can be quite complicated, I will explain here only the five root Samayas, which are of primary concern to contemporary practitioners. From the *Secret Essence Tantra*:

> Do not abandon the unsurpassable and respect the Lama.
> Do not break the use of mantra and mudra.

Develop loving-kindness towards others on the path.
Do not speak of the secret meaning to others.
When practiced and guarded, these five roots
Are the supreme Samayas.

First, an explanation of how to avoid abandoning "the unsurpassable." By developing supreme Bodhichitta and realizing the union of the two truths, all appearances arise as the three mandalas that are perceived through the three doors of the body, speech, and mind. By abiding constantly in this pure view, we do not "abandon the unsurpassable." Coming back to the Union of Dzogchen and Bodhichitta, we can see once again why developing Bodhichitta is so crucial to our realization. The development of Bodhichitta is part of the foundation for keeping the root Samayas, which enable us to attain the result of the path.

Second, an explanation of how to respect the Spiritual Friend. Just as there are outer, inner, and secret Spiritual Friends, so there are also different ways of showing respect to a Spiritual Friend depending on the relationship. But most importantly, we should respect a Spiritual Friend who has granted us any or all three kindnesses. In terms of thinking kindly about our Lama, with gratitude, respect, and devotion, an easy way to remember why this is necessary is that the Lama does not need the student. Lamas give instructions and care for students out of their own kindness and wish to benefit others. Although I have told you from my own experience that at times it was hard for me to face the various appearances presented by my own Lama, I know without a doubt they were always for my benefit. So we should cultivate pure perception of a teacher we have thoroughly examined and accepted. Although we may not yet be able to see our Lama as the Buddha, as did many of the great yogis we read about, at the very least we should be wary of seeing them as suspect, and never doubt that their motivation in giving us Teachings is strictly to benefit us.

The way to break this root Samaya is through having a materialistic, acquisitive, or utilitarian attitude towards receiving the Teachings. In other words, once we receive the Teachings that we want, we push aside the Spiritual Friend as though they are no longer necessary, believing we can do it all without them. We should not treat Dharma practice like strip mining or deforestation, which only goes after wealth or personal power, and places no importance on the land. As contemporary Buddhists, we should always keep the supreme example of Yeshe Tsogyal in mind. She chose to receive the Teachings on the yidam of Vajrakilaya from her Lama rather than from Vajrakilaya because of her understanding that deep faith in and devotion toward the Lama, the living embodiment of all the Buddhas, is the source of all blessings.

Third, the way to avoid breaking the use of mantra and mudra. A practitioner of the highest capacity should take up practice on the yidam (or any other practice that they essentially rely upon) like "the flow of a stream." In other words, rely upon the practice every day. Traditionally, such a practitioner might take up six periods of meditation every twenty-four hours; three during the day, and three at night. But how often the practice is done in a twenty-four hour period depends on the individual. The best possible scenario is that the practice would be taken up at least once during a twenty-four hour period. However, the scriptures state that a practitioner of middle capacity should take up the essential practices four to six times per month. And a practitioner of lesser capacity should take up the practices once a month. Each person must evaluate what kind of practitioner they wish to be and decide how much effort they wish to apply to the development of their practice.

Fourth, an explanation of showing kindness to others on the path. Generally, this means that we should show loving-kindness to all sentient beings within samsara. Just as we can say that all sentient beings have been our mothers, so we can also say that they have all been our companions on the path at one time or another. From a more restricted point of view, this applies to all of those who have entered the path of the Indestructible Secret Mantrayana. And for those who receive Teachings from the same Lama or have attended Teachings and empowerment rituals together, we should view them as our very own dear family, and be especially loving and respectful.

Fifth, regarding the way not to "speak of the secret meaning to others." Although I am not quite sure of the reasons behind this, I have noticed a tendency among my Western students to disclose many details about their practice to others. I think one reason might be that our modern world is so given to advertising. It seems like we are always selling ourselves to others. If this is the case, we must think carefully about how to proceed. If our motivation is for others to think that we are something special because of a particular teaching that we have received, then our Dharma has become worldly Dharma. If that is the case, we should gently put ourselves back on track by once again focusing on the two benefits for self and others, which remain our primary purpose as Buddhists.

In terms of the way to keep this particular Samaya, there are four types of outer secrets and four types of inner secrets that should be kept, as well as one thing that definitely must be kept secret, and one responsibility. Outer secrets include things such as the way to practice the profound view, what yidam or meditational deity practice we do, what mantras we recite, or any miraculous accomplishments we may have attained. Inner secrets include things like the place where we practice meditation, when we practice, who we practice with, and what ritual items we use. The thing that definitely must be kept secret is anything that would cause someone to lose faith in the Dharma because of a lack of devotion or general disposition. The one responsibility is adhering to the Spiritual Friend's instructions to keep certain information or Teachings secret once they are received.

The attainment of signs that indicate the level of maturity in meditation, both during our life and after death, are highly dependent on how we have kept our Samaya, and more precisely if we have kept the secret meaning of the Teachings to ourselves. On this note, I once spoke to a woman who had lost her faith in the manifestation of such signs. The story went that her uncle was a practitioner of the Secret Teachings, and she believed that he would attain the supreme result of the rainbow body when he died. However, after he died she kept wait-ing, but no sign came. At that time, I told her that in Tibet it is said that even the greatest Lamas sometimes fail to attain a sign upon their pass-ing away if they have given Teachings to a wide variety of students. This is because every time Lamas give a new student Teachings, a link of Samaya is created between them. The Samaya of a Lama who has many links to others is easily corruptible, since students don't all keep perfect Samaya. I firmly believe that when Samaya is kept pure, it does not matter who the practitioner is, what color their skin is, whether they are male or female, or whether they have straight or curly hair—they will be able to attain the result of the Teachings.

If guarded carefully, the five root Samayas contain all of the others. However, if we feel that even these five are difficult to keep, we should keep in mind Terton Karmalangwa's words:

> Delusion and mistakes are of the nature of sentient beings.
> But because all phenomena are like a dream, there is the
>   possibility of repentance.

If we realize that we have definitely broken one of the root Samayas, it is possible to purify our mistake. First, we must regret what we have done. Then, we should take up the practice of Vajrasattva and recite the hundred-syllable mantra as it is taught in Patrul Rinpoche's *The Words of My Perfect Teacher*. By relying upon these instructions, just like the nature of gold, our Samaya can be hammered and refashioned until it has regained its original purity.

CHAPTER 12
Living the Union

PADMASAMBHAVA

As the supreme holder of the Dzogchen Teachings, Padmasambhava's entire life is an expression of the Union of Dzogchen and Bodhichitta. Of his own birth, Padmasambhava said,

> My father is wisdom awareness.
> My mother is the emptiness of Samantabhadri.
> My birthplace is the unborn Dharmadhatu.
> The lineage I hold is indivisible awareness and emptiness.

There are several different texts that give accounts of Padmasambhava's life, some of which are available in English. Students who are
not satisfied with the level of detail presented here may want to refer
to these translations.

In the Tantra called *The Roots of Mañjushri* (*Mañjushrimulatantra, 'Jam
dpal rtsa rgyud*), Buddha Shakyamuni prophesied the birth of Padmasambhava, saying,

> After I have passed into nirvana,
> Four times two years later,
> In the lake called Dhanakosha,
> One called by the name "The Lotus Born,"
> Whose faculties are superior to all others, will be born.
> He will transmit the Teachings of the Secret Mantrayana.

In the land of Oddiyana, somewhere in the region of present-day
Pakistan and Afghanistan, lies the lake called Dhanakosha. Based on

Padmasambhava

the blessings of the Buddhas, a child who bore all of the major and minor marks of a Buddha was born there in the blossom of a lotus that was growing in the lake. The child was not exactly a baby; rather, he had the body of an eight-year-old boy. In his right hand he held a vajra and in his left, a lotus blossom. The gods and Dakinis who lived near the lake gave him Teachings on the Indestructible Secret Mantrayana.

Around that same time, the king of the land, who was called Indrabhuti, had been wishing with all his heart for a child. He had made many offerings to the Three Jewels and had given away his material wealth to others in hopes that his wife would bear a child. It was based on these prayers, offerings, and generosity that he found Padmasambhava in the blossom of the lotus that was growing in the center of the lake and recognized him as his own son. He brought Padmasambhava back to his palace and gave him the name Tsokye Dorje (1), which means "the indestructible one born in the lake." This is the first of the names Padmasambhava was given during his lifetime because of his extraordinary realization and ability to benefit beings. Although Padmasambhava was given many names, there are eight names that are of primary importance.

Padmasambhava became the king of Oddiyana and looked after the land in the manner of a Dharma king. However, it was not long before he developed deep renunciation of samsara and wished to leave the palace. Although he begged his parents, they would not permit him to step down from the throne. Because he could not leave in an ordinary way, some other factor had to come into play. One day, Padmasambhava dropped his trident. As it fell to the ground, it struck dead the child of a warrior. After the child died, Padmasambhava released the child's consciousness through the practice of consciousness transference, or *phowa*, enabling the child to take rebirth in a pure land. However, the warriors of the land could not perceive this, and they wanted to kill Padmasambhava to avenge the child's death. Padmasambhava's father would not allow this, and instead he sent Padmasambhava away from the kingdom. Although this story may seem a little bit strange to those who have not heard it before, I want to remind you that it is impossible for ordinary beings to try to replicate or understand Padmasambhava's realization and conduct. We should think of him as being one with the Dharmakaya Samantabhadra.

Padmasambhava left the palace grounds and went to practice meditation in cemeteries throughout India. When he had finished, he traveled back to Lake Dhanakosha, where he received Teachings on the Indestructible Secret Mantrayana in the language of the Dakinis, and directly saw the face of the deity Vajravarahi. Next he traveled to Bodhgaya, where he displayed all sorts of miraculous abilities. When people asked him who he was, he replied, "I am the self-arisen Buddha."

However, the people of Bodhgaya did not believe him, and they began to curse him and call him names. It was then that Padmasambhava realized the importance of taking up the union of conventional and ultimate reality when dealing with ordinary beings. It became clear that wisdom alone would not do; some sort of method was necessary.

232 THE UNION OF DZOGCHEN AND BODHICHITTA

So, Padmasambhava went to see Acharya Trabahatu, who gave him full monastic vows, so that he would be able to maintain the proper worldly appearance of a Dharma teacher. Along with the vows, he was given the name Shakya Senge (2), as well as many Vajrayana Teachings. As a result, he directly saw the mandalas of many Tantric deities.

Throughout his life, Padmasambhava taught widely about the necessity of taking up the union of the two truths. Specifically, he taught that a yogi should separate the view of the ultimate from conventional conduct in order to attain perfect realization. By doing so, a yogi is able to fulfill the two benefits for self and others. The benefit of others is developed by paying attention to the aspect of appearance, which allows the yogi's conduct to be perfected. The benefit of self is completed by avoiding all extremes, which allows the yogi's view and meditation to be perfected. Padmasambhava expressed these ideas in the following two passages on the Union:

> The view of the Indestructible Vehicle [that I hold] is as vast as the ocean, but [my] conduct must not follow it. If conduct follows the view, both virtue and nonvirtue will be seen as empty. Because of this mistake, one will come to see [all things] as having no consequence and one becomes like the dark-hearted.
>
> The view must not follow conduct. If the view follows conduct, one will come to see phenomena as substantially existent. Being bound to this view [of permanence], the time of liberation will never come.

and,

> Though the view may be higher than the sky,
> The attention paid to cause and result must be finer than flour.

Soon after, Padmasambhava asked the nun named Kungamo, who was the emanation of a wisdom Dakini, to give him the empowerments. She turned him into the golden syllable HUM and ate him.

While in her stomach, Padmasambhava received the outer, inner, and secret empowerments. When he passed through Kungamo's bhaga, all the obscurations of his body, speech, and mind were purified.

Because Padmasambhava had realized that his conduct must follow that of an ordinary being, he received the lineages of the Eight Kagyed Deities from the eight Vidyadharas. He also received the complete, perfect oral instructions on Atiyoga from Mañjushrimitra and Shri Simha, and gave the appearance of putting these Teachings into practice and realizing them. From Vimalamitra he received the Teachings called "The Heart Essence of Vimalamitra." Notably, he received the perfect and complete oral instructions from the wisdom body of Garab Dorje. Although he did not make any special effort at putting any of these Teachings into practice, he realized them and directly saw the faces of the yidam deities. Thus, he was given the name Loden Chokse (3).

After omnisciently realizing that Mandarava had the perfect qualities of a consort, Padmasambhava sought her out and they traveled together to a cave in Maratika, in present-day Nepal. For three months, they established the yidam called "the Long-Life Buddha." At the end of three months, they directly saw the face of the Long-Life Buddha, who bestowed the empowerments. Based on receiving these blessings, Padmasambhava and Mandarava attained the result of the Immortal Life Vidyadhara.

Then, Padmasambhava realized it was time to subdue Mandarava's father, who was the king of a land called Zahor. They returned to Zahor, and found that the King, as well as the warriors and other members of the kingdom, were furious with Padmasambhava, whom they thought of as the impoverished beggar who had stolen the princess. They thought, "If we do not do something, he will harm our kingdom again and again." So they made a large pile of sandalwood in an open meadow, and Padmasambhava allowed himself to be tied to it. The fact that Padmasambhava allowed this shows that he had, by this time, become a master at working with conventional reality. The warriors poured oil upon the wood and set it on fire, but it did not burn like an ordinary fire. The wood burned for nine days without showing any signs of being consumed. When the King and his men returned to the pyre to see what had happened, they saw that a lake had appeared where the meadow had been, and that there was a lotus growing in the lake. In the blossom of the lotus, Padmasambhava and Mandarava were sitting in the posture of sexual union, shimmering with light. Upon seeing them, the King and his men were filled with regret and vowed to take up the practice of the Dharma. They gave him the name Padmasambhava (4), by which he is widely known.

Padmasambhava returned to Oddiyana to subdue the beings who were living in the kingdom of his birthplace. When he arrived there, the warriors, still angry with him for causing the death of the child, seized him and attempted to burn him alive. In the same manner as had happened in Zahor, the fire caused him no harm and a lake appeared in the meadow where the pyre had been. Padmasambhava and Mandarava appeared in a lotus blossom in the center of the lake. At the sight of them, the King and his men deeply regretted what they had done, and the King offered all of his wealth and power to Padmasambhava. Then, the King gave him the name Pema Gyalpo (5), which means "the Lotus King."

Padmasambhava traveled all around the cemeteries of Southeast Asia, giving Teachings to the Dakinis and subduing dark-hearted beings using both peaceful and wrathful methods. During this time, he was called Nyima Özer (6), which means "light of the sun."

In Bodhgaya there was a gathering of five hundred practitioners who were saying black mantras with the goal of destroying the Buddhist Teachings. Padmasambhava subdued them by two methods: by debate, and by displaying various miraculous abilities. At this time, he was called Senge Dradok (7), which means "the lion's roar."

Finally, in the dens of thirteen tigers, Padmasambhava mastered the ways of using wrathful energy. Based on this, he subdued the gods, cannibals, and other dark-hearted beings in Tibet and made them the guardians of the Teachings and treasures. During this period he was called Dorje Trolo (8).

Throughout Tibet, when Padmasambhava gave Teachings on Indestructible Secret Mantrayana to his uncommon and supreme students,
such as the twenty-five emanation disciples, the eighty who attained
the rainbow body, the 108 great practitioners, the twenty-five Dakinis,
and the seven great yoginis, he always taught the Union of Dzogchen
and Bodhichitta, such as:

> Only one who has perfectly pure wisdom, faith, devotion,
> and pure perception *combined with the method* will be able to
> realize the view [of the Indestructible Secret Mantrayana].

Padmasambhava's most uncommon student was his consort Yeshe
Tsogyal. After realizing the great benefit of giving her the Teachings
on "The Heart Essence of the Dakinis," he passed the Teachings to
her in their entirety.

Before Padmasambhava left the human realm, he prophesied about
the future of the Vajrayana Teachings in the snowy kingdom of Tibet.
One such prophecy concerned Pematsal, the sister of the King of
Tibet at that time, who was named Trisong Detsen. Pematsal died
when she was just seven years old. While Padmasambhava was staying
in retreat at Samye Chumpu, her dead body was brought to him. He
wrote the syllable NRI on her heart center with ink made from red ver-
milion. Then, although Pematsal's consciousness had already left her
body, Padmasambhava was able to call it back based on the strength
of his meditative absorption. Pematsal came back to life, and Padmasambhava gave her the oral instructions on "The Heart Essence of
the Dakinis" through bestowing the blessings of *phowa*. Then, he
prophesied that at some time in the future, Pematsal would take rebirth
as a terton named Pema Ledreltsal, who would discover the treasure
of "The Heart Essence of the Dakinis." But he said that this would
not be the cause for the widespread benefit of beings. However, in
his very next life, Pema Ledreltsal would be born as the omniscient
Longchenpa.

After Padmasambhava had benefited the beings of Tibet in every way possible, he went to the Western Pure Land, where he still abides, working tirelessly for the benefit of ordinary beings.

LONGCHENPA

As we saw in the life of Padmasambhava, the birth of the great master Longchenpa was prophesied many lifetimes before it actually happened. In terms of the Nyingmapa Teachings, and especially the Secret Teachings, Drime Özer (who is also known as Longchen Rabjam and Longchenpa) is known as the supreme master of the lineage called the "Longchen Nyingthig." Like Padmasambhava, we should recognize him as being at one with the Dharmakaya Samantabhadra.

Longchenpa taught widely about the importance of making Bodhichitta the root of all Vajrayana practice, and also of taking up the union of clarity and emptiness as the supreme practice of meditation. In meditation he was surpassed by none, which is one of the reasons why many enlightened beings praised him even before he took birth in Tibet. Padmasambhava prophesied Longchenpa's birth various times, such as in the following, which describes the birth of Pema Ledreltsal and then Longchenpa:

> At the border of Do-Pot in the land called Drangtang
> A boy will be born to parents who are secret yogis.
> The habitual tendencies of the child's past life will be awakened.
> [This child born in] the Year of the Ox, of the element
>   water and the female aspect,
> Will reveal my profound treasures.
> He will open the doors to three or four, but this will not
>   benefit many.
> At this time, he will practice meditation in the secret way
> And become the holder of the profound treasures.
>
> After his passing, he will take rebirth
> In Ge-ne Tsilung Todkor in the land called Monyul Bumtang,

The Omniscient Master Longchenpa

In the Year of the Monkey. He will have a clear mind and
   great intelligence.
He will become the student of my emanation Rinchen
   Langpa.
In the lower lands of Bumtang he will open the doors to
   the treasures.
At that time he will be known to all as Drime Özer.
He will reveal five treasures and benefit beings inconceivably.

Just as Padmasambhava's prophecies foretold, Longchenpa was
born in Ge-ne Tsilung Todkor in 1308 to parents who were masters of
the Secret Mantrayana. One night before Longchenpa was born, his
mother, Sonam Gyen, had a miraculous dream in which radiant rays of
light emanated from the forehead of a lion, dispelling all the darkness
of the world. The light finally dissolved into her own forehead.

From the time Longchenpa was just a young child, he had the heart of a great Bodhisattva. He had a reservoir of uncommonly deep love and compassion, although he had never worked at developing Bodhichitta. He was also said to have had deep faith and devotion, as well as pure perception. From the age of five, when he first began to study, he easily mastered any course of study he took up. Around this time, his father, the secret yogi Denpa Sung, gave him the empowerments, transmissions, and oral instructions on the Eight Kagyed Deities. He also taught Longchenpa the arts of Tibetan medicine and astrology.

At the age of twelve, Longchenpa took monastic vows and was given the name Tsultrim Lodro. His deep understanding of the *Vinaya* led him to begin giving Teachings at the age of thirteen. At the age of sixteen, he received the empowerments, transmissions, and oral instructions of the "Path and Result," one of the most profound paths of the Sakyapa lineage, from Tashi Rinchen. At age nineteen, he became a student at the most prestigious monastic university in all of Tibet at that time, called Sangpun Natang Shedra. There, he studied Sutra, debate, and Madhyamaka logic for six years, especially the five works of Maitreyanatha and the seven great treatises on valid cognition. After completing his studies, he became known as the supreme master of Buddhist philosophy, logic, and debate in all of Tibet. Because of his great skill in debate, he was given the name Lung Mangpo, which means "he who can quote many scriptures." He was also given the name Longchen Rabjam, which described the way his keen intelligence and wisdom pervaded the universe.

During this same period, he directly met the goddess Sarasvati, who is known as the embodiment of eloquence, intellectual pursuit, and clear speech. Sarasvati took Longchenpa in the palm of her hand, and for seven days showed him all of the different appearances throughout the ten directions of the universe.

Because of Longchenpa's unsurpassable intellect and wisdom, the Lamas and Abbots of Sangpun Natang Monastic University asked him to remain as its head after he finished his studies; however, this was not to be. Tibetans believe that difficult circumstances are often what push one to perfect the view, meditation, and conduct, and in just this way Longchenpa began to experience many difficulties after he became a well-known scholar. Many of the students at Sangpun Natang envied him, and they made it impossible for him to remain there.

From that time on, Longchenpa wandered from place to place staying in retreat, with his only goal being to purify his mind. At the cave called Chokla he meditated on the Union in retreat for five months, abiding in the view described in *The Self-Liberation of Phenomena* (*Chos nyid rang 'grol*):

> Appearances are not separate from their empty natures,
> Just as water and dampness are inseparable and are not two.

Just before dawn on the last night of his retreat, he heard music coming from outside the cave. When he looked into the sky, he saw a young girl of sixteen adorned by beautiful clothing and precious jewels and wearing a crown. Her face was covered by a golden veil. She was riding a horse that was ornamented with jewels and tassels. The young girl entered the cave and Longchenpa held fast to her gown, recognizing her as none other than the Goddess Tara. He began to pray to her reverently.

After hearing Lonchenpa's prayer, Tara removed the crown from the top of her head and placed it on his. She proclaimed that from that day forward she would always bestow the blessings and accomplishments upon him. She also perfected the causes and conditions necessary for him to meet his root Lama, Kumarantza, and receive the oral instructions of Atiyoga. From that time on, Longchenpa abided continuously in the Union by recognizing all things as none other than the perfect, uncontrived view of clarity and emptiness.

When he was twenty-nine years old, Longchenpa finally traveled to the land where Lama Kumarantza lived. One day, when Kumarantza was seated before a group of seventy of his students, Longchenpa arrived. Kumarantza was overjoyed to see him. He told Longchenpa and several of his close students that on the previous night he had had an amazing dream in which the God of the Birds, along with his retinue of thousands of birds, arrived in the land. The God of the Birds, followed by the others, picked up bundles of texts on which Kumarantza's Teachings were written and carried them throughout the land. He said that this dream meant that the one who was to become the holder of his Teachings had arrived.

Longchenpa wished to receive the empowerments and transmissions from Kumarantza, but he had no wealth to offer. Because Longchenpa could not follow the custom of making material offerings, several of Kumarantza's close students would not allow him to receive the Teachings he had been promised. On the night before he was to receive the empowerments and transmissions, Longchenpa was filled with sadness. He thought that because he had not perfectly taken up the two accumulations, he would now be unable to fulfill the two benefits for self and others.

Since he had nothing to offer his Lama, Longchenpa decided to leave rather than cause any embarrassment. He planned to leave just before sunrise, when no one would see him. But as he made his preparations, Lama Kumarantza saw what was happening in his mind's eye, and asked that Longchenpa be brought to see him. When Longchenpa was before him, Kumarantza said that even if Longchenpa had nothing to offer him, he would make Longchenpa his heart student.

Because he was a true Siddha, or accomplished yogi, Lama Kumarantza never stayed in one place for long. He and his community of followers would settle in one place for a short time, but just when everyone was getting used to it, Lama Kumarantza would say that it was time to move again. They wandered throughout the high mountain peaks, making their camp here and there for short periods. During the winter, Longchenpa had no warm clothes to wear and had to endure the hardship of the cold weather. His only food for two months was twenty-one blessed pills and three pints of flour. He had already received the empowerments, transmissions, and oral instructions, as well as the direct introduction to the "Secret Heart Essence," and now wished to stay in retreat. However, this was difficult because of the heavy snow and his lack of warm clothing.

Longchenpa had a thick sack made of matted yak hair in which he usually put his belongings. He sat down inside of it and used it as both a carpet and a covering for his body. In this way, Longchenpa endured the harsh conditions of winter while staying in retreat.

The next year, Longchenpa received the lineages, empowerments, and transmissions on the series of three in Atiyoga. The bestowing of oral instructions was so complete that it was described as pouring the contents of Lama Kumarantza's mind into Longchenpa's. After receiving the Teachings, Longchenpa was known as the holder of all of Lama Kumarantza's Teachings, and supreme among all of his students.

Longchenpa then made the unsurpassable secret offering to his Lama: he vowed to stay in retreat for the next six years while taking up the union of the generation and perfection stages in order to complete the two accumulations. Longchenpa expressed this profound method of taking up the Union of Dzogchen and Bodhichitta in *The Self-Liberation of Mind* (*Sems nyid rang 'grol*):

> Appearance is the method and the generation stage is the
>   accumulation of merit,
> Abandon all grasping at conceptual thoughts [and] mental
>   afflictions.
> The empty wisdom of the generation stage is the accumu-
>   lation of wisdom,
> The cognitive obscurations and innately grasped delusions
>   will be self-liberated.

When Longchenpa was thirty-one years old, he began to impart the Teachings on the Union of Dzogchen and Bodhichitta, in the form of the "Longchen Nyingthig," to a very few students of the highest faculties. He gave many Teachings on the way to practice the Vajrayana path, such as this one from *The Self-Liberation of Mind*:

> [A path] that does not rely upon loving-kindness, compassion,
>   and Bodhichitta

Is not the Vajrayana; it is some other path.

No matter how much one meditates,

If one does not tame the mind, it is a sign that the yogi and
the Dharma are not one.

Around that time, his closest student, Özer Goocha, sought long
and hard for a written form of "The Heart Essence of the Dakinis"
and offered it to Longchenpa. Based on the good condition of receiving this text, Longchenpa had a dream in which he was given the actual
volume of Teachings by the Dakini Shenba Trokdrupma. He meditated upon the Teachings in secret and purified the obscurations.

When he was thirty-two, Longchenpa went to meditate in a cave called
Samye Chumpu, one of the principal places where Padmasambhava
had stayed in retreat. One day, while giving Teachings to four female and
four male practitioners on "The Heart Essence of the Dakinis," the
great protector of the Secret Mantrayana, Ekajati, directly entered the
body of one of the yoginis. The other yogis and yoginis could not bear
to be in the presence of Ekajati's wrathful appearance. But Longchenpa
said, "I am a yogi who has realized the perfect play of appearance and
emptiness. No obstacle will come to us." From that day forward, Longchenpa was always surrounded by Dakinis wherever he went.

Also, while Longchenpa was giving the empowerments, the deity
Vajravarahi, blue in color and adorned with jewels and bone ornaments, arrived in the cave. She said that because it was a very auspicious
day, she had come looking for students of the highest birth. Then,
Longchenpa and his students asked her many questions about the passage of the Secret Teachings in Tibet.

Longchenpa asked her, "Is there any obstacle to my long life?"

"How could there be an obstacle to an emanation of a Buddha?,"
she answered. "Did you all not hear that Vimalamitra's emanation had
returned to Tibet?"

Longchenpa asked, "My master Kumarantza said that the time has
come for me to spread the Teachings and benefit many beings. Was he
given this instruction by you?"

"That is right," she replied.

Longchenpa asked, "If I practice alone in solitary retreat, will I attain the rainbow body? Or instead, if I give widespread Teachings, will I be able to benefit many?"

"You will surely attain the rainbow body if you practice in solitude, but it is more important to benefit beings," she replied. "From this day forward, you will be able to benefit countless beings."

"Is it proper for me to give the empowerments, transmissions, and oral instructions on 'The Heart Essence of the Dakinis'?," he asked.

"You are the supreme holder of the Dharma," she replied. "Why would you not give those Teachings? Do not worry, I will gather students together for you to instruct. As for students who are improper vessels, they would even speak badly of the Buddhas."

"Are the Teachings of the 'Heart Essences' that I have received perfectly pure and complete?," Longchenpa asked.

"They are not mistaken, and are perfectly complete," she replied. She bestowed the blessings as well as a great many other prophecies before she left the cave that day.

One day, on the auspicious twenty-eighth day of the month, Padma-sambhava, accompanied by his retinue of Dakinis and protectors, appeared before Longchenpa and dissolved into his body. This was witnessed by a circle of his closest students. Based on this good condition, Longchenpa composed many vajra songs about the union of clarity and emptiness and the play of appearances, which arise from wisdom. As he sang to his students, the seven Dakinis called Dorje Yudronma appeared before them. The Dakinis answered many of Longchenpa's questions, including the ones that follow.

"Many Lamas teach the 'Heart Essences.' Is it absolutely necessary for me to continue to give Teachings?," Longchenpa asked.

"The Teachings of these Lamas of whom you speak are adequate, but they are not completely perfect. You are the supreme holder of the Teachings, so you must continue to teach," they answered.

"I never practiced in order to beckon you here. So why have you come to see me?," Longchenpa asked.

244 THE UNION OF DZOGCHEN AND BODHICHITTA

"We are always with any yogi who keeps the Samaya and has perfectly taken up the Union. We are like your shadow." Then they proceeded to give him Teachings and direct introductions of the Indestructible Secret Mantrayana.

At another time, when Longchenpa was writing down the meaning of "The Heart Essence of the Dakinis" from memory, Padmasambhava, Yeshe Tsogyal, and Tara appeared before him and bestowed the blessings. Yeshe Tsogyal remained with him for six days and nights, and gave him Teachings on "The Heart Essence of the Dakinis" in the form of signs, verbal explanations, and examples. During those six days he received many uncommon ways of giving direct introductions and methods by which the Teachings could be put into practice. Later, Longchenpa also received the Teachings on "The Heart Essence of Vimalamitra" from Vimalamitra himself.

For the remainder of his life, Longchenpa practiced the Union by taking up the view of Trekchod and the practice of Todgyal while staying in retreat in Samye Chumpu and Gangri Todkyar. He also composed many texts on the common and uncommon methods to take up the Union of Dzogchen and Bodhichitta. Finally, he passed away in 1363, and his body dissolved into the great Dharmadhatu.

JIGME LINGPA

Of the birth of the Vidyadhara Jigme Lingpa, Padmasambhava said,

> An emanation of me will take birth in Chunggye
> And cause everyone to exclaim in amazement, "Who is he?"

In line with the prophecy, Jigme Lingpa was born in Chunggye in 1729. When he was six years old, he received monastic vows at the monastery in Palru Tekchoklang. From the time he was a young boy Jigme Lingpa was known for his deep faith in the Three Jewels, and for the pure perception he had towards all Vajra masters, even when merely hearing their names. Although he had never received any instructions

Jigme Lingpa

on the Secret Teachings, he continually examined his mind. After seeing the mind's momentary nature, he was naturally able to rest in the union of clarity and emptiness. From a young age he also showed prodigious ability in his study of the scriptures and prayer.

Jigme Lingpa's uncommonly deep Bodhichitta revealed itself whenever he saw a sentient being experiencing pain or suffering. He seemed to feel their pain in his own body. Based on this deep compassion for the suffering of others, he composed hundreds and thousands of verses on the way to practice Tonglen. He practiced so diligently that after a time he continually exchanged himself for others. Jigme Lingpa once said that of all the events in his life, he most wished to be remembered for taking up the practice of Tonglen and meditation on the Union.

At age thirteen, Jigme Lingpa became a monk and received the novice monk's vow, but he still had not formed an uncommon relationship with a Spiritual Friend. However, knowledge of the way to practice arose naturally in him, so he practiced based on these methods. His scholastic aptitude was also quite astounding. One day, when he saw a drawing of an eclipse in a text, he became fascinated with the movements of the heavenly bodies. After making a brief study of astrology, he composed an entire astrological calendar in just seven days. On another occasion, he was given a book of traditional, metered poetry. He had never studied this complex system of writing; however, after asking a teacher several questions about the first few stanzas, he completely mastered the art of writing poetry and became the finest poet in all of Tibet.

Not long after, Jigme Lingpa met Lama Trupwang Tuchok Dorje. Jigme Lingpa was the type of practitioner who always saw even ordinary monks with pure perception. However, based on karma and prayers said in the past, when he met this Lama, Jigme Lingpa was immediately filled with a feeling of faith so overwhelming it left him speechless. From Lama Trupwang Tuchok Dorje he was given the ripening empowerments and the oral instructions on the methods to self-liberate the obscurations.

Around age twenty-five, Jigme Lingpa was suddenly struck by the feeling that time was quickly passing him by. He realized the nature of impermanence and felt the nearness of death. He felt renunciation of samsara so deeply that it seemed the world had been turned upside down, and that his life up until that point had been completely wasted. He was filled with deep longing for Padmasambhava, and traveled to the southwest, the direction in which Padmasambhava abides. He began to weep inconsolably, but he soon realized that crying would not enhance his meditation. So he turned his mind back to the Dharma. With a feeling of deep longing, he vowed to meditate ceaselessly on the union of clarity and emptiness until he was able to meet Padmasambhava directly, and attain liberation in either this life or the bardo state.

When Jigme Lingpa was twenty-eight years old, he realized how easy it was for obstacles to come to his meditation. Because of this, he made seven promises that he vowed to keep while he practiced in order to attain complete mastery over the mind. First, he vowed to stay in solitary places. Second, he vowed not to meet anyone who came to see him. Third, because speech is the cause for mental afflictions like attachment, anger, and jealousy, he vowed not to speak to anyone—not even his own relatives. Fourth, he vowed not to trade his spiritual knowledge for mere material wealth. Fifth, he vowed to practice the yidam deity and the Union every single day without exception. Sixth, he vowed to be satisfied with whatever situation he had: regardless of whether or not he had food and shelter. Seventh, he vowed to continuously abide in the four great liberations of drolam.

After vowing to uphold these seven precepts as if they were engraved on his heart, Jigme Lingpa stayed in solitary retreat for three years. During that time, he worked continuously with mindfulness in order to examine whether or not his mind was abiding in the uncontrived view. By taking up the union of clarity and emptiness in this way, his feelings of renunciation, faith, pure perception, compassion, loving-kindness, and Bodhichitta increased day by day and many signs denoting the good qualities of the path appeared. Regarding the Union of Dzogchen and Bodhichitta, the great Jigme Lingpa said,

> One must not rely upon emptiness separate from Bodhichitta;
> [Relying on the union of emptiness and Bodhichitta]
> Is the stainless path of liberation,
> The sacred path of the Sons of the Victors.

and,

> To practice the Mantrayana [based on] the generation of
>   Bodhichitta
> Is called the result or the Indestructible Vehicle.

After practicing in this way for three months, he received signs that his meditation was improving in both his dreams and his waking life. Also, he directly recognized the union of appearance and emptiness, describing it as "meeting emptiness within appearance, and appearance within emptiness." From that time on, he gained the ability to directly relieve the sufferings of animals or other beings by taking up the Union when he practiced Tonglen. When commenting on this miraculous ability, he said that he had not attained it because he was especially wise or of a high birth. It was simply because he had taken up the supremely holistic path of the Union:

> The method of compassion and the wisdom of emptiness:
> These two in union are [ultimate] Bodhichitta!

As Jigme Lingpa said, we should recognize ultimate Bodhichitta as the complete realization of the uncontrived view.

When Jigme Lingpa was thirty-one years old, he completed his three-year retreat, having kept the seven precepts without encountering any obstacles. His relatives and the villagers who lived near his hermitage begged him to stay there rather than traveling throughout Tibet. However, Jigme Lingpa contemplated impermanence extensively and, based on this contemplation, he realized that a yogi must be ultimately satisfied. This could only be achieved, he decided, by becoming a wandering yogi who is completely rootless, and is thus forced to accept whatever conditions happen to be at hand.

Because he was going against the wishes of all the people living nearby, Jigme Lingpa waited until late at night before he left in secret, accompanied by two attendants. While traveling, he encountered five self-arisen stupas made of stone on the road to Samye Chumpu. Upon reaching the stupas, Jigme Lingpa made a large feast offering and prayed deeply. Based on the good conditions that arose from making this offering, he experienced an unusually lucid state in which any appearance that arose was effortlessly liberated into the union of clarity and emptiness. After that, he composed many vajra songs about the nature of the Union, such as this one:

The perfection stage is primordially uncontrived.
There is no reason to meditate on empty "nothingness."
The period of meditation and that which follows are
    the union of bliss and emptiness,
Free of abandoning and grasping, [all] is self-liberated.

Soon after, Jigme Lingpa arrived at Samye Chumpu, where he practiced in strict retreat day and night. Based on the meditation he practiced in his retreat at that time, the wisdom body of Longchenpa appeared before him on three different occasions. Using signs, various methods, dependent arising, and blessings, Longchenpa gave Jigme Lingpa the perfect oral instructions on the "Longchen Nyingthig." Upon receiving the oral instructions, which became one with the vast expanse of Jigme Lingpa's mind, he attained accomplishment in the view of Trekchod and the secret practice of Todgyal. From that time forward, Jigme Lingpa continuously received the blessings of Padmasambhava and his consort Yeshe Tsogyal, and the omniscient Longchenpa. As a result, Jigme Lingpa spontaneously developed conventional and ultimate wisdom, and attained complete omniscience without ever taking up a "proper" course of study. Because he always abided in the union of clarity and emptiness, both excellent and hindering conditions were self-liberated into the Dharmadhatu.

In 1762, he built a hermitage at a place called Tse Rangchung, where he spent the remainder of his life in solitary retreat. While continuing to purify the obscurations, he gave Teachings on the Union of Dzogchen and Bodhichitta and the "Longchen Nyingthig" to students who traveled to see him. Whenever he gave Teachings, he always told them that the drubtob yogis, such as Milarepa and Longchenpa, met the Dharma due to bad conditions that had arisen in their lives and that they were able to attain profound results because they underwent great suffering and hardship. Of his own practice, Jigme Lingpa said,

I have realized an ocean of the Victors' Teachings.
I continuously generate supreme Bodhichitta.

Because I have realized the self-arisen natural state,
The essential faults of samsara and nirvana are transformed
    into wisdom awareness.

Along with giving Teachings, Jigme Lingpa also composed many
texts. He passed away and was liberated into the great Dharmadhatu in
1798 after leaving these instructions on the Union of Dzogchen and
Bodhichitta for practitioners of future generations:

Son, the uncontrived [view], free of the eight extremes,
    [which is] apprehended by the mind is not primordially
    pure vastness.
Son, rest without ceasing in the expression of rikpa,
[Which is] the great union of *clarity and emptiness.*
Son, the generation stage [laden with] attachment to ordinary
    stable visualization is not the practice of Mahayoga.
Son, the grasping at faces and hands must be destroyed by
    the expanse!
Rest in the perfect meditation of *awareness and emptiness.*
Son, generating attachment to meditation on the four joys
    is not the practice of Anuyoga.
Bring together the wind energy and the essence in the
    central channel!
Rest in great *bliss and emptiness* that is beyond the mind.

PATRUL RINPOCHE

Patrul Chökyi Jigme Wangpo was born in 1808 in Kham, Tibet. He was
recognized as an emanation of Pagye Samten Phuntsok by Dodrupchen Thinley Özer, who also gave him his name. From the time he
was just a child, Patrul Rinpoche easily mastered his studies and was
known for his clear mind, subdued emotions, deep faith, and pure perception. He also expressed an uncommon level of Bodhichitta. He
received his monastic vows from Khenpo Sherap Zangbo.

Jigme Gyalwe Nyugu

Patrul Rinpoche received the empowerments, transmissions, and oral instructions on the "Longchen Nyingthig" from Do Khentsye Yeshe Dorje, Dzogchen Mingyur Namkhai Dorje, Dodrupchen Jigme Kalzang, Gyaltse Shenpen Ta-ye, Dodrup Jigme Ngotsar, and Shechen Ontrul. However, supreme among all of his teachers was his root Lama, Jigme Gyalwe Nyugu, from whom he received the complete and perfect Teachings of the lineage. Notably, he received the Teachings on the foundational practices of the "Longchen Nyingthig" twenty-five times from Lama Jigme Gyalwe Nyugu, putting them into practice each time he received them. That is, he actually completed the five hundred thousand mantras, prayers, and visualizations of the foundational practices twenty-five times. By taking up listening, contemplation, and meditation on the oral instructions in solitary places such as a cave in Shinje and the "Long-life Cave," he realized the perfect, uncontrived view.

Patrul Rinpoche

Despite his wealth of knowledge and realization, Patrul Rinpoche cared nothing for the high status of monastic life. He completely abandoned worldly life and material wealth, and became a wandering yogi who cared only for abiding in the Union and the three Dharma actions of giving Teachings, debating, and composing texts.

Patrul Rinpoche vowed never to cast the Union of Dzogchen and Bodhichitta from his mind, and never failed to teach Bodhichitta as the supreme foundation for all meditation. Though easy to understand, the depth of Patrul Rinpoche's Teachings can be seen in the way he taught the Union as taking up the practice of Avalokiteshvara, the Buddha of Compassion:

> The wisdom awareness of all deities can be found within
>   the single deity Avalokiteshvara.
> The essence of all mantras is found in OM MANI PADME HUM.

> All Teachings of the generation and perfection stages can
>   be found within the Teachings of Bodhichitta.
> To practice [this] one teaching perfectly leads to complete
>   liberation.
> Recite the six syllables.

As we see in this transmission, Patrul Rinpoche actually taught Bodhi-chitta as "the great perfection," which includes the entire meaning of the Tantras.

At Dzogchen in Tibet, Patrul Rinpoche gave extensive Teachings on the great Shantideva's *Embarking on Bodhisattva Activities.* Although Dzogchen is a high, snowy, mountainous land, where little plant life can survive, based on Patrul Rinpoche's Teachings, yellow flowers with thirty or fifty petals began to cover the mountainsides. Such flowers had never been seen there before, and they were called "Bodhichitta flowers" which bloomed because of Patrul Rinpoche's blessings.

Patrul Rinpoche is known as the "door" to the entirety of the gama and terma of the Nyingmapa School. But especially, he holds the short-est unbroken lineage (and therefore the most important) of the oral instructions of the profound path of the "Longchen Nyingthig." Also, at a time when many of the transmissions and Teachings of the prac-tice of tsa lung of the "Longchen Nyingthig" were in danger of being lost, Patrul Rinpoche practiced and mastered them, and then passed them on to his students. So it is based on the Dharma activity of Patrul Rinpoche that the Secret Teachings began to flourish in Tibet once more. We Tibetans believe that the pristine quality of the "Longchen Nyingthig," as well as the perfectly maintained Teachings on the *Secret Essence Tantra,* are results of Patrul Rinpoche's great kindness.

Patrul Rinpoche was famed throughout Tibet as being a truly non-sectarian yogi and scholar. All of the works he composed, without exception, are accepted by all four schools of Tibetan Buddhism, with-out any contention that Patrul Rinpoche was a yogi of the Nyingmapa sect. His skill as a composer of texts is highly praised for four reasons. From the point of view of a scholar, his texts contain excellent meaning. From the point of view of one without great intelligence, they are easy to understand. Next, not only are all of the pith instructions present, but they are easy to remember. Finally, no matter what type of language he used to describe the Dharma, whether it was soothing or sharp, it all had the "perfect flavor." When Patrul Rinpoche gave Teachings, he emphasized adopting the holistic meaning of the path, without being dismissive of this part or that, or making similar mistakes. He described the failure to take up the Union with this metaphor of a grazing yak:

> Practicing only the Teachings of emptiness is like a yak that can only see out of one eye. He will starve because he can only see the grass on one side of the field.

Tibetan Buddhists regard Patrul Rinpoche as the root of the "Longchen Nyingthig." This is not only because he practiced and realized the Union, but also because many of his close students became very great scholars and yogis. Among his students were Mipham Rinpoche, Dzogchen Thupten Chökyi Dorje, Onbo Tenzin Norbu, Gadok Siddhu Chökyi Lodro, the Second Dodrup Jigme Phuntsok, the Third Dodrup Jigme Tenpai Nyima, Adzom Drukpa Drodul Dorje, Terton Lerap Langpa, and Ngushul Longdok of the Nyingmapa sect, as well as numerous other yogis and scholars from the other three sects of Tibetan Buddhism. Besides composing the oft-quoted *The Words of My Perfect Teacher*, which gives the essential instructions for how to carry out the foundational practices of the Nyingmapa School, Patrul Rinpoche also composed seven volumes on the methods for taking up the Outer, Inner, and Secret methods. He was liberated into the Dharmadhatu in 1887.

PRAYER FOR THE RIPENING OF BEINGS EVERYWHERE

To all the yogis and yoginis of this new age:
Please listen to the wish I make for you!
Through endless dreams of the future,
You will never even benefit yourselves.
How could you cross the ocean of samsara?
The primordial Dharmakaya Samantabhadra,
The clear-light nature of the Sambhogakaya Vajrasattva,
And the all-pervasive retinues of the Nirmanakaya:
These indivisible three kayas are Bodhichitta itself!
Find certainty in the indivisible two truths of the Great
    Middle Way
And inseparable clarity and emptiness
—the Union of Samsara and Nirvana.
Play in the union of bliss and emptiness—the Great
    Mahamudra,
And in the union of awareness and emptiness—Atiyoga
    Dzogchen.
Rest unmoving in the uncontrived, vast expanse.
Establish the two benefits and see the expression of the four
    appearances
In this life, at the time of death, or in the bardo!

—Anyen Rinpoche
Composed at Tomigawa,
"The River of Merit,"
Nagasaki, Japan
Spring 2004